MEDIEVAL PRACTICES OF SPACE

MEDIEVAL
CULTURES

SERIES EDITORS

RITA COPELAND
BARBARA A. HANAWALT
DAVID WALLACE

*Sponsored by the Center for Medieval Studies
at the University of Minnesota*

Volumes in the series study the diversity of medieval
cultural histories and practices, including such inter-
related issues as gender, class, and social hierarchies;
race and ethnicity; geographical relations; definitions
of political space; discourses of authority and dissent;
educational institutions; canonical and noncanonical
literatures; and technologies of textual and visual
literacies.

For more books in the series, see pages 263–64.

MEDIEVAL PRACTICES OF SPACE

BARBARA A. HANAWALT
MICHAL KOBIALKA
EDITORS

Medieval Cultures, Volume 23
University of Minnesota Press
Minneapolis
London

Published by the University of Minnesota Press
111 Third Avenue South, Suite 290
Minneapolis, MN 55401-2520
http://www.upress.umn.edu

Library of Congress Cataloging-in-Publication Data
Medieval practices of space / Barbara A. Hanawalt and Michal Kobialka, editors.
    p. cm. — (Medieval cultures ; v. 23)
Papers from a conference held in April 1997.
Includes bibliographical references and index.
ISBN 0-8166-3544-7 (HC : acid-free paper) — ISBN 0-8166-3545-5 (PB : acid-free paper)
    1. Civilization, Medieval.   2. Space (Architecture)—Social aspects—Europe—
History—To 1500.   3. Public spaces—Europe—History—To 1500.   4. Space and
time—Social aspects—Europe—History—To 1500.   5. Space and time—Religious
aspects.   6. Space and time—Psychological aspects.   7. Literature, Medieval.
8. Space and time in literature.   9. Visual perception in literature.
I. Hanawalt, Barbara.   II. Kobialka, Michal.   III. Series.
CB353 .M424   2000
307—dc21   99-050793

Printed in the United States of America on acid-free paper

The University of Minnesota is an equal-opportunity educator and employer.

11 10 09 08 07 06 05 04 03 02 01 00   10 9 8 7 6 5 4 3 2 1

Contents

ACKNOWLEDGMENTS

In organizing the conference "The Medieval Practices of Space" in April 1997 and in producing the subsequent volume, Barbara A. Hanawalt and Michal Kobialka gratefully acknowledge the support of the College of Liberal Arts, the Center for Medieval Studies, and the Carl D. Sheppard Fund of the University of Minnesota.

Research assistants play a major role in organizing the conferences of the Center for Medieval Studies and in following through later with editorial work on the books that arise from these conferences. The editors thank Anna Dronzek, Amy Brown, Kristen Burkholder, Darren Bayne, Jonathan Good, and Noel Delgado for their work related to *Medieval Practices of Space*. Anne Mattson, the graduate administrative assistant of the Center for Medieval Studies, was particularly helpful throughout the conference planning and the production of the volume.

INTRODUCTION

BARBARA A. HANAWALT AND
MICHAL KOBIALKA

Ever since the word "space" lost its strictly geometrical meaning, it has acquired and been accompanied by numerous adjectives or nouns that defined its "new" use and attributes. Mental space, ideological space, literary space, the space of the imagination, the space of the dreams, utopian space, imaginary space, technological space, cultural space, and social space are some of the terms that have emerged alongside the Euclidean, isotropic, or absolute space. With the publication of Henri Lefebvre's *La Production de l'espace* in 1974 (the English version, *The Production of Space,* was published in 1991), the possibility that space can be produced altered how one talks about and envisions that which used to be an empty area. Lefebvre's triad of *spatial practice* (perceived), which embraces production and reproduction of each social formation, *representations of space* (conceived), which are tied to the relations of production and to the order, hence knowledge, that these relations impose, and *representational spaces* (lived), which embody complex symbolism dominating, by containing them, all senses and all bodies, has changed not only how one studies the history of space but also the history of representations as well as of specific representational practices.

It is therefore not surprising that the uses and definitions of space are proliferating and becoming increasingly important as a subject matter as well as an analytical tool for a number of different disciplines including those studying the Middle Ages. In the area of cartography, for instance, it is quite apparent that medieval maps divided space differently than modern ones. In the great *mappae mundi,* Jerusalem was placed at the center of the map and the crucified Christ was often superimposed on the map to divide the space. The continents were ranged around the circle of the map with important cities or countries noted. Pilgrimage maps depicted the routes in a linear fashion rather than following the actual terrain. In cathedrals, the use of the internal space changed frequently, with perhaps the most dramatic being the erection of rood screens that divided the congregation from the choir, clergy, and high altar.

It is not only the use of space, however, that is engaging medievalists in a reevaluation of how medieval people thought and lived. The realization that people divided space by gender is becoming more apparent: women occupied rooms, houses, quarters in the cities and villages, while men's activities took them farther abroad to streets, highways, fields, cities, oceans, battles, and council tables. Space carried meanings. The king's peace in England, for instance, originally meant that area around his person, but as the king's legal authority expanded, breaking the king's peace meant breaking one of the king's laws anywhere in his realm. Not only did people create uses for space, but having done so, that space could influence the behavior of those who occupied it; defining space tended to prescribe the behavior within it. Words, metaphors, images, signs, poetic illusions, and personally created identities all used space or place to add meaning to the external world.

The chapters in this volume, however, go beyond the current exploration of space in the Middle Ages and explore the nuances of medieval practices of space in heterogeneous places and at specific times. Historians, theatre historians, art historians, and literary scholars have all explored the implications of medieval spatial practices and in the process have crossed disciplinary boundaries. All of the chapters touch on the varieties of use of space as metaphor, language, and definition but group into three main categories. The mapping, uses, and definitions of urban space are found in the chapters by Michael Camille on Paris, Daniel Smail on Marseille, and Charles Burroughs on Florence and Rome. The ecclesiastical and theological practice of space are explored in the chapters by Andrzej Piotrowski, Michal Kobialka, and Valerie Flint. The use of space for performance and staging of one's belonging appear in chapters by Donnalee Dox, Jody Enders, and Kathleen Biddick. Finally, the volume ends with another view of medieval Paris in which Tom Conley completes the analysis of space by taking the readers back to Paris with words rather than signs as a guide to the medieval city.

As the essays presented here unequivocally indicate, the practice of space in the Middle Ages was never homogeneous, but always in flux, and depended on how its attributes were defined at the time and disseminated by the historical agents. Drawing on the philosophical thought of Michel Foucault, Michel de Certeau, and Pierre Bourdieu, some of the people who contributed to our knowledge of the subject, the authors problematize the notion of space that, since the times of Newton's *Principia* (1687), has been perceived to be absolute and empty. They ask what is revealed when space is viewed as an open and mutable field of specifiable relationships and structures; as a site actuated by the ensemble of movements deployed within it; as a structure that is determined by the distribution of economic, social, cultural, ideological, and theological capital.

By focusing on the practices within a heterogeneous space, it becomes apparent that space is thoroughly imbued with quantities and qualities marking the presence of bodies, signs, and thoughts that had disappeared from view or a discourse in the topography of the medieval landscape. By emphasizing the multiple understandings of the notion of space as well as the heterogeneity of the practices positioned in it, we hope to draw attention to a different configuration of knowledge that will lead to new alignments of thoughts regarding medieval practices of space.

Michael Camille's chapter sets the stage for the volume by exploring the use of urban signs to define the city and the spaces within it. Urban signs advertised businesses and were the equivalent of street numbers for identifying individual houses. They were distinct from heraldic or sacred signs that were also abundant in any medieval city, and they also functioned in different ways from modern signs. He explores the oldest extant sign in Paris, a sign reflecting the story of St. Julian as told in the *Golden Legend*. St. Julian's penance for killing his parents was to ferry travelers across a river. Because everyone knew the story, the sign was an appropriate one to announce a hostel for travelers. As Camille points out, "Signs are indicators of lived social place, not disembodied abstract space." He argues that "place" might be a better guide to medieval thinking about their lived environment than our modern and abstract notion of space. His investigation of signs shows how they functioned to define place, status, and gender within the city of Paris.

Using the verbal descriptions of the location of houses and shops in Marseille that notaries recorded in making deeds of sale, Daniel Smail develops a notarial cartography for the city. In the absence of plot maps, the verbal descriptions indicate the mental pictures that people used to identify the place in which they lived and distinguish it from surrounding places. But the notaries took the information that the buyers and sellers gave them and turned them into cartographic statements. Thus when a smith gave his address as Esperon, the notary wrote that he lived on the street of Esperon. The inhabitants also identified their residences as a vicinity, a practice of space that did not refer to a limited geographical area but concentrations of trade: the fruitery, fishmongery, jewelery, goldsmithery, and so on. One long street, New Street, consisted of segments, each for a different trade. But notaries translated all these vicinities into New Street. The notaries, in translating local descriptions, committed what Smail has called "notarial violence" on local perceptions of space. When they moved out of the trade area, notaries adopted the ancient usage of *insulae,* or islands, to describe the holdings of the church or a noble family. Thus the notarial verbal record mapped the power structure of the city and tended to repress the local divisions of space.

Using records and visual evidence, Charles Burroughs investigates spaces of arbitration between the internal and external worlds of house and street. Porticos or loggias permitted the enactment of social memory along with the legal transactions that occurred there. Thus a marriage contract could be announced from the portico in full view of the public and thereby create a social memory of the terms and the alliance of two houses through marriage. The use of this public space that was part of the house produces a theatre for the notarial culture that presided over the betrothal as the priest did over the actual marriage. Likewise, arbitrated disputes were announced from the porticos and reconciliation ceremonies were announced and performed there. So useful was the loggia that the notaries encouraged Florence to build a public loggia adjacent to the city hall where these useful judicial transactions could have a full viewing public. But by the early fifteenth century aristocratic culture began to withdraw from the interface of the private house and the public street, which the loggia represented, and instead houses were remodeled with the loggia facing the central courtyard of their palaces. The final blow to the tradition came with the destruction of the public loggia for the entrance of Pope Leo de Medici into the city. The dialogue between legal and architectural language had come to an end.

Faced with the prohibition of representational images of Jesus and the saints during the Iconoclastic controversy between 726 and 843, Byzantine architects attempted to evoke the mysterious and the holy through the play of light, solid matter, and time in the sanctuary. Andrzej Piotrowski explores both the figurative and nonfigurative representation in Byzantine architecture that defined the viewers' experiences of the internal space in churches. As Piotrowski argues, "buildings do not make arguments," they structure experiences in order to imply thoughts in viewers. If such a proposition is tangible, the representation of the divine, as his examples show, was constructed in a manner different from how it is presented in current architectural publications. That is to say, the play of light through translucent marble inserts in windows directed attention to the theological sense and symbolic meaning of light and darkness in the churches. All parts of the internal space of the churches, be they squinches or domes, added to the process by "heightening the interactions between figurative depiction and the void space." By simply being present in the church, a believer was a part of this different spatial reality affirming the existence of the divine.

Another way to use space within the sanctuary of a church was through the use of its space for liturgical practice. Michal Kobialka discusses liturgical drama of the early Middle Ages in terms of the shifts and transformations in monastic practices that institutionalized specific representational places for the staging of the presence/absence of Christ in the Easter Sunday service. The eleventh-century copy of the tenth-century monastic code, the *Regularis concordia,* often quoted to explain the emergence of liturgical drama in England in the tenth century, is used to suggest that this text was part of the instability of spatial practices that arose from the Norman conquest and the theological discussions regarding the Eucharist. As such, unlike its tenth-century equivalent, the eleventh-century *Regularis concordia* raised serious questions about the representation of the Eucharist: was God really present in the bread and wine, and if so, how does one represent this? How could the use of sacred, monastic space interpret the drama? By asking these questions, the document partook in the process of constructing new practices embodied in the text and in the images produced. These practices destabilized the approved convention and exposed a space where the theological controversies about the presence of Christ in the Eucharist, the monastic customs in post-Norman conquest in England, and new forms of meditation established unexpected tensions and new alignments. By the fourteenth century, as we shall see in the Dox and Enders chapters, such qualms had disappeared entirely.

Monastic use of space was important not only for liturgy, but also for monastic discipline. Valerie I. J. Flint has done a thoughtful reading of the practice of spatial separation in monastic orders and has extended these to the secular use of distancing the perpetrator from the crime through pilgrimage. Her chapter shows that a sense of space within the community was part of the identity of belonging to a monastery. Novices had their spaces at the refectory, in work assignments, and in the choir. Monks also had their place in these hierarchies of space and place. While Benedict's monastic code permitted the use of corporal punishment to discipline monks, it is apparent in practice and in subsequent codes that the strong preference was to impose a temporary, spatial distance from the community. Often the space was such that the miscreant would be able to observe as an outsider but could not move into the inclusive worship or repast of the community. He was made to understand the fellowship he had lost. The rules hoped to encourage the misbehavers to mend their ways and return to the community. Only extreme recalcitrance would put a member permanently out of the order. Among secular governments, penitential pilgrimages, Flint suggests, were also a way of removing the thorn in the flesh of the victims by sending the offender off. Secular governments, she suggests, learned to use spatial distance as a healing device for conflict.

Dox, Enders, and Biddick move the argument for the use of space into a consideration of how membership can be inclusive and non-membership exclusive. Lines, both blunt and subtle, were drawn on stage and in pictures to create the idea of distance and assimilation of the Jewish population. Even in England, where Jews had been expelled in the 1290s, the Croxton *Play of the Sacrament* could convincingly raise the image of the exclusion of Jews from the Christian majority—the right-believing, dominating community. The plot involved the appropriation of the Host (wafer in the Eucharist) for the experimentation of the Jews. The Croxton play was part of a genre that included the *Mistere de la Sainte Hostie* in France. In both plays Jews experiment with destroying the miraculous powers of the Host. Burning, boiling, nailing, and otherwise trying to destroy the thin wafer fail. Both plays end with conversion, although the chief offender in the French play is executed in a space that is particularly repugnant to a Jew—the slaughter area for pigs. The Christian betrayers also have different fates, although both involve spatial separation. In the Croxton play the merchant who sells the Host is ordered by the bishop to go on a pilgrimage, a punishment that Flint suggests may have derived from monastic practice. In the French version a woman who wants to appear in her best at Easter mass secures the

Host by faking her communion in order to redeem her outer garment *(surcoat)* from the Jew. Her exile takes her out of the country and to an unhappy end. Finally, Biddick discusses how in two views of Nuremburg the Jewish quarter disappears only to be replaced with new city buildings that all but obliterate the space the "other" occupied.

In the performance of the Croxton play, an elaborate set with scaffolds, blazing fires, boiling cauldrons, and an exploding oven divide the stage space and the actors from each other. The space, however, is mutable in that the scaffolds convert to altars and Jews convert to Christianity. Dox explores the medieval scientific and theological concepts of space and the void and argues that the space of the stage could be considered the bounded cosmos in which God is omnipresent. Thus the play can represent Christian salvation history occurring in God's time and space. The exit of the Jews and Christians singing the *Te Deum* into the church of Bury St. Edmunds confirms the power and presence of God.

Despite the similarity of the Croxton play and the *Mistere de la Sainte Hostie,* Enders points out that the denouement is really very different. The violence of the Jews to the Host is similar, but the violence of the Christians to the Jews in the French version is very different. In taking over the Jew's house to become an ecclesiastical place for celebration of the miracle of the Eucharist and in the execution of the Jewish father of the family, the play reflects a colonization of Jewish space. She juxtaposes the acts of violence to the Host in the private space within the Jew's home (his hearth) to the very public expulsion of him and his public execution in the pig butchery. Preceding his own eviction, he throws his rebellious family into the streets to gain help from the Christians that they now propose to join in communion. The play suggests to its audience that Christians should be suspicious of what occurs in the privacy of Jewish homes and keep a surveillance on Jewish space. The play conveyed a "sinister message of anti-Semitism" to any community viewing the play.

Biddick explores the local ethnography of Nuremberg, including views of local aspects of gender, age, class, dress, and fabric. She has used city views that were presented in the 1493 *Nuremberg Chronicle* and the 1575 cityscape from the *Civitates orbis terrarum.* While it was usual of medieval cartography, particularly the *mappae mundi,* to place Jerusalem in the center of the map, the *Nuremberg Chronicle* has displaced Jerusalem as the center of time in favor of the new center, Nuremberg. They also went to great lengths to establish the heterosexuality of the new city as well as disconnect it from the old concept of Jerusalem as the center of the world. In the later version, the city becomes a backdrop for the display of citizens themselves as they pose in sartorial splendor before their city. The new, nonmedieval spatial regime required cutting off ancient Israel from the present space Jews inhabited in Nuremberg.

Bringing the readers back to cities and to Paris in particular, Tom Conley analyzes Villon's ballad, "Contredictz de Franc Gontier," as a map of the city. Conley considers the literary space of the Middle Ages first as the shape of the manuscript and the words on the page, "the spaces described in and through the writing," and then as "poetic space." The latter is the sense of the whole that the reader gets from the experience of reading, but which is more evocative than a direct reading of the language and words of the poem. Mapping the poetic space and the real or physical space, the poem describes a city view of Paris and, like the *Nuremberg Chronicle*, removes the theological center of Jerusalem and posits the possibility that Paris is either a modern Jerusalem or a Babylon. The poem also plays with the mapping of seasons and odors, rural and rustic, and the security of the inside of a brothel compared to the threatening outside world. While Camille's view of Paris is very much the streets, the commerce, and the signs of what lies within buildings, Conley has shown the inside of the brothel/hostel. But the inside is permeable space in which the winds of seasons invade.

The chapters on the medieval practices of space draw attention to the shifting uses of space and the lack of stability of concepts of space in the Middle Ages. The practice of space encompasses its uses, but can also be abstracted in concepts such as mental, physical, social, political, real, or imaginary. The staging of space and how space allows itself to be staged can be observed in chapters in this volume that deal with the uses of urban space for signs, plays, theological and scientific writing, notarial records, and poetry. Architectural space in churches directed the attention of worshipers to particular parts of the church, and liturgical uses of space dramatized the different phases of the mass. The uses of space came to have words and metaphors associated with them that elevated some spaces and debased others. The coronation chair connoted a very different status than the gallows. Even in a prison such as Newgate in London, the worst chamber in which to house prisoners was ironically named the Paradise room because one was closer to death there. Images of space such as boats, castles, walled cities, city panoramas all took on meaning that the viewer could interpret on shields, tavern signs, churches, and in books. The policing of special spaces, both personal and public, became important in defining social structure. One wore special gowns, enclosing the body's space, at a New Year's celebration at court or at an urban parade on the election of a new mayor. The space occupied by those in these distinctive clothes was protected from those who did not have the right to wear the costume—even the trade in such ceremonial garments was regulated so that no mistake could be made from year to year. Those who violated the rules regulating access and egress to special spaces were punished with expulsion from the community or public humiliation. Space in itself, in the form of excommunication, exile, and pilgrimage, was used for punishment and for expressing the behavior and practices that were included and those that were excluded.

We would like these essays to function as gestures of thinking that are positioned in a dynamic field of discourse about the medieval practices of space. Each and every one of them pays homage to an order before it passes through it to question the past and present rationalizations that constructed it. Each and every one of them travels through a landscape, traces the imaginations that formed it, and tries to restore the elements that could bestow visibility on a thought that is no longer possible. Finally, each and every one of them engages in a historiographic practice of exploring a complex network of social, political, ideological, economic, and theological relationships and structures that stabilized a space into a well-defined place. It is our hope that each and every one of these essays perturbs that which history supposedly laid to rest.

Readers interested in the topic may consult the following sources for further discussion of the production and representation of space:

Bachelard, Gaston. *The Poetics of Space.* Trans. Maria Jolas, with a foreword by Etienne Gilson. New York: Orion Press, 1964.

Bourdieu, Pierre. *The Field of Cultural Production.* Edited and introduced by Randal Johnson. New York: Columbia University Press, 1993.

Boyer, M. Christine. *The City of Collective Memory.* Cambridge: MIT Press, 1994.

Chaudhuri, Una. *Staging Place: The Geography of Modern Drama.* Ann Arbor: Michigan University Press, 1995.

Cresswell, Tim. *In Place/Out of Place: Geography, Ideology, and Transgression.* Minneapolis: University of Minnesota Press, 1996.

de Certeau, Michel. *Heterologies: Discourse on the Other.* Trans. Brian Massumi, with a foreword by Wlad Godzich. Minneapolis: University of Minnesota Press, 1986.

———. *The Practice of Everyday Life.* Trans. Steven Rendall. Berkeley: University of California Press, 1984.

Deconstruction and the Visual Arts. Edited by Peter Brunette and David Wills. New York: Cambridge University Press, 1994.

Deleuze, Gilles. "Nomad Art: Space." In *The Deleuze Reader.* Edited and with an introduction by Constantin V. Boundas. New York: Columbia University Press, 1993.

Derrida, Jacques. *On the Name.* Edited by Thomas Dutoit. Stanford, Calif. Stanford University Press, 1995.

Displacement, Diaspora, and Geographies of Identity. Edited by Smadar Lavie and Ted Swedenburg. Durham, N.C.: Duke University Press, 1996.

Foucault, Michel. "Of Other Spaces." Translated by Jay Miskoviec. *Diacritics* 16, no. 1 (spring 1986): 22–27.

Garner, Stanton B. *Bodied Spaces: Phenomenology and Performance in Contemporary Drama.* Ithaca, N.Y.: Cornell University Press, 1994.

Gregory, Derek. *Geographical Imaginations.* Oxford: Blackwell, 1994.

Jackson, Peter. *Maps of Meaning: An Introduction to Cultural Geography.* London: Unwin Hyman, 1989.

Lefebvre, Henri. *The Production of Space.* Trans. Donald Nicholson-Smith. Oxford: Blackwell, 1991.

Place, Power, Situation, and Spectacle: A Geography of Film. Edited by Stuart C. Aitken and Leo E. Zonn. Lanham, Md.: Rowman & Littlefield, 1994.

Sexuality and Space. Edited by Beatriz Colomina. Princeton Papers on Architecture, 1. Princeton: Princeton University Press, 1992.

Spain, Daphne. *Gendered Spaces.* Chapel Hill: University of North Carolina Press, 1992.

Streets: Critical Perspective on Public Space. Edited by Zeynep Celik, Diane Favro, and Richard Ingersoll. Berkeley: University of California Press, 1994.

Women and Space. Edited by Shirley Ardener. London: Croom Helm, 1981.

1

Signs of the City

PLACE, POWER, AND PUBLIC FANTASY IN MEDIEVAL PARIS

Michael Camille

One of the oldest streets in Paris on the Left Bank is the rue Galande, between rue St. Julien le Pauvre to the east and the corner of the Place Maubert to the west. Approaching this corner on the north side of the street, one comes upon number 42 rue Galande, one of those ubiquitous little cinemas that make the French capital such a haven for lovers of the moving image. Most cineasts entering the building and most passersby do not notice the little static image placed high above on its graffiti-covered facade (figure 1.1). A stone relief carving only a few feet high, it depicts the legend of St. Julian the Hospitaller, who along with his wife is shown ferrying their mysterious and divine passenger across a raging river (figure 1.2). It blends in so well with the multiplicity of other signs in the commercial hubbub that this little stone carving is literally a forgotten part of the city, floating out of time and place. For a long time this piece of fourteenth-century sculpture was thought to be a fragment of the nearby church of St. Julien le Pauvre, whose tympanum was destroyed in 1675. But this is not the case. Unlike so much of the medieval sculpture we see today in museums, this is not a piece of a lost, larger whole and, as documents show, has not been moved. Nor is it like the numerous Gothic statues on the exterior of the cathedral of Notre Dame just across the Seine, which were heavily restored in the last century and more recently scrubbed clean for the tourist gaze. This little carving,

Figure 1.1. 42 rue Galande, Paris. Photograph courtesy of the author.

Figure 1.2. Sign of St. Julian, stone relief, 1373–80, 42 rue Galande.
Photograph courtesy of the author.

though weathered, is unrestored, in its original site, and still performing its original function—it is a house sign.[1]

This sculpture cannot be a fragment from the destroyed tympanum of the nearby church of Saint Julien le Pauvre, demolished in 1675. First, the church was probably dedicated to a different Julian, either the Martyr or the Confessor and not the Hospitaller. Second, and more important, in 1380 the house on the rue Galande was already described in a document as "Maison ou au-dessus est l'ansaigne de saint Jullien" (the House above which is the sign of Saint Julian).[2] Seven years before, the same building is also described as the "Maison de la heuse" (House of the Boot), which gives us a fairly clear date as to when this particular sign was placed over the door. Another document of 1441 describes the material, position, and subject matter of the sign: "Maison ouquel est à present élévée en pierre de taille l'ymaige de Sainct-Jullian, sur l'uisserie dudict hostel" (The house where there is at present raised in carved stone the image of Saint Julian on the door of the said hostel).[3] Today, two houses to the west, at number 48 rue Galande is a restaurant called the "Auberge des deux signes," an example of what we might at first assume is a modern linguistic sign referring to lost visual markers. But already in 1360 this was known as the "Maison des deux signes." To confuse matters, the house appears in a 1429 document as the "Hostel des deux cignes" (the House of the Two Swans), possibly part of the veritable menagerie of animal signs surrounding the sign of St. Julian. There was the "Maison du cheval rouge" and the "Maison des lyons" on one side, and at the corner, "La Corne de cerf" (the Ram's Horn), a famous sign attested in 1435, marking a house that belonged to the Picard Nation of the University. The various Nations of the University of Paris, needing lodgings for visitors and students, owned many of the houses on this street, which at its east end abutted one of the most famous streets of the quarter, the rue du Fouarre or the Street of Straw, where students of the liberal arts crowded to hear lectures. We do not know who owned the house with the image of St. Julian, only that it was an important and valuable property transferred in 1413 for the substantial sum of more than 80 "ecus d'or."[4]

The last time I photographed the cinema at number 42, not only had its owners restored and cleaned the modern concrete facade around the medieval sign, they had put up their own new, eye-catching, painted and projecting sign reading "Studio Galande," incorporating an image of movie-camera projection. In the modern metropolis we negotiate space almost totally through the grid of language. Nineteenth-century photographers like Charles Marville and Eugène Atget show that Paris was the first great city of signs in the modern sense with billboards and the bombardment of written words on every wall and surface, and, as Molly Nesbit has shown, the first studies of older signs in the city were part of a modernist and surrealist construction of the urban phantasmagoria.[5] I shall return to this issue, but it is important to first understand how medieval signs functioned in radically different ways from modern ones. In contemporary Paris, for example the green cross of the pharmacy is a visual sign, but the word "pharmacie" is necessary for it to dispense drugs. Not only in maps and road signs, street signs announce our location as pedestrians, painted words guide us during the day and neon ones at night. Most of these textual signs are commercial. We find individual houses through similar linguistic and numerical means, a number and a street address.[6] Street names existed in Paris during the Middle Ages, but numeration of houses was not standard until quite recently, imposed by law only in 1805.[7] Until then one located inhabitants and businesses through a system of purely pictorial signs, three thousand of which were still listed in the seventeenth century. In the tax registers of 1292, houses are indicated by the name of their proprietor, which suggests that the imposition of signs was a relatively late medieval phenomenon.[8] As late as 1599 the foreign visitor Thomas Platter described how "if one is searching for a person it is necessary to know the exact house where he lives, the sign of that house, and the floor which he inhabits."[9] The rue Hirondele just off the old rue Git-le-coeur, also on the Left Bank, still has the old eighteenth-century incised street name below one of the famous nineteenth-century blue plaques that itself has been replaced today by an even more modern one (figure 1.3). In our current urge to historicize, now we tend to name streets after famous people, events in the past, or even dates, but this street was named after a sign, an image of a bird on one of its houses. The house sign often created the street name in this way. The rue Galande, however, was named after one of its noble owners, Mathilde de Garlande, wife of Matthew of Montmerency, who received the land as a fief of the abbey of St. Geneviève in 1202 in order to build *hospitibus ad hospitias*.[10] But many streets in Paris whose names date back to the Middle Ages refer to a more impersonal imposition of signs.

The image of St. Julian on the rue Galande is not only the oldest extant street sign in the city, it is the only Parisian sign of any antiquity that is not now housed in the Musée Carnavelet, which has an extensive collection of house signs, most postdating the medieval period.[11] The subject represented here is taken from the dramatic story of one of the three Julians recounted in the *Golden Legend,* that of St. Julian the Hospitaller.[12] Out hunting one day, a noble youth is chasing a stag, which turns to him and says, "Why do you hunt me, you who are destined to kill your own father and mother?" In order to escape fulfillment of this awful prophecy, the young man wandered to a country far away from his home where he married and became a prosperous householder. Returning to his house one day, he saw what he thought was a stranger in bed with his wife under the covers. Drawing his sword, he slew the two who turned out, to his horror, to be none other than his long lost parents, who had come in search of their son and whom his wife had taken in for the night. In order to expiate himself from the sin of having killed both his parents, he built a hut by the side of a perilous river where he and his wife ferried travelers across. Long after this a stranger appeared and begged to be ferried across the river on the night of a terrible storm. As the story ends in the *Golden Legend,* the man "who was eaten with

Figure 1.3. Rue Hirondelle, Paris. Photograph courtesy of the author.

leprosy and horrible to look upon" turns into a shining angel who announces their repentance has been accepted so the couple can die peace-
fully. The sculpted image focuses on the latter part of the narrative and
not the scene of Julian's sin. The earlier image of Julian's terrible mistake takes up the main space of the miniature in a full page dedicated to
the saint in the fifteenth-century *Hours of Peter of Brittany* (figure 1.4).[13]
But in the *bas-de-page*, we see a similar composition to that in the Paris
sign with the saint and his wife on either side of a small boat and a
standing, nimbed figure, not just an angelic messenger but Christ himself, in the middle. In the manuscript the figure is clearly Christ with a
cruciform nimbus, but in the sculpture he has a more ambiguous

Figure 1.4. Legend of St. Julian in the boat, *bas-de-page* of the *Hours of Peter of Brittany.*
Fifteenth-century Paris, Bibliothèque Nationale Ms. lat. 1159 fol. 155v. Copyright Bibliothèque
Nationale de France, Paris; reprinted courtesy of the Bibliothèque Nationale de France.

human appearance, the "cliquette" or "clapper" carried by lepers to announce their coming hanging around his neck. That Christ appears with
the most highly stigmatized physical illness of the Middle Ages—
leprosy—is also significant in terms of the spaces of medieval Paris,
where leprosaria, most notably the hospital of St. Lazare, their patron
saint, were located at the periphery of the urban space.[14] Here near the
center of the city, the most feared leper appears in the most-loved body
of Christ. According to the *Golden Legend,* it had been a particularly
stormy night when Christ appeared in the guise of a leper *(qui sic*

infirmus et quasi leprosus apparuerat) and asked to be transported across
the river. On the left of the scene is the goal of the journey, the safe
haven of the hostel on the far shore, which metonymically also represents the house over which the sign stands. The scene depicts that climactic moment of recognition as their mystery passenger reveals his
identity and, in return for their charity, promises the two astonished sinners eternal salvation.

With its thematics of wandering hospitality—the young saint leaving
his home after the prophesy, his wife giving up her own bed to the old
couple, and the penance of running a hostel for travelers—Julian became
the patron saint of hostels or more general lodging places in the later
Middle Ages. The French poem "La Paternostre saint Julien" was a prayer
recited by travelers in the hope they would receive hospitality on their
journey.[15] Chaucer describes the generosity of the Franklin by allusion to
the saint: "An householdere and that a greet was he; Seint Julian he was
in his contree." As Gawain sees Bertilak's castle in the distance in
Gawain and the Green Knight, he associates the same two sacred figures
we see on the Paris sign, thanking "Jesus and sayn Gilyan, that gentyle
ar bothe, that cortaysly hade hym kydde and his cry herkened. 'Now
bone hostel,' coth the burne, 'I beseche yow yette!'"[16]

An internationally understood and not just a local image promising
hospitality, the rue Galande example also shows not an otherworldly
saint but a contemporary and functioning economic unit—a married
couple—who ran the hostel. Many medieval signs show a man and wife
as an economic unit, either the "first" couple, Adam and Eve, or other
couples.[17] The rue Galande is not far from the Petit Pont and the great
river artery of the Seine, so this example has a topographical as well as a
symbolic logic. First, a ship was on the seal of the merchants and a crucial emblem for the city.[18] Saint Julian was also patron of fishmongers,
as evidenced in an elaborate stained glass window at Rouen cathedral
dedicated to the multiple Saint Julians described in the *Golden Legend.*
Fish were not only a major source of food for Parisians, but they also
appear carved against the running water, once probably painted blue, on
the sign.[19] But the central emphasis in the carving upon the leprous and
therefore abject nature of the mysterious traveler/Christ suggests that
this image did not function as a shop sign but rather that here was a safe
resting place. Today more often a verbal logo, "Holiday Inn" welcomes
the tired driver from a distance, and in a similar way this sign was com-

monly used for pilgrimage hostels to suggest comfort, spiritual as well as physical. It may have been designed especially to contrast to commercial signs, like the wisp of straw or greenery on a pole that often signaled a public house or a tavern.[20] Signs like that of St. Julian suggest a nucleated concept not of persons but of place, in which each house had its own centrality and significance, not just a numbered element in a sequence as in our modern cities, but with its own identity in an image. While the recent historical research on the city has emphasized the importance of images in the performative rituals that animated the streets during special festivals, the more quotidian tactics of these static signs have for the most part been ignored.[21] Many historians of the city, as a mode of experience as well as an architectural site, have described how urban life puts more emphasis upon visual recognition, and the importance of visual signs certainly suggests another kind of quotidian literacy, based not upon textual learning but another system of understood symbols and structures.[22] I want to explore in the rest of this chapter the function of such an image—its use of a hagiographic legend to advertise a commercial and not a spiritual location and what this little vestige of the medieval city can tell us about the status of signs in the urban spaces of medieval culture.

SIGNS AND SPACES

I say spaces and not space quite deliberately. There was no such thing as "space" for medieval people. The word "espace" meant an interval of time or distance, and, as Edward S. Casey has described in his recent book *The Fate of Place: A Philosophical History,* the hotly debated issues among Parisian philosophers of the time concerned place *(locus)* and not our modern abstract notion of space, which is a postmedieval category. In this respect architectural historians who talk about the "space" of the great Gothic cathedrals are imposing an anachronistic notion of experience on these structures.[23] Signs are indicators of lived social place, not disembodied abstract space. Modern theorists and semioticians often fall into what I see as a trap of overstratifying what they call medieval urban space into two distinct and separate registers, one embodied in the sculptural complex of the cathedral of Notre Dame and its multifaceted and complex sign system (figure 1.5) and the other represented by the little

Figure 1.5. Notre Dame Cathedral, Paris: north transept with projecting gargoyles (mostly restored). Photograph courtesy of the author.

sign of St. Julian only a couple of stone's throws away (in medieval spatial terms) across the river (see figure 1.2).

Françoise Choay made such a stratification in her influential essay in *The City and the Sign: An Introduction to Urban Semiotics*:

> The system of the medieval city can be defined especially by closure (inside its surrounding walls) and by the differential relations between two types of elements: functional cellular mini-elements (individual houses), and semantically charged maxi-elements (cathedral or church, palace, squares). The former are opposed to the latter (in a relation of transcendence) and to each other by distinctive features, in particular the slope and pattern of their roofs, the windows of their facade: their heterogeneity displays itself along the street in a relationship of proximity that will here be called syntagmatic.[24]

This analysis is, in my view, misplaced. Sacred sites were not the only places that were "semantically charged." Choay's interpretation gives power only to those sculpted signs on sites of ecclesiastical control like the cathedral or aristocratic privilege, like the *hôtel* or palace, totally neglecting what she calls the "mini-elements." Just as the maxi-elements contained important signs around doorways, windows and entrances, so too did ordinary house facades. Similarly, just as there were signs on the cathedral of Notre Dame that jutted out into the street itself, in the form of gargoyles that kept rainwater off the roof (see figure 1.5) and that had no individual significance, the streets of medieval Paris were penetrated by countless projecting signs, usually belonging to shops or trades, of quite specific significance and meaning. So it was not only at Notre Dame that the Parisian could see saints and sinners, devils, angels, and fantastic animals cavorting and projecting out into the profane world beyond. That profane world was itself marked by the same forms. Whereas the signboard is in a sense a framed picture, a plane set into the grid of geometrically observable signs in the modern city, the old sculptural signs, jutting out as they did onto the street-space itself, became one with the rubbed-up-against, quotidian chaos of the urban body-politic. It is not surprising that they have not survived in large numbers. As well as this important material aspect, the way such signs create a kind of mental map of modes of power is also important. The medieval imaginary was teeming with signs that differentiated one mini-element, that is, one house, from another. If the monument, the great cathedral for example, commands bodies and orders space, what of these smaller, vernacular signals? Do they too project their messages in order to construct conformity and identity?

In addition to ecclesiastical complexes, I also want to contrast these small urban signs to the sign systems of the aristocracy that were appearing all over the city in the same period—heraldic arms and blazons, which were the personal property of particular families and which announced more radically than any other sign in medieval culture the elision of image and identity.[25] The great town house of the nouveau-riche merchant Jacques Coeur in Bourges is all about the great ego of an "I." Life-size statues of servants look out of windows onto the street in expectation of the arrival of their master, like apostles waiting for the Last Judgment on a church tympanum, and the whole facade was filled with representations of the owner's mottoes, emblems, and arms.[26] The use of heraldry as a spectacular public form of visual display might, I think, have played a role in the creation of what Brigitte Bedos-Rezak has termed "the civic liturgies" developing in towns at the same time, but in resistance to rather than collusion with these aristocratic signs of self.[27]

Signs were of three types: the first two usual for house signs, the third for shops. The first type was sculpted three-dimensional wooden or sometimes stone images integral to the architecture because they functioned as either imposts, lintels, or corner buttresses known as *poteaux-cornieres*. In Paris the only extant example of such a sign in wood is a vertical sculpture nine meters high and now on display in the Musée Carnavelet, representing the Tree of Jesse surmounted by the Virgin Mary. An old drawing shows that it once formed part of the timber structure on a house at the corner of the rue Saint-Denis and the rue des Prêcheurs when it was known as the "Maison de l'arbre-aux-prêcheurs" (House of the Tree of the Preachers). This nomenclature suggests that it was viewed from a nonsacred subject position by the urban population.[28]

The second, less elaborate type was smaller, sculpted images that were either set above the door against the wall or placed in specially designed niches, known as "montjoies."[29] The third type consists of a flat board or sometimes an object suspended on a pole projecting out into the street. This type, traditional for commercial establishments like shops and taverns, will be discussed later.[30] One obvious function is to mark the dwelling, to make its location distinguishable and memorable. But whereas in the artificial *ars memorativa* one imagined houses or buildings and placed mnemonic signs within them in order to recall chains of words, the house signs served as actual mnemonic markers of space. Like all memory images they were supposed to be striking, even obscene, and sometimes involved puns and wordplay. As recently described by Francesca Canadé Sautman, signs were "a silent language of urban people," a "network of allusions and stories and popular experience that one cannot decipher without respecting the oral articulation of the pun." Sautman gives as an example the inn called "Au lion d'or" (The Golden Lion), which represented the shining beast, but when sounded out phonetically also meant "au lit on dort" (in bed where one sleeps).[31]

Another function would be magical, the sign seeking the protection of certain saints or even pre-Christian symbols like the sun.[32] Placing an animal skull over a doorway as protection was common in the earlier Middle Ages for domestic dwellings and the use of house signs has been related to this talismanic tradition. In contrast to this archaic residually magical function, there is the "modern" function of articulating a space of selfhood—the sign as identifying private property. In the case of house signs, the image usually did not refer to a particular person but to the place itself, which different individuals and generations could inhabit, taking on the associations of the place/sign while they dwelt there. In this respect, to use current terminology, signs were subject-positions to be assumed from within and not identities that were imposed from outside.

If there were three basic structural types of signs, there was an infinite variety of signs themselves. Almost all the signs in Paris are long since gone, but fiscal documents (mostly for tax purposes), beginning in the fourteenth century and continuing into the sixteenth, list houses by their names, providing historians with evidence of their spectacular variety.[33] Religious signs were the most common, most images of particular saints. Yves Papin, in what remains the only modern study of signs, in an article in *Archeologia* called "Les Enseignes médiévales: Un Langage pittoresque et médiévale," starts with the St. Julian image and makes an argument for extending it into the urban realm, Emile Mâle's notion of the "évangile de pierre" (gospel in stone). "Nothing was more familiar to the eyes of the Middle Ages," says this author, "than the Virgin, Christ, the angels, and saints."[34] But their transposition onto the facades of houses or in niches on corners of streets is surely more complex than extending the Bible metaphor to encompass the whole city. When a deranged soldier who sought to destroy one of these street-corner statues of the Virgin in 1418 was miraculously repulsed by the Virgin, her more sacredly secure sisters inside the church commemorated the Virgin's triumph over his outrage by burning him in effigy at that site each year on the anniversary of the event.[35]

I would argue that these signs actually present an alternative, protective population to those on altars in chapels inside or in niches outside the church. In Paris there was even a House of the Three Living and the Three Dead, a popular subject of church frescoes, but surely different in meaning once transposed onto the streets, where it was a sign without specific funerary associations.[36] Part of this difference can be seen in nomenclature itself. The Maison du sabot or the Maison du cheval blanc—both examples from the seventy-six known house names on three city blocks of the Ile de la Cité—make a direct association with a visual sign. But religious designations like the Maison de l'ymage Notre Dame or the Maison de l'ymaige Saint-Kristophe cannot directly designate site and saint. The house of Our Lady would be a church dedicated to the Virgin Mary, so that the phrase "image of" played a crucial role in drawing attention to the sign itself as representation of that saint. Two other interesting issues are raised in an examination of names in this part of Paris. First, the names of houses can change. One even suspects that the same visual sign, as it got worn and battered, perhaps less legible, was given a different designation. In this way a house called "des trois chandeliers" in 1257 received a new sign in 1423 when it became the "Cheval à louer," but when it was referred to as "des Sagittaires" in 1509, it may have been the same equestrian image that evoked a different name. The same is the case with the "chastel" (1369) getting a new coat of paint and becoming the "Chateau d'or" in 1613.[37] The proliferation of signs also meant that there was more than one sign of many of the saints. Another Maison de l'imaige Saint Julian existed on the rue de la Juiverie in this part of Paris, for example, as well as the Left Bank. His statue also graced the portal of the chapel of the hôpital Saint-Julien-des-Ménétriers, where he served to embody the boundaries of a sanctified space.[38] By contrast the saint on the house stood in a different relation both to his divine prototype and to the viewer, who came toward it not in pious contemplation but crossed its path in everyday, banal experience.

Such signs became the property of those they protected. Paris was also divided according to different trades practiced in various quarters and streets, each with their popular saint-protectors. Signs like those of St. Catherine or St. Julian functioned in a totally different way in the space of the street than they would in a church, watching over wheel makers in the case of St. Catherine and intimately linked with bodily production. Less iconic points of devotion than public stamps of approval, these images formed a network of interconnections related to trade and family associations rather than the text of the Bible or the golden legend. The sign of St. Julian is unusual in depicting not a single figure of the saint but a complex narrative in which Christ is in fact the central figure. Performing Christ's blessing for every visitor to the hostel, for every passerby, for the house and its caretakers (who occupy the subject-position of the saint and his wife), this sign worked on a far more practical and performative level in the economy of daily life than did similar images carved on or in the church. For in the church the sacred sign served to police the sacred space and delimit its boundaries.

Many houses had sculptural signs that did not partake of the aura of the sacred. A good example is the famous House of the Musicians at Reims. Here some of the very same sculptors who created the hundreds of statues for the cathedral in the middle of the thirteenth century also made life-size images of elegant courtly minstrels, which sat in their niches facing the street until the street was destroyed during the First World War (their remnants are now in the cathedral museum).[39] But in Reims as well as in Paris, after the images of saints the most common category of signs were those of animals, which included "au lion" and "au singe vert," and horses of all colors, because they carried persons, were commonly used for inns and hostels. Many described a fantastic menagerie of fabulous beasts using monstrous or mythological forms such as the Maison au griffon and the House of the Unicorn. There were at least two houses in Paris called the "Maison des marmousets." There was a *domus marmosetorum* already in the early thirteenth century, "ubi sunt duo marmoseti lapidei" or "marmouset," a word meaning a monkey-like idol or grotesque humanoid form and used to describe the figures squatting under the jamb on Gothic cathedrals like Notre Dame.[40] On the Île de la Cité there was a "rue des Marmousets" from 1206, so named after what a document of 1280 described as "two marmosets in stone."[41]

Quite remarkably, the monster rather than the saint creates place and has jurisdiction. This focus on the monstrous in the space of the city clearly has repercussions for how we think about the role of marginal images on sacred edifices. It was considered that such images usually went unnoticed and, significantly, compared to the named saints and narratives of the center, unnamed. But in the space of the city these forms take on as much valency and protective power as those on the church.

A number of known house signs were astrological or cosmological, such as the ubiquitous sun "au soleil d'or" and "à la lune." Others were more esoteric and referred to literary traditions like the God of Love (*Dieu d'amours*). But many of the wood-carved signs visible on houses were of animals and also had strongly sexual aspects, related to their magical or apotropaic function. An exotic bestiary of golden lions, dancing bears, fiddling cows, spinning sows, and green monkeys—the menagerie of the city—mingled the beasts of the fields for the trades of the metropolis in rich and complex ways. With their origins as animal skulls and other symbolic objects placed over thresholds, the house sign was part of a much older system of symbolic beliefs. Old houses were thought to be the abode of evil spirits, and in 1476 the Maison de l'ours et du lion on the rue des Marmousets was said to be haunted by a demon.[42] The distorted body of fantasy, the gargoyle and the chimera, thus could serve to protect the house, just as it did the cathedral. Similarly one finds obscene or scatological images on houses or boundary markings. A wooden carving of a man "mooning" passers-by did not give his name to the house in Angers where he performs his rude self-display, but he was part of the erotic dynamic of urban life that was also visible in Paris.[43] According to a description of the city written by Gilbert de Metz (ca. 1407–32), some of the city's most significant markers were not churches but carved stones like the "great stone of marvellous workmanship" on the Right Bank, "which is called the *Pet au Diable* (Fart of the Devil)."[44] One of the postmedieval signs in the Musée Carnavelet depicts a theme that we know from documents existed earlier, the sign of the "Truie qui file" (The Spinning Sow) from a house on the rue Saint Antoine. New apprentices and artisans from the neighborhood were "forcibly brought to kiss this sow, care being taken to smash their noses against the stone, and then until nightfall there was nothing but dancing, shouting, masquerades and bouts of drinking all through the neighbourhood."[45] Kissing the pig with all its associations of leprosy, death, and sex was part of an archaic *rite of passage* still played out on the streets of Paris in the early modern period.

Examples like this suggest that in thinking about the place that was the medieval city we have to enlarge our conception of public space to include this shared system of signs. As Steve Pile has described in his recent study of the modern metropolis *The Body and the City,* "Through fantasy, whether conscious or unconscious, the urbanized subject creates an imaginary urban landscape, which is constructed partly by the materiality of the city, partly by the modalities of identification, partly by defensive processes and partly by the 'contents' of the unconscious." [46] There was a taste in the fifteenth century for fantasies made up from street names and house signs, as evidenced in fiction called *Le Mariage des quatre fils Hémon et des filles de Dampsimon.* The four sons of Aymon was in fact a house sign as were their three brides, "The Three Daughters of Dan Symon," while other characters in the story were represented on religious signs like "The Three Kings," "The Man with Two Heads" (Janus), as well as the more popular ones like "The Wild Man" and "The Spinning Sow." [47] Just as statues are often described as the ghostly second population of the baroque city, the medieval city was peopled by signs; in this story the signs come to life for a great wedding so that the bride and bridegroom can appropriate the various good things they represent, the *couronne* (crown) from the courtyard of the Porte de Paris, the *gans* (gloves) from the rue des Asis, and being carried by three signs of strongmen, including Saint George de la rue des Barés in an interesting interplay of sacred and profane signs. The religious signs "The Cardinal" and "The Preacher" come into play during the ceremony itself, while for the wedding feast many of the fruits and animals form the fabulous food. Although there is no role for the little sign of Saint Julian on the rue Galande to play in this ritual of the representations, this work provides clear evidence of the currency of house signs of all types in Parisian culture.

Signs were also associated with status. That they carried powers of jurisdiction and were taken more seriously than decorations is suggested by the affair of the "Pet au Déable" that was celebrated by the poet François Villon. Police records also attest to the stealing of this infamous boundary stone from its owner, Mademoiselle de Bruyère, by students who carried it from the Right to the Left Bank. [48] An elaborate sign on one's house signaled wealth and status. A miniature of Dives and Lazarus, where the rich man's dwelling is open like a shop to reveal the riches within, has on its exterior marmosets and monsters in roundels (figure 1.6). As cities became more complex, the effort at social differentiation became more marked. This was not, as in our modern cities, a matter of property horizontally segregated by neighborhoods structured around property values, race, and class. Medieval Paris was not divided into rich and poor districts because every quarter had its poor, and people and families of very different means lived within a single building.[49] Except for the very rich like Dives, who could afford whole buildings, most small shopkeepers and workers rented tenement apartments. One of the most infamous of medieval Parisians, Nicolas Flamel, who made his will in 1416, made his vast wealth not as an alchemist as popularly thought, but, as Geremek showed, as a slum landlord, who built cheap housing for poor folk at exorbitant rents. Interestingly, Flamel inscribed edifying maxims on the front of his houses. One of them, engraved on a house built in 1407 on the rue de Montmerencey, contained a sculpted frieze containing images of himself and his wife Pernelle kneeling before the Trinity as well as French verses reminding those living in the upper floors that they were obliged to say the Pater Noster and the Ave Maria for the salvation of poor sinners.[50] Is it any wonder that modern advertising has utilized the imperatives of language, following Flamel's example, to make us buy and has not depended upon the open valency of the pictorial sign? Flamel's houses were typical of Parisian dwellings of the time; the ground floor was occupied by a shop, workshop, or inn, and the upper stories (of what were often three- and four-story buildings) were rented out to poorer people. A much later house on the rue Volta is one of the very few still extant that shows us how high medieval Parisian structures actually were.[51] The higher one lived in medieval Paris, the lower one's social position. On the wealthier street level, the place of productivity and of public life, or just above it, signs served to propagate the image of the urban fabric as rich and productive.

If we look at the "image" of the city as represented in medieval art, it is interesting to see how signs appear mostly in French and English contexts as part of the standard way of representing urbanity.[52] In the famous city labeled "Constantine" in the Luttrell Psalter, actually a depiction of a Rogation Day procession around the walls of the city of Stamford in Lincolnshire, the mercantile signs of the inn and projecting signs of shops actually compete with the cross that surmounts the church at its center.[53] Another interesting manuscript image, this time made in Paris

Figure 1.6. The rich man Dives and the poor man Lazarus. Paris, Bibliothèque Nationale Ms. fr. 178 fol. 67. Copyright Bibliothèque Nationale de France, Paris; reprinted courtesy of the Bibliothèque Nationale de France.

itself, is a miniature from Thomas de Saluce's romance, *Le Chèvalier errant* and shows well-dressed courtly couples out shopping on the cobbled streets and markets of Paris (figure 1.7).[54] The cross here has become just another marker among a multiplicity of signs and is no longer at the center of the space. It marks a site where a vender of chickens and onions can present her wares for sale and is overshadowed by both the bustle of the stalls and shops and the circular sign representing a tavern or cabaret on the right that juts out before the door.[55]

SIGNS AND COMMERCE

Compared to house signs, which were for the most part arbitrary in their signification, shop signs had to announce things for sale or services offered. Originally the merchants suspended the actual objects produced as signs: a loaf of bread for a baker, a *plat a barbe* for the barber, or a pot on the end of a long pole for a potter. Throughout Europe branches of vegetation had long been wound in a circle and suspended on a pole to indicate places where wine was sold, such as that visible in the fifteenth-century Parisian miniature (see figure 1.7).[56] These natural objects of decomposable material gradually came to be replaced by more permanent images. Shops were structured as an opening, with shutters coming down to form the counter *(étal)* while the top shutter *(auvent)* protected goods from sun and rain. The main reason for names not being used, in my view, was not the lack of literacy among the urban population, but the way in which signs were organized to articulate occupation and social position, rather than personal identity. Signs of métiers could be quasi-religious, such as the sign of St. Lawrence's grill by roast-meat sellers and the sign of St. Martin for inns, but most were based upon the similitude of services or goods sold, such as a shoe for a cobbler.[57] In distinct areas of the city where similar shops were grouped together, the spicers, armorers, and furriers often gave their names to streets. The famous *Vie de Saint Denis* manuscript of 1316, showing the bridges of Paris, also shows various trades but with no signs in sight.[58] In a sense, these laboring artisans represented performative signs using their own bodies because they produced their goods in open view of passersby. One did not need to see the sign of three platters hanging up to signal a barber because he was visible, just as in a famous miniature of a street scene from a manuscript of Gilles de Rome's *Livre du gouvernement des princes*.[59]

This late fifteenth-century miniature shows the introduction of written signs advertising "Bon Ipocras" (sugared wine) at the stall of a "confiseur" patissier. Artisans and shopkeepers lived on the ground floor and, according to the ordinance of the city's guilds, worked "on the street, their window or door ajar." [60] The 120 regulated crafts are described in the *Livre de métiers* of Étienne Boileau in 1268, and interestingly the manuscript of this important document contains marginal signs alongside each craft, which shows how this association of certain images with certain crafts had already created something of an industrial iconography by the thirteenth century. [61] The fact that these tradesmen also had their own corporate and sometimes even individual signs in the form of seals is also something that needs to be explored more fully in relation to this self-signaling mercantile association. [62] The tax list of 1292 lists 366 shoemakers, 151 barbers, 45 purse makers, 33 painters, 24 sculptors, 21 woodcarvers, and the proliferation of signs must have surely had something to do with the increasing competition between the 151 barbers, who would have sought to make each particular establishment significant and different from others by using a vivid sign or appropriating one in a rented dwelling that already existed. [63]

Figure 1.7. Thomas de Saluces, *Le Chevalier errant* (Atelier du maître de la Cité des dames). Paris, 1400–1405, Bibliothèque Nationale Ms. fr. 12559 fol. 167. Copyright Bibliothèque Nationale de France, Paris; reprinted courtesy of the Bibliothèque Nationale de France.

Other reasons for the increasing number of projecting signs in late medieval cities include the darkness and narrowness of many streets that made it difficult to see either craftsmen at work in the dark recesses or any signs placed flat against the buildings. Such a narrow passageway, sometimes only a few feet wide, would make it difficult to see an individual house or where one began and the other ended. Sometimes there was an overproliferation of signs. A London act of 1375, repeated in the *Liber albus* compiled in 1419, ordained that

> [W]hereas the ale stakes projecting in front of taverns in Chepe, and elsewhere in the said city, extend too far over the king's highways to the impeding of riders and others, and by reason of the excessive weight, to the great deterioration of the houses on which they are placed; to the end that opportune remedy might be made thereof, it was by the mayor and alderman granted and ordained and upon summons of all the taverners of the said city, it was enjoyed upon them, under pain of paying forty pence unto the Chamber of the Guildhall, on every occasion upon which they should transgress such ordinance, that no one of them in future should have a stake bearing either his sign, or leaves, extending or lying over the King's highway of greater length than seven feet at most . . .[64]

Another great source of evidence about house signs in the later Middle Ages are the title pages of early printed books (figure 1.8). The advent of printing in the late fifteenth century did not result in what Victor Hugo described in *Notre Dame de Paris* when he said "the book will kill the building."[65] Indeed, the book pointed to the building in a system of early advertising. The house sign of the printing establishment was often depicted on the title page of the printed work, linking social place with the book. Once again the proliferation of signs caused problems. Jocodus Badius of Paris wrote, "We beg the reader to notice the sign, for there are men who have adopted the same title, and the name of Badius, and so filch our labour." For Benedict Hector of Bologna: "Purchaser, be aware when you wish to buy books issued from my printing office. Look at my sign which is represented on the title page, and you can never be mistaken. For some evil-disposed printers have affixed my name to their uncorrected and faulty works, in order to secure a better sale price for them."[66]

Figure 1.8. Title page of a book printed by Geoffroy Tory in Paris "at the sign of the Pot Casse," 1530.

All this evidence suggests that for urban dwellers in the Middle Ages signs were a part of the texture and negotiation of everyday life. In the very spaces of the Left Bank traversed by these images, students and masters at the University of Paris debated the nature of signs in the philosophical sense. Roger Bacon in his *Compendium of the Study of Theology* and his *De signis* used the example of the street sign in discussing the relationship between the imposition of signs by human agency and natural signs imposed by God. "A foreign traveler, seeing a circle, goes into a wine shop and, granted there would be no wine, yet the circle was a sign for him. Therefore, whether there be wine or not, the circle remains in the character of a sign." [67] But Bacon rejects this explanation because it assumes the theory that signs "at pleasure" (ad placitum) are imposed without reference to the existence or nonexistence of their significates and offers the counterclaim that reimposes the circle for what he only imagines to be wine. "Rather, the traveler, unaware of the absence of wine, would imagine wine in the shop, and once, granted, false wine is imagined, he constitutes the circle a sign for himself by his new intuition; and hence the character of a sign is renewed." Bacon's explanation is an appeal to equivocal signification because the significates of the original imposition are radically different, i.e., real and imagined wine. In De signis Bacon adds a further note that the new imposition is an act of imagination.[68] Here are signs then that go against the whole Augustinian notion of intelligibility—for they are signs that can point at nothing, leading only to themselves. As opposed to the sacred signs, discussed elsewhere by Bacon, these have forgotten themselves and no longer point to paths of eschatological or exigetical order in the imaginary. It is not by accident that Bacon, who taught at the University of Paris from 1245, chose this particular form of visual signification to make his argument about the conventionality of certain kinds of signification, living as he did in the city of signs par excellence.

One navigated in the medieval city not only through visual signs but also using other sensory pathways—most notably sound and smell. Sounds, such as those of the interminable "crieurs de Paris," filled the streets as well as the Latin jabber of students signaling that one was on the Left Bank.[69] Certain districts were pungent: fish merchants along the river, butchers on the Right Bank, and most of all the stink of the tanners. The best place to go today to get a sense of what a medieval city like Paris felt and smelt like—its flows of pedestrians, donkeys, and bright colors— is a city like Fez, in Morocco, where the tanning district spreads its distinctive odors through the whole quarter. Dyed skins are pounded by half-naked workers in vats hollowed out of the streets themselves and are laid on roofs to dry. But there is one thing not visible in the intense odoriferousness of the labyrinthine streets of Fez that is crucial to my argument about Paris. Françoise Choay describes how in spite of apparent similarities with the medieval syntagma

> the fundamental difference consists in the lack of difference among Moroccan facades. . . . Poor and rich have the same facades and doors, so that a foreigner has no means of identi-

fying the district where he strolls (he would have to decipher the symbolic positions of the women standing on the thresholds of the houses). This visual homogeneity corresponds to the fact that in Arab society there is no pattern of authority . . . nothing but chains of influence connected with polyfunctional individuals whose powers and abilities are numerous and not clearly defined.[70]

Already, then, the Western medieval city is a system of clear demarcations and controlled perimeters, its signs producing spaces where particular classes congregate and do business. Signs not only indicated place but also position and caste; butchers are lower than goldsmiths because of the status differences between blood and gold.

SIGNS AND DESIRE

One of the most evocative of all Atget's photographs of old Paris, of a postmedieval sign, is one he took as part of a series recording "Enseignes et veilles boutiques de Paris," inspired by the antiquarian publications on Parisian signs by Fournier and Beaupaire. It shows the "Maison a l'homme armée" at 25 rue des Blanc Manteaux in which the waiter stares out at us from behind the glass, the new transparent medium.[71] Here the shop window overtakes the opaque sign as the locus of the gaze of desire and commodification in what Walter Benjamin immortalized as the Paris of the nineteenth century. This juxtaposition leads me to ask one final question: were street signs of the medieval imaginary like our own urban spaces where desire is stimulated and played out? When I photographed the St. Julian sign in 1989, the little cinema on the rue Galande was showing the film version of Jean Genet's *Querelle,* and below it the poster displayed for this movie set up some interesting tensions between fourteenth-century nautical imagery and the twentieth-century homoerotic image of the sailor. The tempestuous sea of the world becomes a site of endlessly deferred desire for the modern Parisian flaneur, as opposed to the resting place of the medieval pilgrim.

Paris, described by many historians as the first Western metropolis in the modern sense, was already a center of commodification, fashion, and self-display in this period and did not have to wait until Benjamin's

Paris of the arcades in order to display conspicuous consumption on its streets.[72] The miniature, from as early as 1400, includes in the top right corner an inn with its circle of leaves and in the middle many commodities being sold in various stalls, but also in the right foreground two nobles, a man and a woman dressed in their finery, who are out "window" shopping in an age before shops had windows (see figure 1.7). This spectacular commodification is already evident in Jean de Jandun's *Tractatus de laudibus Pariisus* of 1323, which contains, along with a description of the university area and the churches, a description of the merchandise for sale in the Halles des Champeaux that is of such variety that the writer does not know the words in Latin to describe them.[73] Desire is always in excess of language, which is what makes the street sign crucial evidence in the history of desire. Are these two medieval flaneurs?

According to Susan Buck-Morss, the flaneur is seduced by the world of appearances, by the ever-increasing frenzy of movement of capital, people, and commodities. "Trapped in the spectacle of the urban modern as a child in the mirror, the flaneur could not see beyond the glass to bourgeois values etched into the tain of the city. The streets had become a hall of mirrors, of shop windows, which framed, reproduced, and distorted every desire and pleasure: this is commodity fetishism, the erotics of consumption, produced in situ."[74] The commercial signs of the medieval city were surely part of this new capacity of images to evoke desire for material goods, to promise what Roger Bacon had described, by imposition of the imagination.

Finally, I want to return to the rue Galande, but also to a text written by one of its inhabitants in the thirteenth century, Jean de Galande, better known as John of Garland. A chapter of his treatise on student behavior, the *Morale scolarium*, opens with his admonition to students to "Regard as models of deportment the graven images of the churches which you should carry in your mind as living and indelible pictures."[75] Garland was here advocating the use of images as models of behavior and desire in a way that suggests that people modeled themselves on the fashionable forms and poses of images. The only comparable models in modern Paris would be the fashion mannequins in the store windows, which strike me as the phantasmic equivalents of the stone Gothic virgins and saints, like the statue of an apostle now in the Musée de Cluny from the facade of St. Jacques de l'Hopital, 1326–27.[76] The mannequin and the statue are models of action in the way that the house signs were not; rather than dictating fashion or deportment they are open for constant redefinition. Were the sculpted house signs like that of St. Julian and his wife similarly models of and models for bodily comportment and social interaction? Surely the very closeness of such images to people's everyday experience makes them more available, not only as signs for the body, but also as articulations of the dwelling as itself a kind of corporeal container.

This observation brings me to another aspect—how space is gendered. In a recent discussion of the house and home as the domestic sphere of women, architectural historian Mark Wigley makes much of the metaphor of the body as a building. He cites the fourteenth-century Parisian physician Henri de Mondeville who describes the body as a house, "the house of the soul, which like any house can only be maintained as such by constant surveillance of its openings. The woman's body is seen as an inadequate enclosure because its boundaries are convoluted . . . turned inside-out."[77] Peter Stallybrass has argued that "the surveillance of women concentrated upon three specific areas: the mouth, chastity, and the threshold of the house. These three areas were frequently collapsed into one another."[78] Entrances and interiors are female, especially churches, and even whole cities.[79] If sacred and enclosed space was coded feminine as a number of studies have shown, the unexplored area of the street, I would argue, was masculine. Not only because it was where public men went out to do business leaving wives and daughters at home, but because its very signs were art of a network of phallic significations; the only women who could roam freely in Paris were the "women of the streets," the "filles de joie," and then only in certain regulated and prescribed areas. One of these very near the rue Galande was on or near the "Abreuvoir de Mascon," a fountain or drinking trough that marked the area where in 1419, according to tax documents, there lived many "filles de joie et amoureuses."[80]

Not everyone had equal access to the streets, nor did everyone share the same license to look. Although the fifteenth-century poet Françoise Villon was fascinated by street signs and often wrote about them, he was no Baudelairian flaneur, a position only really possible in Haussmannian boulevards and spectacular Benjaminian arcades of modern metropolis. The flaneur's gaze is one of nostalgia, of loss, in which the constant search for gratification is never assuaged, the very opposite of the semisacral and certainly magical signs that made the medieval city a quite different site of spectacle and desire. Its signs were not only cut in stone but also marked on bodies, moving through the space itself: the yellow triangle or circle signaling a Jew, the stripes a prostitute, the brown habit and rope belt a Franciscan.[81] In addition to these signs of surveillance and ominous "marking-out," the general population also wore badges, often of a highly suggestive sexual nature made of lead or pewter that are an enormous undisclosed category of visual evidence about medieval self-presentation in terms of race, class, and gender that scholars are just beginning to explore.[82] In a space so inhabited by static signs, the living inhabitants become signs too. In an early fifteenth-century English miniature of the travels of Marco Polo, a prostitute is painted using her body as a signal to entice a male traveler into an inn, or, as one scholar has suggested even more explicitly, a brothel, which was identified by a white signboard that was obviously not enough.[83] The relation between the body and private versus public space, studied by Diane Shaw from medieval London documents, also suggests that "the body was part and parcel of the private landscape of property."[84]

In his analysis of the postmodern city, Henri Lefebvre, the most influential theorist and historian of space in our century, describes the radical transformation of signs in modernity into what he calls "the world of signs and images": "Images and signs of history, of authenticity, of style. Signs of the world: of the other world . . ." He uses very negative terms where "talk of beauty refers to brand images." "The world of images as signs," he goes on, "exercises a fascination, skirts or submerges problems, and diverts attention from the 'real'—i.e., from the possible. While occupying space, it also signifies space, substituting a mental and therefore abstract space for spatial practice—without, however, doing anything really to unify those spaces that it seems to combine in the abstraction of signs and images. Differences are replaced by differential signs, so that produced differences are supplanted in advance by differences which are induced—and reduced to signs."[85]

This bleak regime of the empty sign perfectly describes the workings of modern advertising, but I would see this system as quite different from the way signs functioned in the medieval metropolis and in the medieval urban imaginary. While we might see relations between multinational advertising and the messages that made up the exterior and interior place that was the cathedral of Notre Dame, the city streets were a realm of more elastic and self-generated signification. The spectacular signs of modernity do not create a truly shared public space but are always geared toward the private psyche, the monadic consumer caught up in his or her own desire. The fantasy that is generated in the medieval city is, in contrast, not rooted in subjectivity nor is it akin to the "group fantasy" by which Deleuze describes the mesmerization of the "great gregarious masses" in modernity.[86] We might refer to what is created here as "public fantasy," not in opposition to anything in the private realm, but in the medieval sense of the word "public" that sees the *res publica* as that which belonged to the community as a whole and was exempted from commercial exchange.[87] The materiality of the medieval house sign provides us with an alternative paradigm of the image and its construction of place and subjectivity in medieval culture, one that is quite distinct from other regimes of the sign, either sacred or heraldic. Before their eradication by the centralizing and ruthlessly quantifying urban grids constructed by the modern French state, the house signs of medieval Paris marked sites of multiple and shifting identities, places and communities, shared structures of the imaginary, which were not imposed from above or outside, but which were articulated from within the teeming multiplicity of the body politic itself.

NOTES

This chapter is part of an ongoing larger project to be entitled *Sculpture, Signs, and Streetlife in Medieval France.*

1. The sign is most fully discussed and its historical documentation presented in Adolphe Berty, continued by Lazare Maurice Tisserand, *Topographie historique de Vieux Paris: Region centrale de l'université* (Paris: Imprimerie Nationale, 1897), p. 166, where the sign is reproduced in an engraving on p. 167. Other important early literature includes Clément de Ris (comte L.), *Les Veilles Enseignes de Paris extrait des Mélanges de la Société des Bibliophiles, 1869* (1877), pp. 6–7; Charles Fegdal, *Les Vielles enseignes de Paris* (Paris: Figuière, 1913), pp. 185–86; *Procès-verbaux de la Commission municipale du Vieux Paris* (16 June 1909), pp. 68–69; François Boucher, *Les Enseignes de Paris, gravées à l'eau forte par Jean-Julles Dufour* (Paris: Le Goupy, 1924), pp. 12–16; Amédée Boinet, *Les Eglises Parisiens* (Paris: Éditions de Minuit, 1958), pp. 203–6. Two recent descriptions that reproduce the relief are Jean-Pierre Willesme, *Enseignes du Musée Carnavelet—histoire de Paris: Catalogue raisonné* (Paris: Musées, 1995), no. 3, pp. 19–20; and, most recently, Laure Beaumont-Maillet, *Guide du Paris médiéval* (Paris: Hazan, 1977), pp. 95–96.

2. For the erroneous view that the sculpture once decorated the church, see Berty's original assertion, in *Topographie historique*, p. 301, corrected by Tisserand in a footnote on the same page; see also, Georges Poisson, *Évocation du grand Paris*, ed. Jacques Hillairet, 3 vols. (Paris: Editions de Minuit, 1956–61), p. 549; for the 1380 document see Berty, p. 166.

3. Berty, *Topographie historique*, p.166.

4. Berty, ibid., cites a 1413 document giving "quatre vingts escus d'or à la couronne, de vingt deux solz, six deniers tournois chascun."

5. See Molly Nesbit, *Atget's Seven Albums* (New Haven and London: Yale University Press, 1992), pp. 382–96; Naomi Schor, "*Cartes Postales:* Representing Paris 1900," *Critical Inquiry* 18 (1992): 188–244; and Alice Kaplan and Kristen Ross, *Yale French Studies*, no. 73 (1987), special issue on "Everyday Life."

6. Paul Arthur and Romedi Pasini, *Wayfinding: People, Signs, and Architecture* (New York: McGraw-Hill, 1992).

7. For the regulations on street names in Paris, see le Cler-du Brillet, *Continuation du traité de police*, IV (Paris, 1738), pp. 327, 347, and the useful chronology presented in Willesme, *Enseignes*, pp. 12–14.

8. For house signs in Paris see Adolphe Berty, *Etudes archéologiques*, 12 (1855), pp. 5–6, and the literature cited above in n. 1, but most usefully Edouard Fournier, *Histoire des enseignes de Paris* (Paris: E. Dentu, 1884), p. 30, who describes their explosion in the fourteenth century. An abridged but less useful edition has recently been published, *Paris par ses enseignes* (Paris: Editions La Bibliotheque, 1994). For house signs in general in the Middle Ages, see E. de la Querière, *Recherches historiques sur les enseignes de maisons particulières* (Paris, 1852) and Jean-Pierre Leguay, *La Rue au Moyen Age* (Rennes: Éditions Ouest-France, 1984), pp. 104–10. The best illustrated discussion is Yves d. Papin, "Les Enseignes médievales: Un Langage pittoresque et universel," *Archeologia* 69 (1979): 37–42. The use of signs is of course an ancient precedent, see Roger Ling, "Street Plaques at Pompeii," in *Architecture and Architectural Sculpture in the Roman Empire*, ed. Martin Henig (Oxford: Oxford University Press 1990), pp. 51–56.

9. Louis Sieber and Edgar Maruse, "Description de Paris par Thomas Platter le Jeune de Bâle [1599]," *Mémore de la Société de l'histoire de Paris et de l'Ile-France* 23 (1896): 189.

10. For the rue Galande, in addition to Berty, *Topographie historique*, p. 156, see Auguste Andre Coussillan, *Dictionnaire historique des rues de Paris, par Jacques Hillairet*, 8th ed. (Paris: Editions Minuit, 1985); and Jean Lebeuf, *Histoire de la ville et de tout le diocese de Paris*, I (Paris: Fechoz et Letouzey, 1883), p. 299.

11. See Willesme, *Enseignes*.

12. *Acta Sanctorum*, Jan., tom. II, col. 974. For the saint's legend, see *The Golden Legend of Jacobus de Voragine*, translated and adapted from the Latin by Granger Ryan and Helmut Ripperger (1941; reprint, New York: Arno Press, 1969), pp. 130–31; Paul Perdrizet, *Le Calendrier Parisien a la fin du Moyen Age d'apres le Breviares et les Livres d'Heures* (Paris: Les Belles Lettres, 1933), pp. 95–96, who reproduces the St. Julian sign as figure 9; and Louis Réau, *Iconographie de l'art chrétien*, II (Paris: Presses Universitaires de France, 1958), pp. 766–69.

13. See Victor Leroquais, *Les Livres d'heures manuscrits de la Bibliothèque Nationale*, vol. 1 (Paris: Macon Protat Freres, 1927), p. 79, plate LIII.

14. For the social meaning of leprosy, see the useful treatment by Francesca Canadé Sautman, *La Religion du quotidien: Rites et croyances populaires de la fin du Moyen Age* (Firenze: L. S. Olschki, 1995), pp. 182–93. A leper appears at the gate of the Right Bank in the *Vie de Saint Denis*, Paris BN fr. 2090–92, reproduced in Virginia Wylie Egbert, *On the Bridges of Medieval Paris: A Record of Early Fourteenth-Century Life* (Princeton: Princeton University Press, 1974).

15. See the list of examples from French texts given in Paul Meyer, "De l'alliteration en roman de France," *Romania* 11 (1882), p. 577.

16. Chaucer, general prologue to *The Canterbury Tales*, in *The Riverside Chaucer*, ed. L. D. Benson (Boston: Houghton Mifflin, 1987), ll. 339–40; and for Sir Gawain, *The Poems of the Pearl Manuscript*, ed. Malcolm Andrew and Ronald Waldron (Berkeley: University of California Press, 1978, 1982). I am grateful to David Wallace for these references.

17. Two examples would be the so-called "House of Adam" at Angers, which has a depiction of Adam and Eve as a couple on the "poteaux cornière," described in Péan de la Tuillere, *Description de la ville d'Angers* (Angers, 1778; Marseille: Laffitte Reprints, n.d.), pp. 148–49; and the later carving of the House of Vannes and his wife at Vannes, Brittany.

18. See Brigitte Bedos-Rezak, *Corpus des sceaux francais du Moyen Age. I: Les Sceaux des villes* (Paris: Imprimerie Nationale, 1980), p. 515; H. H. Brindley; "The Ships of the Seal of Paris," *Proceedings of the Cambridge Antiquarian Society,* (1915–16), pp. 120–47.

19. Georges Ritter, *Les Vitraux de la cathedral de Rouen: XIIIe, XIVe, et XVe siècles* (Cognac, Charente: Impression d'art des établissements FAC, 1926), p. 42, plates IX–XI.

20. For inn signs as distinct from sacred signs, see Barrie Cox, *English Tavern Names* (Nottingham: Center for English Name Studies, 1994); and Bryant Lillywhite, *London Signs* (London, 1972). For other countries, see Hans Conrad Peyer, *Viaggiare nel Medioevo dall'opsitalità alla locanda* (Hannover: Editori Laterza, 1990), pp. 245–47; on the importance of inns more generally, Philippe Wolff, "L'Hôtellerie, auxiliaire de la route; Note sur les hôtelleries toulousaines au Moyen Age," *Bulletin philologique et historique,* 1 (1960): 189–205; and the essays collected in Hans Conrad Peyer, *Gastfreundschaft, Taverne, und Gasthaus im Mittelalter* (Munich: R. Oldenbourg 1983).

21. I am thinking of Lawrence M. Bryant, *The King and the City in the Parisian Royal Entry Ceremony* (Geneva: Libraire Droz, 1986) and the essays collected in *City and Spectacle in Medieval Europe,* ed. Barbara A. Hanawalt and Kathryn L. Reyerson, (Minneapolis: University of Minnesota Press, 1994); especially Elizabeth A. R. Brown and Nancy Freeman Regalado, "*La Grant Feste:* Philip the Fair's Celebration of the Knighting of his Sons in Paris at Pentecost of 1313," pp. 56–89.

22. Louis Wirth, "Urbanism as a Way of Life," in *Classic Essays on the Culture of Cities,* ed. Richard Sennett (New York: Appleton-Century-Crofts, 1969), pp. 143–64, at p. 155.

23. Edward S. Casey, *The Fate of Place: A Philosophical History* (Berkeley: University of California Press, 1997), pp. 103–15.

24. Françoise Choay, "Urbanism and Semiology," in *The City and the Sign: An Introduction to Urban Semiotics,* ed. M. Gottdiener and Alexandros Ph. Lagopoulos, (New York: Columbia University Press, 1986), p. 165.

25. The best pathway through the vast literature is that provided by Michel Pastoureau, *Traité d'héraldique: Grands manuels* (Paris: Picard, 1979).

26. See Michael Camille, *Gothic Art: Glorious Visions* (New York: Abrams, 1997), figures 45 and 46; and Michel Mollat, *Jacques Coeur, ou L'Esprit d'enterprise au XVe siècle* (Paris: Auber, 1988).

27. Brigitte Bedos-Rezak, "Civic Liturgies and Urban Records in Northern France 1100–1400," in *City and Spectacle in Medieval Europe*, ed. Barbara A. Hanawalt and Kathryn L. Reyerson, (Minneapolis: University of Minnesota Press, 1994), pp. 34–56.

28. Jean-Pierre Willesme, *Sculptures médiévales (XIIe siècle–début du XVIe siècle)* (Paris: Musée Carnavelet, 1979), no. 8, pp. 28–29; and Willesme, Enseignes, no. 3.

29. See Leguay, *La Rue au Moyen Age*, pp. 98–10.

30. Jacob Larwood and John Camden Hotten, *The History of Signboards from the Earliest Times* (London: Chatto and Windus, 1898); Ernst Grohne, *Die Hausnamen und Hauszeichen* (Gottingen, 1912).

31. Sautman, *Religion du quotidien*, pp. 2–3.

32. Christopher A. Faraone, *Talismans and Trojan Horses: Guardian Statues in Ancient Greek Myth and Ritual* (Oxford: Oxford University Press, 1992), pp. 22–23, for guardians of the house.

33. See, for example, *Comptes du domaine de la ville de Paris: 1 (1424–1457)*, ed. A. Vidier, L. Le Grand, and P. Dupieux (Paris: Imprimerie Nationale, 1948).

34. Papin's statement in "Les Enseignes," p. 38, is surely influenced by the work of Emile Mâle, *L'Art religieux du XIIIe siècle en France* (Paris, 1898), translated by Harry S. Bober as *Religious Art in France, the Thirteenth Century: A Study in Medieval Iconography and Its Sources*, ed. H. Bober, Bollingen Series 90 (Princeton: Princeton University Press, 1984).

35. Edouard Fournier, *Chroniques et légendes des rues de Paris* (Paris: E. Dentu, 1893), pp. 364–65; Sautman, *Religion du quotidien*, p. 3; Gilles Corrozet, *Antiquitez de Paris* (Paris: N. Bonfons, 1586), p. 138v. For a 1633 engraving of the 1418 event, see Yvan Christ, *Eglises Parisiennes actuelles et disparues* (Paris: Tel, 1947), plate 96.

36. For the House of the Three Living and Three Dead, see Berty, *Topographie historique*, 1: 160; and for the theme in art, P. Chihaia, "Le Roman de Barlaam et Joasaph et l'origine de 'la recontre des trois vifs et des trois morts'" in his *Immortalité et decomposition dans l'art du moyen âge* (Madrid, 1988).

37. These examples are taken from the study by Adolphe Berty, "Trois Ilots de la Cité," *Revue archeologique* 14 (1860): 197–215.

38. See Yvan Christ, *Eglises Parisiennes*, plate 89.

39. Georges Boussinesq and Gustav Laurent, *Histoire de Reims*, tom. I (Reims: Marot Braine, 1933), pp. 348–49; Luke Demaison, *Congrès archéologique de France*, tom. I, 87th session (Paris: Société française d'archeologie, 1911), pp. 127–37; and Christoph-Hellmut Mahling, "Das Haus der Musikanten in Reims," *Festschrift für Walter Wiora, zum 30 Dezember 1966*, ed. L. Finscher and C.-Hellmut Mahling (Kassel: Bärenveites, 1967), pp. 250–63.

40. G. de Poerck, "Marmouset: Histoire d'un mot," *Revue belge de philologie et d'histoire* 37, no. 3 (1940): 615–44.

41. Benjamin Guérard, *Cartulaire de l'église de Notre-Dame de Paris* (Paris: Imprimerie de Crapelet, 1850), 3: 278.

42. Paris, Arch. Nat., X ia 4817 fol. 176v, discussed in Pierre Champion, *François Villon: Sa vie et sons temps*, 2 vols. (Paris: H. Champion, 1913), p. 211.

43. Tricouillard, as he is called, is reproduced in Claude Gaignebet and Jean-Dominique Lajoux, *Art profane et religion populaire au Moyen Age* (Paris: Presses Universitaires de France, 1985), p. 201.

44. Le Roux de Lincy and L. M. Tisserand, *Le Paris de Charles V et de Charles VI vu par des écrivains contemporains* (Paris: Imprimerie Impériale, 1867), p. 201; also discussed by Champion, *François Villon*, p. 55, and Jean Favier, *François Villon* (Paris: Fayard, 1982), pp. 145–51.

45. Edmond Beaurepaire, "Les Enseignes de Paris," *Le Carnet* (October and December, 1902), p. 26; Willesme, *Enseignes*, p. 79, no. 123. For the ritual, see Jubinal, *Mystères inédits, du XVe siècle* (Paris: Techener, 1837), 1: 375; *Le Marais: mythe et réalité* (Paris: Hôtel de Sully, 1987), p. 255; and Sautman, *Religion du quotidien*, p. 40.

46. Steve Pile, *The Body and the City: Psychoanalysis, Space, and Subjectivity* (London: Routledge, 1996), p. 236.

47. First published by Achille Jubinal, *Mystères inédits du XVe siècle*, 1: 369–76; it is also discussed in Fournier, *Histoire des enseignes*, pp. 57–64; and Champion, *François Villon*, 1: 61–64. In addition to the analysis by Sautman, *Religion quotidien*, p. 8; see also Nancy Freeman Regalado, "Effet de Réel, Effét du Réel: Representation and Reference in Villon's *Testament*," *Yale French Studies* 70 (1986), p. 72.

48. Champion, *François Villon*, p. 54; and Jean Favier, *François Villon* (Paris: Fayard 1982), pp. 145–51.

49. Bronislaw Geremek, *The Margins of Society in Late Medieval Paris* (Cambridge: Cambridge University Press, 1987), pp. 69–79.

50. Le Roux de Lincy and L. M. Tisserand, *Le Paris de Charles V et de Charles VI vu par des écrivains contemporains* (Paris: Imprimerie Impériale, 1867; reprint, Caen: Paradigme, 1992), pp. 457–58; Marcel Aubert, *La Maison dite de Nicholas Flamel rue Montmorency à Paris* (Nîmes: C. Lacour, 1992), p. 13; Geremek, *Margins of Society*, pp. 80–81.

51. For the house on the rue Volta, see Beaumont-Maillet, *Guide du Paris médiéval*, p. 61; for the size and height of medieval structures, see S. Roux, "L'Habitat urbain au Moyen Age: Le Quartier de l'Université à Paris," *Annales, Économies, Sociétés, Civilisations* 24 (1969): 1195–219; and the richly illustrated handbook by Pierre Garrigou Grandchamp, *Demeures Médiévales: Coeur de la cité* (Paris: Desclee de Brouwer, 1994).

52. Chiara Frugoni, *A Distant City: Images of Urban Experience in the Medieval World*, trans. William McCuaig (Princeton: Princeton University Press, 1991); Pierre Lavedan, *La Répresentation des villes dans l'art du Moyen Age* (Paris: Vanoest, 1954). Other general studies include Andre Chedeville, Jacques Le Goff, and Jacques Rossiaud, *La ville médiévale des Carolingians à la Renaissance*, vol. 2 of *Histoire de la France urbaine*, ed. Georges Duby (Paris: Seuil, 1980–85); and the section on urban space in Georges Duby, *A History of Private Life II: Revelations of the Medieval World* (Cambridge and London: Harvard University Press, 1988), pp. 438–505.

53. See Eric Millar, *The Luttrell Psalter* (London: The British Museum, 1932), plate 162; and Michael Camille, *Mirror in Parchment: The Luttrell Psalter and the Making of Medieval England* (Chicago: University of Chicago Press, 1998), pp. 273–74.

54. For this manuscript, see Millard Meiss, *French Painting in the Time of Jean de Berry: The Limbourgs and Their Contemporaries* (London: Phaidon, 1974), p. 381.

55. H. Martin, "La Fonction polyvalente des croix à la fin du Moyen Age," *Annales de Bretagne et des Pays de l'Ouest*, 90 (1983): 95–113; on crosses in Paris see Michael Camille, *Master of Death: The Lifeless Art of Pierre Remiet Illuminator* (New Haven and London: Yale University Press, 1996), p. 239.

56. See the documents listed in Sautman, *Religion quotidien*, pp. 4–5; and Pierre Turpin, "L'Escoive ou l'escouve dans la language juridique et de la toponymie du Nord de la France," *Revue du Nord* XXII (1936): 204–16.

57. For St. Lawrence, see Sautman, *Religion du quotidien*, p. 3; for a stone sign of a cobbler in Cordes, see Chedeville et al., *La Ville medievale*, p. 255.

58. *Vie de Saint Denis*, Paris, BN fr, 2090–92; Egbert, *Bridges of Medieval Paris*.

59. Henry Martin, *Les Principaux Manuscrits à peintures de la Bibliothèque de l'Arsenal* (Paris: Imprimerie Nationale 1929), plate LXXXV, p. 61.

60. R. de Lespinasse and F. Bonnardot, *Les Métiers et corporations de la ville de Paris, XIIIe siècle : 'Le Livre de métiers' d'Etienne Boileau* (Paris: Imprimerie Nationale, 1879), LXI.

61. Ibid., planche II (Facsimile du BN fr. 24069 fol. 1), p. 232; Elizabeth Sears, "Métiers and Merchandise in the Margins of Parisian Manuscripts," paper delivered at the International Congress of Medieval Art, Kalamazoo, Michigan, 1994.

62. See Brigitte Bedos-Rezak, "Towns and Seals: Representation and Signification in Medieval France," in *Town Life and Culture in the Middle Ages and Renaissance: Essays in Memory of J. K. Hyde*, ed. Brian Pullen and S. Reynolds, *Bulletin of the John Rylands Library of Manchester* 72 (1990), see especially pp. 45–47.

63. See H. Géraud, *Paris sous Phillipe le Bel, d'apres des documents originaux et notamment d'apres un manuscrit contenant le rôle de la taille imposé sur les habitants de Paris en 1292* (Paris: Imprimerie Nationale, 1837); for an analysis of artists and sculptors from these records, see F. Baron, "Enlumineurs, peintres et sculpteurs parisiens des XIIIe et XIVe siècles d'apres les rôles de la taille," *Bulletin archéologique du Comité des travaux historiques et scientifiques, nouvelle série*, 4 (1969): 37–121.

64. Cited in Jacob Lawrood and John Camden Hotten, *The History of Signboards* (London: J. C. Hotten, 1866), p. 6.

65. Victor Hugo, *Notre Dame of Paris*, trans. John Sturrock (London: Penguin, 1978), p. 196.

66. These examples are from Lawrood and Hoten, *History*, but see also Philippe Renouard, *Répetoire des imprimeurs Parisiens, libraires, fondeurs de caractères en exercise à Paris au XVIIe siècle* (Magent-le-Roi: Librairie des arts et métiers, 1995).

67. Roger Bacon, *Compendium of the Study of Theology*, ed. Thomas S. Maloney (Leiden: Brill, 1988), p. 107.

68. Ibid., p. 169, and Jan Pinborg, "Roger Bacon on Signs: A Newly Recovered Part of the Opus Maius," in *Medieval Semantics: Collected Studies* (London: Vavorium, 1984), p. 407.

69. Alfred Franklin, *Les Rues et les cris de Paris au XIIIe siècle* (Paris: Leon Willem-Paul Daffis, 1874); and Massin, *Les cris de la ville: Commerces ambulantes et petits métiers de la rue* (Paris: Albin Michel, 1978), pp. 28–33. For this century, see Adrian Rifkin, *Street Noises: Parisian pleasure, 1900–40* (Manchester: Manchester University Press, 1993).

70. Choay, "Urbanism and Semiology," p. 170.

71. Molly Nesbit, *Atget's Seven Albums* (New Haven and London: Yale University Press, 1992), pp. 382–96.

72. Willibald Sauerländer, "Medieval Paris, Center of European taste: Fame and Realities" in *Paris: Center of Artistic Enlightenment*, Papers in Art History from the Pennyslvania State University, IV (1989), pp. 13–24.

73. See Le Roux de Lincy and L. M. Tisserand, *Paris et ses Historiens* (Paris: Imprimerie Nationale, 1867), p. 50; discussed in Serge Lusignan, "La Lettre et le travail: L'Impossible point de recontre des arts mécaniques au moyen age," in *Le Travail au Moyen Age: Une Approche interdisciplinaire*, ed. J. Hamesse and C. Murraille-Samaran (Louvain: Universite Catholique de Louvain, 1990), pp. 129–39. For the Parisius Paradisus metaphor, see Charlotte Lacaze, "Parisius-Paradisus, An Aspect of the Vie de St. Denis Manuscript of 1317," *Marsayas* 16 (1972–73): 60–66.

74. Susan Buck-Morss, "The Flâneur, the Sandwichman, and the Whore," *New German Critique* 39 (1986): 116.

75. Louis John Paetow, *Morale Scolarium of John of Garland (Johanes de Garlandia), A Professor in the Universities of Paris and Toulouse in the Thirteenth Century* (Berkeley: University of California Press, 1927), p. 174.

76. See *Les Fastes du Gothique: Le Siècle de Charles V* (Paris: Réunion des Musée Nationaux, 1981), no. 10, pp. 68–69.

77. Mark Wigley, "Untitled: The Housing of Gender," in *Sexuality and Space*, ed. Beatriz Colomina (Princeton: Architecture Press, 1992), pp. 337–55. See also Roberta Gilchrist, "Medieval Bodies in the Material World: Gender, Stigma, and the Body," in *Framing Medieval Bodies*, ed. Sarah Kay and Miri Rubin (Manchester: Manchester University Press, 1994), pp. 43–61. For cities and gender, see Elizabeth Grosz, "Bodies-Cities" in *Space, Time, and Perversion: Essays on the Politics of Bodies* (London and New York: Routledge, 1995), pp. 103–11.

78. Peter Stallybrass, "Patriarchal Territories: The Body Enclosed," in *Rewriting the Renaissance: The Discovery of Sexual Difference in Early Modern Europe*, ed. Margaret W. Ferguson et al. (Chicago: University of Chicago Press, 1986), p. 126.

79. A seminal study is F. Choay, "La Ville et le domaine bâti comme corps," *Nouvelle revue de psychanalyse* 8 (1974): 239–52.

80. Berty, *Topographie historique*, p. 275; Jacques Rossiaud, *Medieval Prostitution*, trans. Lydia Cochrane (Oxford: Blackwell, 1985). For sites of prostitution in medieval Paris, see Geremek, *Margins of Society*, p. 77.

81. See Ulysse Robert, *Les Signes d'infamie au Moyen Age: Juifs, sarasins, hérétiques, lepreux, cagots, et filles publiques* (Paris: H. Champion, 1891); and Michael Camille, *The Gothic Idol: Ideology and Image-Making in Medieval Art* (Cambridge: Cambridge University Press, 1989), pp. 180–83.

82. See Malcolm Jones, "The Secular Badges," in *Heilig en Profaan 1000 Laatmiddeleeuwse insignes uit de Collectie H. J. E. van Beuningen* (Cothen: Rotterdam papers: A Contribution to Medieval Archeology, 1993); and the essays collected in *Heilig en Profaan: Laatmiddeleeuwse insignes in cuilturhistorisch perspectief*, ed. A. M. Koldeweij and A. Willemsen (Amsterdam: Van Soeren, 1995). The same types of material exist in Paris, see Arthur Forgeais, *Collection de plombs historiés trouvé dans la Seine*, vol. 3 (Paris: Aubry et l'Auteur,

1864); and Denis Bruna, *Enseignes de pèlerinage et enseignes profanes* (Paris: Musée National de Moyen Age, 1996).

83. Oxford, Bodleian Library MS Bodl, 264, *Travels of Marco Polo*, fol. 283, discussed in this context of prostitution by Hans Peter Duerr, *Intimität: Der Mythos vom Zivilisationprozeß, II* (Frankfurt: Surkamp, 1988), Abb 167, p. 303.

84. Diane Shaw, "The Construction of the Private in Medieval London," *The Journal of Medieval and Early Modern Studies* 26 (1996): 447–67.

85. Henri Lefebvre, *The Production of Space*, trans. Donald Nicholson-Smith (Oxford, Basil Blackwell, 1991), p. 389. See also Edward S. Casey, *The Fate of Place: A Philosophical History* (Berkeley: University of California Press, 1997).

86. Gilles Deleuze and Félix Guattari, *Anti-Oedipus: Capitalism and Schizophrenia* (Minneapolis: University of Minnesota Press, 1983), p. 30.

87. Georges Duby, "Private Power, Public Power," in *A History of Private Life II: Revelations of the Medieval World*, ed. G. Duby (Cambridge: Harvard University Press, 1988), pp. 4–6.

2

The Linguistic Cartography of Property and Power in Late Medieval Marseille

Daniel Lord Smail

Angevin Marseille, like any medieval European jurisdiction, generated enormous quantities of legal contracts and other records involving property and property conveyances from the thirteenth century onward. Medieval property sites were rarely mapped by means of graphic representations, and Marseille's records are no exception to this general rule; in thousands of pages of documentation from late medieval Marseille, one will never find an image even remotely like a map.[1] All the same, these records betray the shaping presence of sophisticated linguistic maps, for verbal descriptions of property sites can signify real property only if a cartographic science, whatever its technological form, mediates between word and thing. To put the matter simply, all property sites, in any legal discourse, are assigned plat descriptions, not unlike addresses.[2] These "addresses" conform to certain templates, such as the nesting template of street, city, and state typical of the United States. The discourse of cartography was not foreign to a nominally mapless world like medieval Marseille; in the minds of its notaries, lords, property holders, and citizens, Marseille was a world that was richly mapped.[3]

Mapped it was, but in diverse ways. It is this very diversity of cartographic forms that is so striking. The modern Western address form, after all, is fairly universal; it is structured by a single template whose

most basic unit is the street. The verbal maps found in the records of
Angevin Marseille, by contrast, convey four distinct templates, the basic
units of which vary widely from one interest group to the next.[4] The public notaries primarily used the street template that would, in time, become the urban norm. Among artisans and other citizens, however, the
basic unit for identifying both residence and plat was not the street but
the neighborhood or "vicinity," as I shall call it. Third, the template used
by powerful landlords and the city council was based on what the records call an "island" *(insula, isla)* or city block; within the insular template, property sites were located on islands that usually bore the name
of the most notable resident, and adjoining streets were rarely named.[5]
Use of landmarks constitutes a fourth and less significant template often
favored by artisans. These templates were mutually exclusive; they had
different ideas about what should be the basic unit of the plat or address,
and hence it is rare to find a plat description in medieval Marseille
defined according to two or more templates. They were, in effect, distinct
cartographic grammars or fundamental grids of reference, a distinction
that is effaced if we privilege one "official" form over the others. Curi-
ously, these competing grammars usually agreed on basic lexical terms or
spatial vocabularies. In the mid-fourteenth century, for example, notaries
typically referred to a certain place near the port as the Street of the
Moneychangers (carreria Cambiorum). Artisans and laborers, in turn,
preferred to call it simply the Change (Cambio), as it was known in the
vernacular. Third, the officials associated with powerful landlords invariably called it the Island of the Moneychangers (insula Cambiorum).
Here, the lexical term remains the same. It is the structure of the space—
imagined as a street, as a vicinity, or as an island—that shifts. Although
this appears to be a rather trivial linguistic distinction, it is significant
for several reasons. First, members of these three interest groups were
fairly consistent in following a single style, suggesting a certain degree
of collective consciousness or group consensus on cartographic practice.
Second, there is a functional correlation between each of the three major
templates and the political awareness and goals that we can impute to
each of the three groups. These different cartographies reflected different practices of space. Third, a single template, the street template favored by the notaries, was gradually coming to dominate cartographic
discourse, eliminating its rivals in the process. In so doing, it unhinged
the linguistic and epistemological basis for alternative practices of space,

most notably in the case of artisans and laborers. The overall process was part of a universalizing agenda sponsored, in this case, by a relatively small group of notaries, usually numbering no more than thirty or thirty-five in any given generation. It was a cartographic transformation but in linguistic form, preceding the graphical *furor geographicus*. The mapping of urban space, according to this argument, was unthinkable before the development of a universal cartographic language.

The most authoritative cartographers in Angevin Marseille in the thirteenth and fourteenth centuries were the public notaries.[6] The public notariate of medieval Marseille was composed of men licensed by the count of Provence, a title held, after 1251, by the Angevin king or queen of Naples. The notaries wrote contracts for the general public that included marriage acts and testaments, commercial agreements, land transactions, and debts and loans of various descriptions. Notaries were also required to keep abbreviated copies of their contracts in casebooks, most of which included a year's worth of activity, and to transmit these casebooks as an element of the public record from father to son or from master to apprentice. Casebooks from fourteenth-century Marseille have survived at a rate of two to three per year, out of an original total of perhaps thirty per year. Even so there are great drifts of them. By the mid-fifteenth century, there are about seven surviving casebooks per year, some of them 400 folios in length.[7]

Used often to study family practice, piety, commerce, and related topics in social and economic history, notarial casebooks also reveal a great deal about late medieval urban cartographic science. They do so by virtue of the many references to property sites found in sales, leases, donations, and a variety of other contracts involving the conveyance of rights over urban property.[8] A given contract must identify the property in question, and it does so by means of a property site clause. Marseille's notaries customarily introduced these clauses with the adjective *sitam* or *situm,* depending on whether the property was a feminine *domus,* a neuter *hospicium,* or some other kind of building or site. Several examples of site clauses follow.

Example 1
... *sitam in civitate Massilie in carreria St. Martini* ...
... situated in the city of Marseille in the Street of St. Martin ...

Example 2
. . . sitam in Malocohinac del Temple . . .
. . . situated in Malocohinac del Temple . . .

Example 3
. . . sitam ante valvas inferioras ecclesie beate Marie de Acuis . . .
. . . situated before the lower doors of the church of B. M. de Acuis . . .

Example 4
. . . sitam ad cantonum Triparie . . .
. . . situated at the corner of the Tripery (tripers' quarter)

Example 5
. . . sitam ante Fontem Judaycum . . .
. . . situated before the Jewish fountain . . .

Example 6
. . . sitam retro domum Bondavini . . .
. . . situated behind the house of Bondavin . . .

Example 7
. . . sitam in carterio Sancti Johannis in carreria Figueria . . .
. . . situated in the quarter of St. Jean in Figueria Street. . .

Example 8
. . . sitam in carreriam Bernardi Gasqui ad partem bodii carreriam
Botoneriorum . . .
. . . situated in the Street of Bernat Gasc with the Buttoners' Street
right behind . . .

The site clause, in turn, was followed by an abutment clause in
which the neighboring properties were identified. In Example 1 above,
the ensuing abutment clause went as follows:

> . . . abutting *(confrontatam)* on one side the house of Raymon
> Borier, and on another side the house of the heirs of the Gen-
> tleman Guis and the house of Symon de Sant Masel, and in
> front the public street and behind another public street.[9]

These examples reveal a diverse range of possible site descriptions,
from streets (examples 1 and 8) and intersections (example 4) to districts and vicinities both large and small (examples 2 and 7). Adjoining

landmarks (examples 3, 5, and 6), especially churches and other public buildings, were also used frequently. We are not in the presence of a modern administrative science that has, with few exceptions, created a universal cellular address template.

Yet within this array of options, notaries had clear preferences. Table 2.1 is based on a sample of 479 of these property site clauses from conveyances notarized between the years 1337 and 1362. The table reveals that notaries in mid-fourteenth-century Marseille used streets, alleys, or similar public spaces as the first term in site clauses 59 percent of the time.[10] Street alone, moreover, was five times more popular among the notaries than suburb, the next most commonly used geographic designation. Over time, the dominance of streets in notarial cartography would grow. By the mid-fifteenth century, we find that streets are used in 78 percent of all site clauses, and by the sixteenth century the use of streets in site clauses was nearly universal.[11]

Table 2.1. Geographic usage in notarized site clauses, 1337–1362

TYPE OF LABEL	PRIMARY USAGES IN SITE CLAUSES	
	No.	%
Street (carreria)	248	
Market	16	
Alley (transversia)	11	
Quay (rippa portus)*	4	
Intersection (cantonum)	4	
Stairway (deyssenduda)	1	
Total streets	**284**	**59**
Suburb (suburbium, burgum)	55	
Artisanal vicinity	29	
Provençal vicinity	22	
Sixain, quarter, or parish	19	
Sub-city**	10	
Jewish quarter (Jusataria)	10	
Island (insula)	7	
Total districts	**152**	**32**

(continued)

| | PRIMARY USAGES IN SITE CLAUSES | |
TYPE OF LABEL	No.	%
Church	25	
Oven	9	
Fountain	4	
Notable man or woman	3	
Gate or wall	1	
Mill	1	
Total landmarks	**43**	**9**
Grand total	**479**	**100**

*This is an ambiguous category that I have included with streets (rather than landmarks) because the quay was a long, public space, unlike the circumscribed sites that typify landmarks. Furthermore, houses are typically described as being *in rippa portus*, similar to the expression *in carreria*, and as being *iuxta*, *subtus*, or *super* churches, ovens, and other landmarks.

**Either *ville inferioris* or *ville superioris*.

Sources: ADBR 351E 3–5, 642–45; 355E 1–12, 34–36, 285, 290–93; 381E 38–44, 59–61, 64bis, 72–75, 79–87, 384, 393–94; 391E 11–18; Archives Municipales de la Ville de Marseille, 1 II 42, 44, 57–61.

The nearly universal use of streets in addresses and plats, however, was still a thing of the future in Angevin Marseille, and a revealing feature of the table is that 41 percent of all notarial site clauses do not use streets. The exceptions are telling. Many of the property sites in question were located in parts of the city where notarial presence was weakest; notaries, as a result, were more or less forced by circumstances to use alternative templates. This is particularly true of property sites located not in Marseille's lower city, the busy commercial port where most notaries did business, but in the upper or episcopal city, whose houses and gardens had been under the dominion of the bishop of Marseille possibly since the time of Gregory of Tours.[12] Although the Angevin crown had taken over possession of the upper city,[13] the bishop remained the major property lord in the upper city and the template long used by the episcopal court, based on islands, was so powerful that many streets in the upper city simply did not have names in the mid-fourteenth century and remained nameless for centuries to come. Hence, notaries were often forced by circumstances to use the episcopal template of islands or large districts. Thus, we hear of properties being sold that were located "in the island of Bertran Montanee," "in the island of Guilhem Andree," and "in the island of the Lavandier." These islands bore names of powerful individuals or families, and episcopal usage of the names suggests a tacit acknowledgment of their authority over "their" blocks. When notaries did insist on mentioning streets in site clauses, we get tortured descriptions of fundamentally nameless entities, such as "the street that goes to the oven," "the street that goes to Sedis," "the alley that goes to the sea," "the street above St. Antoine," "the street that goes toward the episcopal compound and toward the gate called Johan de Massilia." The large percentage of property sites not defined by streets in table 2.1, in other words, does not always indicate notarial inconsistency and cartographic ineptitude. It also reveals the latent tension between competing visions of city space.

The other area where notarial cartography did not hold sway was in the suburbs or faubourgs *(suburbia, burgi)*. The suburban cartography was unique in one regard: it was the one area of the city where there was a great deal of confusion and uncertainty in lexical usages. Most fundamentally, there was no agreement on the very names of the suburbs, let alone their boundaries. In all available records, we find references to a total of eighteen suburbs. Many of these overlapped, some turning up as streets located within the boundaries of another. The lexical confusion itself is extremely interesting because it surely reflects not just notarial uncertainty but inconsistencies in common usage more generally. Inhabited chiefly by agricultural laborers and pastoralists—only three craft groups, the tanners (and they for reasons of public hygiene), the cordwainers, and the tile-makers, lived and regularly practiced their trade outside the walls of the city—it was an area of the city that had little political voice and experienced considerable population turnover. These factors may have contributed to the cartographic confusion.

More intriguing is the fact that few notaries lived in the suburbs. Although notaries sometimes traveled to the suburbs to practice their trade, of those whose casebooks have survived only one, Peire Aycart, lived there, and Peire himself had moved inside the city walls by 1359. For most notaries, their suburban practice was rather limited. The notaries, in sum, were almost certainly less informed about the suburban map than they were about the map of the city in which they lived, and therefore were much less able to impose a cartographic norm. The suburban cartographic confusion reflects both the relative weakness of notarial knowledge and the failure of what we might call notarial surveillance and stewardship.

For the notaries, perhaps the most mysterious space of all was the Jewish quarter,[14] the Jusataria. In a modern map produced by one of the many local historians who have worked on Marseille's medieval topography, the Jusataria is presented as a large space crisscrossed by several unnamed streets that were clearly hopeful attempts on the part of the author to draw what he assumed must have been there.[15] Another map is equally revealing: a more careful scholar, Bruno Roberty, left the Jusataria largely blank and only drew in a few well-documented streets in the northeastern corner and two intersections, one coming off the New Street to the south and the other cutting in on the western edge.[16] The enormous cartographic uncertainty reflected in both these maps is a fair reflection of what the archives have left us, namely a good understanding of the northeastern corner of the Jusataria and little else.

The reasons for this are interesting and have to do not just with an aesthetics of disappearance.[17] Houses located within the Jusataria, according to our exact geographic terminology, are identified in twelve notarial acts. In five site clauses, the district constituted the entire site description *(domum . . . sitam in Jusataria)*, and in another seven the site—the well-documented northeastern corner—was further delimited by reference to streets or alleys.[18] From these acts we learn that the northeastern corner, located near the church of St. Martin and the home of Marseille's cosmopolitan Jewish property lord and moneylender, Bondavin, was interpenetrated by a large Christian population.[19] This Christian presence, and the acts that result, made the space knowable by Christian notaries. Significantly, only one of the twelve site descriptions comes from an act involving a transfer between two Jewish parties. It is extremely unlikely that this single act represents all the property conveyances between Jews between 1337 and 1362, and hence we are forced to conclude that many property conveyances between Jews were simply not notarized and that notaries were only called in to deal with conveyances in the Jusataria involving Christian clients. With the Christian property-owning population limited to the northeastern corner, there are simply no extant acts from which we might reconstruct the cartographic lexicon of the remainder of the Jusataria.

The margins of the notarial world were harder to map in terms of streets. The response of the notaries was not to people these mysterious spaces with monsters, as did the authors of the *mappae mundi*, but instead to borrow more freely from alternative templates. In site descriptions involving property conveyances in the lower city, the heart of notarial activity and presence, the predominance of street-based usage is more noticeable: in 249 conveyances of lower city property in this sample, streets and related terms (intersections, alleys) are used 161 times, or 65 percent of the total.

To argue for an intimate association between notaries and streets, however, is to duck an important question: was this explicitly a notarial cartography? After all, notaries worked for clients who brought them sets of facts and asked them to arrange those facts in a legally binding form. There may be nothing particularly "notarial" about the resulting pattern. To address this question, we need some kind of document that offers grounds for comparison, a document that conveys the cartographic imagination of ordinary men and women directly to us, unmediated by the notaries.

Extraordinarily enough, there is such a document. Between the years 1349 and 1353, a city-wide confraternity, largely composed of artisans and laborers, kept a register that listed the names of its 560 members, the amount of support each person gave, and, in 376 cases, the person's place of residence (table 2.2). The register is in Provençal, the everyday tongue of medieval Marseille. As we can tell from its peculiarly angular handwriting, the register was written by a literate merchant or perhaps an artisan, not by a notary. In these 376 descriptions, we find that only 13 percent of the men and women of this confraternity used streets to define their addresses. They never used islands. Most significantly, fully 54 percent referred to vicinities bearing either Provençal names or the names of trade groups. To give some examples, we find residential areas bearing Provençal names like Bella Taula, Cola, Corregaria, Crotas, Enquant, Esperon, Lansaria, Malcohinat, Peyra que Raja, and Riba. Vicinities bearing the names of trade groups include Fustaria (Carpentery), Pelisaria Estrecha (Narrow Furriery), Sabateria (Shoemakery), Veyraria (Glaziery), and so on. Notarial usage of artisanal and Provençal vicinities, by contrast, stands at 11 percent. Similarly, use of adjoining landmarks drops from 24 percent among the artisans to 9 percent among the notaries.

Table 2.2. Labels identifying property sites or places of domicile

	CONFRATERNITY OF ST. JACQUES DE GALLICIA		NOTARIAL SITE CLAUSES (FROM TABLE 2.1)	
TYPE OF LABEL	No.	%	No.	%
Street, alley*	50	13	284	59
Suburb	27	7	55	11
Sixain	6	2	46	10
Landmark	89	24	43	9
Artisanal vicinity**	101	27	29	6
Provençal vicinity**	103	27	22	5
Total	**376**	**100**	**479**	**100**

*In ADBR 2HD–E7, any address prefaced by *quariera* or *cariera*, followed by *de*.
**In ADBR 2HD–E7, any address beginning with the prepositions *en la, a, a la,* or *als* and not including the word *quariera* or *cariera*.
Sources: ADBR 2HD–E7 and as for Table 2.1.

The difference in usage involves transformations that were both linguistic and historical. To begin with, the public notaries, in creating site clauses, always had to translate the Provençal of their clients into Latin. Thirteenth- and fourteenth-century Provençal, at least in Marseille, did not even have a word for street, and the simple act of translating Provençal into Latin involved the creation of a street template where none existed before.[20] This comparison clarifies the degree to which notaries were consciously abandoning both the vicinity and the landmark as units of artisanal cartographic awareness and were replacing it with the street. The addresses found in this Provençal register are the closest approximation we have to what people actually said in the fourteenth century when asked by a notary to name a place of domicile or identify a property site, and we are in a better position to measure what the notaries did with this information. To judge by the confraternal register, ordinary men and women, confronting a request that they identify a property site, would have normally (78 percent of the time) answered by identifying the site in terms of landmarks or vicinities. Yet only 20 percent of all no-tarial site clauses ended up using the templates of landmark or vicinity.

Specific examples make the general pattern clearer. The Provençal vicinity of Esperon or Speronum was invariably called the Street of Esperon (carriera Speroni or carreria de Sperono) by the notaries, and sometimes the name was changed entirely, such as to the Street of Guilhem Folco (carreria Guillelmi Fulconis). The Fruitery (Frucharia) comes out in notarial casebooks as the Street of the Fruitery. In a similar way, Steps (Escalas) was turned into the Street of the Steps by the notaries; "near" Guilhem Folco (costa Guilhem Folco) ended up as the Street of Guilhem Folco; the market area known as the Tripery (Triparia) became, in notarial hands, the Street of the Tripery; the Palace (Palays), the Street of the Palace; the Shoemakery of the Temple (Sabateria del Temple), the Street of the Shoemakery of the Temple; the Arches (Crotas), the Street of the Arches; and so on.

We can see the translation process at work in the cases of specific individuals. The prominent buckler Johan Englese, a member of the confraternity of St. Jacques de Gallicia, gave his address to the scribe as "Fons Judayca" (Jewish Fountain). In 1359, in the midst of a kind of miniterritorial expansion, he purchased two houses adjoining his prop-erty. The notary who registered the transaction, Peire Giraut, listed the site as the Street of the Jewish Fountain. In another case, a baker and confraternal member named Guilhem Bidorlle, who identified himself as living "en la Frucharia" (in the Fruitery), was for unspecified reasons the host to a ceremony in 1352 in which a vineyard was being leased. Johan Silvester, the notary who drew up the contract in Guilhem's house, identified the transaction site in the subscription clause as the Street of the Fruitery. In a third case, Rostahn de Mayron, who gave his address to the confraternal scribe as "Frache" (the name of a gate), was named by a third person in a notarized house sale as owning a house located in the Street of Frache. Last, the smith Esteve Bernat, who gave his own ad-dress as "Esperon," was identified in a notarized property sale as living on the Street of Esperon.

One could multiply these examples at length, and all would illus-trate how notaries habitually translated vicinities and landmarks into streets. The process carries the appearance of an innocent and relatively minor act of translation, made necessary perhaps by language difference but not otherwise meaningful. Yet I would argue against this complacent solution. One need not ascribe sinister motives to the notaries to appreciate that languages carry ideologies, as Benjamin Whorf might observe, and that acts of translation invariably compromise meaning.[21] In this light it is worth noting that popular Provençal usages that consistently resisted the notarial model could have an effect on notarial practice. Thirteen members of the confraternity described their address, using the landmark template, as the "Font Jueva" or "Fons Judayca" (the Jewish Fountain) and never defined it as a street. In seven site clauses referring to the same area, the notaries called it a street on three occasions ("carreria Fontis Judaycum") but used the landmark template on four occasions ("Fontem Judaycum"). Similarly, the Carpentery (Fustaria), used five times in the confraternal register and never called a street, was translated by notaries into a street only four times in nine site clauses referring to the area. The historical process whereby Provençal cartography gradually gave way to notarial cartography was uneven; what we have here is a snapshot taken in the mid-fourteenth century in which we find certain vicinities still capable of resisting reduction to streets.

They could do so, clearly, whenever they were seen as markers of status and identity, and the powerful ideologies attached to the idea of vicinity are manifest and, in some respects, statistically demonstrable. A vicinity was a social construct or, perhaps, to borrow from de Certeau's language, a practice of space.[22] The words, as labels, did not refer to rectilinear streets but instead to socially cohesive but geographically indeterminate areas. In the special case of trade groups, the Provençal names defined a living and working space ideologically organized around a single trade. The social nature of the vicinity is made clear by the obvious preference on the part of many confraternal members for seeing themselves as living within clearly defined vicinities. Fruitery, Fishmongery, Jewelery, Goldsmithery, Cobblery, Carpentery, Shoemakery of Sant Jacme, Furriery, Cavallion, Esperon, Steps, Corregaria, Colla, Prat d'Auquier, Tripery: each of these fifteen vicinities was named as a place of residence by five or more people and account for 43 percent of the addresses given in the confraternal register. Only three of the suburbs and two other areas—the Negrel Street and the Jewish Fountain—were mentioned five or more times by members of the confraternity.[23] Heavy recruitment from these areas surely played a role in their greater-than-average representation, but even this is telling, for, by this argument, it is primarily in vicinities such as these that social solidarity and vicinal identity was sufficiently strong to make such confraternal recruiting efforts successful. The socially dysfunctional nature of streets, in turn, is attested to by the thinness of representation from each street. Excluding Negrel Street as a special case because of the great concentration of shoemakers found there, the twenty-six streets averaged 1.42 inhabitants.[24] The forty-three vicinities, by contrast, averaged 4.74 inhabitants. Even the forty-three landmarks, which averaged 2.07 inhabitants, did better than the streets.

The act of translation did not involve only a shift in template from vicinity or landmark to street. Sometimes the spatial vocabulary preferred by ordinary Provençal speakers was abandoned by the notaries. Take the example of the carreria Nova (the New Street). Running from the gate of Tholoneum to the Street of the Upper Drapery, it was one of the longest streets of the lower city. But it was a new street, at least in name, and maybe for that reason was *never* used by artisans and other members of this confraternity. Consider the men and women of the confraternity who, in the notarial template, could be said to have lived on the New Street. When these people described their place of residence to the confraternal scribe, they all, without exception, cut the street into its constituent segments, using names based on Provençal usage such as Jewish Fountain, Jewelery, Fruitery, and Tholoneum. In using the expression "New Street," notaries were incorporating these four vicinities into an entirely different, and much larger and longer, spatial entity. Other examples include the Street of the Lower Drapery, which was enfolding two vicinities known as the Spicery (Speciaria) and Corregaria, and the Street of Lansaria (carreria Lansarie), which was similarly enfolding the Nettery, the Coopery, the Slipperery and the Brassery. In so doing, Marseille's notaries were anticipating Baron Haussmann by some 500 years in creating ever longer streets, bulldozing their way verbally through Provençal and artisanal vicinities as they did so. The practice also had contemporary parallels in the architectural transformations of Renaissance Italian cities, as Charles Burroughs remarks in this volume.[25] Communal interest in the maintenance of public spaces encouraged both wider and straighter streets, an architectural transformation that eliminated noble encroachments. In Marseille, perhaps owing to the failure of communal ideology and the political dominance of an oligarchy comprised of nobles and great merchants, there were few architectural transformations before the sixteenth century.[26] The physical transformation of urban space came decades or even centuries after its linguistic transformation.

In other cases, we find notaries linguistically relocating their subjects. In a court case from 1380, for example, the defendant, a fishmonger named Ugueta Provinciala, described herself as living in the "Piscaria" (Fishmongery). Next to the name of the neighborhood, however, a notary has written, in slightly different ink, *in transvercia sive carreria Petri de Serveriis* (in the Alley or Street of Peire de Serviers).[27] It is a telling distinction. This fishmonger thought of her living space in professional terms: it is the area where she and her colleagues sold fish and made their residence. Some court notary figuratively took her off the main street and stuck her in an alley.

Other examples illustrate a similar kind of violence. Johan Aymari, who gave his address as the Fishmongery, was placed by the notary Jacme Aycart in the Street of Johan Sancholi. From other records we know that Johan Sancholi was a merchant who lived on a street located below the Fishmongery. A woman named Covinens Raymbaud, who gave her address as Quay (Riba), was in 1359 located on an alley running northward away from the quay named after the nobleman Laugier de Soliers. The brothers Bertomieu and Guilhem Estaca, both prominent shoemakers, gave their address as "Speronum" to the confraternal scribe but are always located on the Street of the Glaziers in notarized acts from the period. Salvaire Rogon identified his address as "Peyra que Raja," the name for a portion of a longer street called the Street of the Cobblery, but another document places him on the "transversia Nicolai Griffedi prope Curatarie" (the alley of Nicolau Grifen near the Cobblery). The most interesting history may be that of the clothier Antoni Gras, who gave his address to the confraternal scribe as the "Draparia" (Drapery) and elsewhere gave his address as the "carreria Draparie Superioris" (Street of the Upper Drapery) but in several notarial acts was consistently identified by the notary Jacme Aycart as a resident of the "carreria Elemosine" (Street of the Almoner), a street that ran northward from the Street of the Upper Drapery.

Why this notarial hostility to vicinities? To answer this question we need to explore more carefully what these vicinities were. As mentioned above, vicinities were social constructs. In the case of vicinities named after trade groups, the social, commercial, and political nature of the entity is particularly evident. The usage has deep roots in Marseille's political culture. A hundred years earlier, before 1250, representation on the city council was determined by craft membership and not by quarter or status, and artisanal vicinities were to some extent territorial units of governance.[28] For this reason, artisanal vicinities are found more commonly in the records from the period—not yet translated, as it were, into streets. This artisanal political order was suppressed by Charles of Anjou when he came to power in Provence in the 1250s. By 1349, when the confraternal register opens, this political order had already been in decay for a century; council membership was determined by larger administrative quarters called *sixains* and above all by membership in the city's ruling oligarchy. The mid-fourteenth-century usage of artisanal vicinities, in other words, reflected a vanishing political order, and the habit of naming vicinities or even streets after craft groups would, with a few exceptions, disappear completely by the seventeenth century.

In the case of other vicinities that bore Provençal names like Esperon or Peyra que Raja, it is less easy to define their social or political role. We must assume that the name carried connotations of decency and good repute. What is nonetheless clear from all these examples is that vicinities had indeterminate borders and were defined not according to a scientific cartography, but instead by those who thought of themselves as living within them. As social constructs, they were not easily mappable entities and did not readily fit into the notarial or legal vision of the city as a tracery of streets. The gradual ascendance of the notarial street-based model, to hypothesize on the basis of this evidence, eliminated one of the linguistic bases of social cartography and social identity in Marseille. This is not to say that social groups could not find other means of creating and expressing their identities. It is only to say that changes in linguistic cartography were making it discursively, or cartographically, more difficult.

We have, then, two kinds of notarial violence. One was grammatical, occurring whenever notaries translated vicinities or landmarks into streets. The other was lexical, occurring whenever notaries dissected ungainly artisanal vicinities into an array of adjoining or overlapping streets, each with a different name, or enfolded hitherto distinct vicinities into ever longer streets. Both kinds of violence, grammatical and lexical, could happen every time a notary drew up a contract relating to a conveyance

of property. Yet there was also a historical process afoot, because the
street template, over time, was itself becoming increasingly normative
in notarial practice. A sample of 241 site clauses in notarial casebooks
between 1445 and 1455 reveals that usage of streets and similar public
spaces had increased considerably (table 2.3). Although usage of adjoining landmarks such as churches did not drop significantly in notarial
usage,[29] districts, especially Provençal and artisanal vicinities, diminished by half. By the mid- to late sixteenth century, when Provence had
been incorporated into the kingdom of France and the Provençal tongue
itself was on the wane, both vicinities and landmarks were vanishing
from cartographic discourse.

Table 2.3. Geographic usage in notarized site clauses, 1337–1455

	1337–1362		1445–1455	
	No.	**%**	**No.**	**%**
Street	284	59	188	78
District	152	32	35	15
Landmark	43	9	18	7
Total	**479**	**100**	**241**	**100**

Sources: as for Table 2.1 and ADBR 351E 285, 330, 333, 344, 367, 378, 379, 402, 408, 409,
435; 352E 7; 355E 108, 133, 142; 358E 7, 283; 373E 6, 15, 37; 381E 90, 107.

All this evidence shows that notaries did not passively replicate
some universal verbal cartography in late medieval Marseille. Instead,
the street template was bound up with and even promoted by notarial
culture. But why were public notaries in Marseille so interested in
streets? In contemporary Italian cities, the architectural reengineering
of streets was associated with communal interests. In Marseille, where
this reengineering was linguistic before it was physical, the major agent
of change was the public notariate.

One possibility is that notaries were simply conforming to some
legal norm imposed by the continental common law, and that the transformation from Provençal cartography to Latin notarial cartography was

the result of the penetration of Roman law into everyday practice. Yet it is not as easy as this. First, the Roman legal forms used by the notaries demanded a property site clause, but these forms—judging by the very diversity of possible plat descriptions in the mid-fourteenth century—do not seem to have specified the cartographic template used in the clause.

In theory the phrase "located in Marseille" could have served the legal form quite well, and in fact site clauses were sometimes as vague as this. The geographical designation that figures in two notarial formularies from the first half of the thirteenth century, in fact, is the parish *(parrochia)* and not the street; hence, Marseille's notariate in the fourteenth century was departing from Italian notarial custom.[30] Second, site clauses were never used in courts of law to prove or disprove ownership; as a result, it is not clear that their actual form mattered a great deal.[31] Both of these points are sustained by the simple fact that site clauses were occasionally left blank in notarized property conveyances and on other occasions were clearly filled in after the fact. Last is a simple but absolutely funda- mental point: the vicinal and insular templates were in fact no less precise, in their legal description of a property site, as the street template. When appearing in property conveyances or rent registers, all three templates listed a site—street, vicinity, island—and all used abutment clauses to delimit the precise location of the property, the abutment clauses serving much the same function as street numbers do today.[32] Streets were not the unique solution to some legal demand for precision in the verbal representation of space; the law, understood crudely, cannot explain why notaries preferred a street template.

To explore this issue of precision in greater depth, let us turn to the third major template found in Angevin Marseille, the template used by two of the city's major property lords, the bishop and the crown. Both were committed to a usage of truly antique status, that of *insulae* or islands. The origin of insular usage may lie in the Christian habit of carving up Christian spaces into discrete territories such as bishoprics or sees.[33] It may also be an echo of the ancient Roman administrative language of islands surviving in the bureaucratic language of western Christendom, or, for that matter, some combination of the two.[34] Whatever the source, islands occur in the earliest episcopal rent register from the late thir- teenth century and dominate episcopal records throughout the four- teenth and early fifteenth centuries. In the bishop's rent registers from the mid-fourteenth century, upper city properties owing ground rents to the bishop were grouped neatly into forty-one islands, and in one register these islands were conveniently listed in an opening rubric.[35] The crown, in turn, controlled some fifty islands scattered throughout the city.[36] In their registers we find that property sites are identified by island and, within the island, by means of abutment clauses that include streets. Strikingly, these streets are almost never named in episcopal records, and royal records are markedly less than consistent; in both, abutment clauses usually refer generically to a public street *(carreria publica)*. Many islands were named after resident notables of the island, and in certain cases, in both royal and episcopal records, we find that the name of the island changes as the son succeeds to the father. This suggests continuing family control or patronage. In some cases, the eponymous resident owned numerous houses on the block and may have either leased out those he did not use himself or used them to form a family compound in the Genoese style.[37] The sources, regrettably, do not allow us to take a closer look at how this patronage may have operated in practice.

Some islands changed their eponymous family entirely as noble or patrician lineages failed or relocated to other parts of the city. A crown register from 1377, for example, tells us that the island of Gautelm Malet used to be named after Guilhem d'Ancona, and another, now called after Giraut Lort, was once named after Raymon Pisan.[38] This name change created certain problems of identification because any rent collector needs to know how to find present-day properties in past records. The solution, tellingly, was *not* to identify these new islands by describing scientifically where they were situated, i.e., not by naming the streets that surround the island. Instead, more simplistically, record keepers just gave the old names, as in the cases above. Here, a genealogy of prominent families prevails over the impersonal naming pattern based on streets. An island newly named in 1377 after the nobleman Johan de Cuges has a particularly interesting history: the register says that the island, in earlier records, was called "the island of the Lower Tannery." This reveals a drift in the lexical term away from artisanal groups and toward noble patrons, a drift that reflects, in a small way, the political defeat of craft guilds in the thirteenth century and the gradual process whereby the craft guild order was expunged from what were quite literally sites of memory.[39]

Islands were rational and, by the standards of the time, relatively precise ways to describe property locations. Yet notaries, in their casebooks, rarely used the language of islands. This is not because the islands found in seigneurial records were architecturally distinct from spaces that normally drew notarial attention: there is no reason to believe that any of these islands had central courtyards or interior passageways, and in any event the areas of the lower city that were mapped as islands in royal records were invariably mapped as streets in notarial records.[40] In a few notarized property conveyances, it is true, we do find reference to the bishop's islands. A truly remarkable feature of these transactions is that all involved property under episcopal lordship, and all of the conveyancing ceremonies were performed inside the episcopal compound before representatives of the bishop. By controlling the venue of the transaction, in other words, these officials were also able to control how the property site was identified in the notarial record of the transaction. The bishop so thoroughly dominated the naming practices of the upper city, in fact, that it is very difficult to map that city's fourteenth-century topography. Property site clauses based on the insular template do not mention other islands and often do not identify adjoining streets, and therefore it is difficult to figure out where one island stood in relation to another. Even in the seventeenth century, a hundred years after record-keeping practices in the episcopal court had begun to adopt a street-based format, we find a number of streets with no names.[41]

The coupling of the use of islands with patrons or family lineages may be the key to explaining their popularity among lords in Marseille and elsewhere. Domestic architecture allowing, the implied sociability of the island focuses inward, toward a courtyard or shared living space dominated (in ancient Rome, medieval Genoa, and certain modern cities in Islamic areas) by a kin-group or a patron, and turns a blank wall to the exterior.[42] A similar sociology may operate even in a place like Marseille where courtyards were uncommon. With the very idea of an island, the street itself becomes merely a space between compounds, not a street in the sense of a thoroughfare, a public space permitting urban circulation.[43] Medieval lords or family lineages exerted control most effectively through chains of patronage; the template of the island fit their political goals.

Because islands, like neighborhoods, provided a rational and useful template for the identification of property sites, the gradual triumph of street-based usage from the thirteenth to the sixteenth century could not have been simply the result of some growing concern for legal precision. The fact that the notaries did not arrive at the solution developed by their counterparts in ancient Rome—the island as the basis for administrative cartography—is tribute enough to their innovation, especially when we consider that to use streets in these clauses was to depart from the powerful spatial discourse of the church.

We return, then, to the question: why were notaries interested in promoting streets as the basic unit of the cartographic practice of space? The answer I will offer here is that the street template was part of a civilizing agenda from which Marseille's notaries, as a group, benefited. Notaries in Marseille, with a few exceptions, were rarely associated with prominent noble lineages, factions, or patrons of any sort. The extant casebooks reveal a remarkable diversity in a given notary's clientele: the notary Jacme Aycart, for example, encountered more than 4,500 different men, women, and children in his twelve extant casebooks written between 1348 and 1362. Similarly, prominent nobles worked indiscriminately with all available notaries. The great merchant and squire Peire Austria, for example, did business with five of the eleven notaries whose casebooks are extant from the mid-fourteenth century, and the nobleman, city councillor, and faction leader Amiel Bonafos used the services of nine. In the absence of any form of patronage, Marseille's notaries had to cast their nets wide. They relied on income derived from transactions made between people who did not know each other very well, certainly not well enough to trust either in an oral guarantee, the suasion offered by a patron, or the constraints imposed by the culture of honor and shame. Notaries competed with both patrons and with artisanal groups in acting as brokers, providing their clients with access to resources. Notaries thrived on the kind of exchange promoted by the free circulation of individual men and women throughout the city. It suited their political and social agenda to develop a cartography that depicted the civic body as a network of communicating streets. This cartography was antithetical to the patronal model of the island and the artisanal model of the vicinity, both of which envisioned social relations as intimate relationships based on personal acquaintance, the kinds of relations that obviated the need for notaries and the contracts they offered. Streets, in short, are associated with civility, the kind of *gesellschäftliche* society imagined by Ferdinand Tönnies.[44] The small fortified villages around Marseille, tellingly, rarely had named streets in the fourteenth century; site clauses from village property transfers typically say that a house located "in the said *castrum*" was sold to so-and-so. This fact helps explain why urban notaries often did not bother to identify streets in the suburbs that ringed the society: these suburbs, like rural villages, were outside the walls that demarcated civil society. Notaries profited from civility. However sociological the argument—one could not expect to find a contemporary document actually recording a sentiment like this—it would be extraordinary if this remarkable fit between notarial sociology and notarial cartography were merely coincidental, given that notarial cartography promoted the very values on which notaries depended for the profitable exercise of their profession and for their own self-promoting endeavors.

Yet this alone does not explain why the notaries, in a sense, won the battle to define urban space. To explain this we must return to the law. The law indirectly effected a change in cartographic understanding, not through its formal rules but because the property site clauses demanded by legal contracts forced people to create a language for something they simply may not have thought about a great deal before. It is a question of conversation. Imagine, if you will, the following scenario. A husband and wife, accompanied by another man, come to a notary, lounging outside his house in the hope of attracting some business, and ask him to draw up a contract of sale. He sets to work. Arriving at the site clause, he asks where the house is located; the woman whose house it is explains that her family has always called it the "Sabateria" (Shoemakery), even though her father was a cobbler, and tries to recall the names of the current neighbors. As she ponders, her husband suggests that it is not too far from the church of St. Jacques de Corregaria, and the buyer, disagreeing a little with the woman, says that the house is in the vicinity known as "Corregaria." The notary has always found this area a little confusing, especially because the shoemakers themselves have moved away from the vicinity toward the east. He knows that the lord who collects the ground rent on the property calls this area the Island of Jacme Jaucenne in his records, but the lord isn't present and is not constraining the notary in any way. He eventually compromises by writing down that the house is located on the Street of Corregaria near the church of St. Jacques.

Now although the sellers and the buyer may be experiencing this sort of conversation for the first time, the notary goes through it several times a month and will have hundreds of these conversations over the course of his career. The repeated conversations make the notary an expert in urban cartography, and it is an expertise he shares not only with his apprentices but also with his fellow notaries, as he witnesses their acts, and they witness his, and as they discuss their professional attitudes at guild meetings. The notaries become, in effect, the official cartographers of the city, and the template they develop, by its growing clarity, gradually becomes the city-wide template, forcing out those used by ordinary citizens and by the great lords. The law, then, was responsible for this development only insofar as it promoted the legal contracts that entailed cartographic conversations. The results of those conversations were shaped by notaries who, for self-interested professional reasons, guided their clients toward a cartography based on city streets.

Cartographic conversations were not particular to Marseille; they were taking place wherever scribes or notaries drew up contracts related to the conveyance of rights in property, in the north as well as in the south of Europe. They were becoming increasingly more common across the fourteenth and fifteenth centuries, as property holdings, especially after the Black Death, were turning over more rapidly, spurred by vacancies and urban immigration.[45] The template that emerged out of these conversations may have become the bureaucratic norm in most places of western Europe by the end of the fifteenth century, if not earlier. There was surely a great deal of diversity in the way this process unfolded in different regions of Europe. Elsewhere, notaries may not have been the major agents of change, as in the case of Italian cities where the universalizing process seems to have been more closely associated with communal interest.

By the mid-sixteenth century, as we know, graphic representations of urban space from a bird's-eye view and eventually from the perpendicular became commonplace. Part of their novelty, compared to their medieval antecedents, was their awareness of streets. As streets grow straighter and more prominent in maps and artistic renderings of cities, and as the city itself appears increasingly neat and tidy, the buildings in elevation that dominated medieval urban representations become uniform, shrink in proportion, and eventually disappear altogether. The elimination of houses and buildings was a dehumanizing process, an extension of a dehumanizing process inaugurated in Marseille by notaries in the fourteenth century as they progressively replaced vicinities and landmarks with streets.[46] To reiterate a key point, the agent of change in this new awareness of streets, in Marseille, did not consist of new cartographic technologies and a growing awareness of scale in and of themselves. Nor did it lie in the interests that Marseille's civil leaders may have had in defining urban spaces. The awareness of streets developed first in Marseille's notariate.

"In general the production, transmission, and acceptance of scientific knowledge are not the consequence of the application of some set of universal standards or procedures, but the outcome of an open-ended process of socially negotiated judgments by practitioners who are struggling to make their own views and skills credible and authoritative." So observes David Turnbull, summarizing, from a cartographic angle, recent work in the sociology of scientific knowledge.[47] In late medieval Marseille, the practitioners were the members of several local interest groups of incommensurate size and status—a small notariate, even smaller episcopal and royal curias, a large array of artisans and workers— each contemplating a heterogeneous array of physical sites and each preferring to represent these sites according to a favored linguistic template. In a largely contingent universalizing process, a single template, the street template favored by the notaries, crowded out the others and became the administrative and scientific norm. It is an interesting sequence, for the elaboration of a consistent verbal map preceded the development of graphical maps.[48] Evidently the plurality of medieval cartographic grammars made it difficult to imagine a single map form: only when the street emerged as the universal template did it become easy or possible to imagine a graphic map of a city. In this regard it is important to observe that the interest groups were not mutually exclusive. Medieval notaries worked for themselves and for great lords. Virtually all notaries and seigneurial officials were also native speakers of Provençal. For this reason, the template one used on any occasion depended on the context and on one's interlocutors.

Notaries, in a cartographic arena, were adhering to well-known scientific processes of making heterogeneous entities standard and interchangeable. They were, as an institution, engaged in an act of classification.[49] They were doing so before large-scale state sponsorship of graphic cartography, or indeed before state interest in any form of cartography, verbal or graphic. To argue for the agency and significance of late medieval notarial culture is not to diminish the subsequent role of state interest in the ensuing *furor geographicus*. It is to say only that the relationship between power and geography is indeed long-standing,

and that some of the linguistic and mental roots of the early modern
cartographic revolution lie in the play of power and interest in the late
medieval city.

NOTES

I am grateful to Charles Burroughs and Maryanne Kowaleski for their helpful advice on an
earlier draft of this article, and I would also like to thank Michal Kobialka and Barbara
Hanawalt for inviting me to participate in this project.

1. P. D. A. Harvey, "Local and Regional Cartography in Medieval Europe," in *Cartography in Prehistoric, Ancient, and Medieval Europe and the Mediterranean*, vol. 1 of *The History of Cartography*, ed. John B. Harley and David Woodward (Chicago: University of Chicago Press, 1987), pp. 464–65, 470. Notaries elsewhere in Europe could and occasionally did produce maps in an effort to clarify property locations; see *Il notaio nella civiltà Fiorentina: Secoli XIII–XVI: Mostra nella biblioteca medicea laurenziana, Firenze, 1 Ottobre–10 Novembre 1984*, ed. Arnaldo D'Addario (Florence: Vallecchi Editore, 1984), p. 300.

2. Plat descriptions (legal descriptions of property sites) and addresses (elements of the clauses used to identify people) in medieval Marseille were virtually identical in form, although addresses did not use abutment clauses.

3. It is equally possible to map rural space in this way; see Jean Coste, "Description et délimitation de l'espace rural dans la campagne romaine," in *Sources of Social History: Private Acts of the Late Middle Ages*, ed. Paolo Brezzi and Egmont Lee (Toronto: Pontifical Institute of Mediaeval Studies, 1984), pp. 185–200.

4. Templates are underlying codes that structure the language whereby space is described. They are imbued with values developed at relatively small sites of production or within discrete groups. Turnbull speaks of "knowledge spaces" and "modes" in ways that are reminiscent of my use of templates; see David Turnbull, "Cartography and Science in Early Modern Europe: Mapping the Construction of Knowledge Spaces," *Imago Mundi* 48 (1996): 7.

5. In Marseille, the parish is almost nonexistent as a geographical entity in records relating to property or in identity clauses, even in episcopal records. This stands in marked contrast to England and other regions in both northern and southern Europe where parishes, as administrative divisions, became part of the public cartographic imagination.

6. For a helpful introduction to the notaries see Lauro Martines, *Lawyers and Statecraft in Renaissance Florence* (Princeton: Princeton University Press, 1968), pp. 34–38. Especially important for the historical study of notaries in southern France and Italy is Roger Aubenas, *Étude sur le notariat provençal au moyen-âge et sous l'Ancien Régime* (Aix-en-Provence: Editions du Feu, 1931); Louis Stouff, "Les Registres des notaires d'Arles (début XIVe siècle–1460). Quelques problèmes posés par l'utilisation des archives notariales," *Provence historique* 100 (1975): 305–24; Brezzi and Lee, eds., *Sources of Social History;* John Pryor, *Business Contracts of Medieval Provence. Selected "Notulae" from the Cartulary of Giraud Amalric of Marseilles,*

1248 (Toronto: Pontifical Institute of Mediaeval Studies, 1981); D'Addario, ed., *Il notaio nella civiltà Fiorentina;* and Thomas Kuehn, *Law, Family, and Women: Toward a Legal Anthropology of Renaissance Italy* (Chicago: University of Chicago Press, 1991).

7. For southeastern France in general, see Robert-Henri Bautier and Janine Sornay, *Les Sources de l'histoire économique et sociale du moyen âge,* 3 vols. (Paris: Centre National de la Recherche Scientifique, 1968–84). Notarial holdings are described in volume 2. For Marseille, see my "Notaries, Courts, and the Legal Culture of Late Medieval Marseille," in *Medieval Urban and Rural Communities in France: Provence and Languedoc, 1000–1500,* ed. Kathryn L. Reyerson and John Drendel (Leiden: E. J. Brill, 1998), pp. 23–50.

8. Such contracts are discussed in Kathryn L. Reyerson, "Land, Houses, and Real Estate Investment in Montpellier: A Study of the Notarial Property Transactions, 1293–1348," *Studies in Medieval and Renaissance History* 6 (1983): 39–112.

9. Archives Départementales des Bouches-du-Rhône (hearafter ADBR) 381E 79, fols. 100r–v, 30 October 1353.

10. Ninety-nine clauses in this sample include two or more terms (see examples 7 and 8). The first term in the site clause is arguably the most significant. Secondary terms, moreover, follow a pattern of usage essentially identical to the pattern typical of first terms, and for ease of interpretation I have left them off the table.

11. See table 2.3.

12. See Philippe Mabilly, *Les Villes de Marseille au moyen-âge: Ville supérieure et ville de la Prévôté, 1257–1348* (Marseille: Astier, 1905), pp. 3–4.

13. On the political history of Marseille see Victor-L. Bourrilly, *Essai sur l'histoire politique de Marseille des origines à 1264* (Aix-en-Provence: A. Dragon, 1925).

14. I discuss the status and location of mid-fourteenth-century Marseille's single Jewish quarter in "The Two Synagogues of Medieval Marseille: Documentary Evidence," *Revue des études juives* 154 (1994): 115–24.

15. Octave Teissier, *Marseille au moyen âge: Institutions municipales, topographie, plan de restitution de la ville, 1250–1480* (Marseille: V. Boy, 1891).

16. ADBR 22F 140.

17. On this see Kathleen Biddick, "Paper Jews: Inscription/Ethnicity/Ethnography," *Art Bulletin* 78 (1996): 594–99.

18. In two of these cases the Jusataria was not mentioned at all.

19. On Bondavin see Joseph R. Shatzmiller, *Shylock Reconsidered: Jews, Moneylending, and Medieval Society* (Berkeley: University of California Press, 1990).

20. The word in the standard medieval Provençal dictionary is *ruta* or *ruda,* cognate with the French *rue,* but it never appears in documents from Marseille, and on those occasions when a Provençal document speaks of a street, the scribe used a transliterated version of the Latin *carreria.* For the Provençal word, see Pierre Pansier, *Histoire de la langue provençale à Avignon du 12e au 19e siècle* (1924; reprint, Geneva: Slatkine Reprints, 1974 and Marseille: Laffitte Reprints, 1974), p. 150.

21. See, for example, Benjamin Lee Whorf, *Language, Thought, and Reality: Selected Writings of Benjamin Lee Whorf,* ed. John B. Carroll (Cambridge, Mass.: MIT Press, 1956).

22. Michel de Certeau, *The Practice of Everyday Life,* trans. Steven F. Rendall (Berkeley: University of California Press, 1984), pp. 117–18; see also Michel Foucault, "Of Other Spaces," *Diacritics* 16 (1996): 22–27.

23. The latter two clearly display the social characteristics of vicinities, and the Font Jueva (Jewish Fountain), in particular, should probably be included among the vicinities, even though, in some dry technical sense, it fits the landmark template.

24. The carreria Negrelli (Negrel Street) was one of the few areas of the city where a great density of shoemakers did not result in the appellation "Sabateria." The reason may be that Negrel Street was a major thoroughfare for traffic between the upper and lower cities. Nonetheless, the consistent and seemingly proud usage of the address by shoemakers attests to the sense of shoemaker identity with the carreria Negrelli.

25. Charles Burroughs, "Spaces of Arbitration and the Organization of Space in Late Medieval Italian Cities," this volume. See also Paula Lois Spilner, *"Ut Civitas Amplietur": Studies in Florentine Urban Development, 1282–1400* (Ph.D. dissertation, Columbia University, 1987).

26. On the political ascendance of this oligarchy in fourteenth-century Marseille, see Georges Lesage, *Marseille angevine: Recherches sur son évolution administrative, économique, et urbaine de la victoire de Charles d'Anjou à l'arrivée de Jeanne 1re (1264–1348)* (Paris: E. de Boccard, 1950); Christian Maurel, "Structures familiales et solidarités lignagères à Marseille au XVe siècle: Autour de l'ascension sociale des Forbin," *Annales: Économies, sociétés, civilisations* 41 (1986): 657–681; and idem, "Le Prince et la cité: Marseille et ses rois . . . de Naples (fin XIIIe–fin XIVe siècles)," in *Marseille et ses rois de Naples: La Diagonale angevine, 1265–1382,* ed. Isabelle Bonnot-Rambaud (Aix-en-Provence: Édisud, 1988), pp. 91–98.

27. ADBR 3B 96, fol. 96r, 29 Aug. 1380.

28. Bourrilly, *Essai sur l'histoire politique de Marseille.*

29. The space around churches was, cartographically speaking, very conservative and resisted incorporation into the street-based template for some time. Whether this is because of the awkward shape of the public spaces that surrounded churches or because ecclesiastical discourse itself resisted the change is an open question.

30. For formularies using parish *(parrochia)* see Salatiele, *Ars notarie,* ed. Gianfranco Orlandelli, 2 vols. (Milan: A. Giuffrè, 1961), 2: 229, and Bencivenne, Ars notarie, ed. Giovanni Bronzino (Bologna: Zanichelli, 1965), p. 38.

31. Property transfers were far more significant as a means for proving the existence of debts and trails of ownership, and the site clause, once it was set on paper, appears to have had absolutely no future relevance in law.

32. Few houses in Marseille bore names that could serve to delimit precise locations. This is in marked contrast to Paris, among other places; see Michael Camille, "Signs of the City: Place, Power, and Public Fantasy in Medieval Paris," in this volume.

33. Robert Bartlett, *The Making of Europe: Conquest, Colonization, and Cultural Change, 950–1350* (Princeton: Princeton University Press, 1993), pp. 5–23.

34. Oswald A. W. Dilke, *Greek and Roman Maps* (Ithaca: Cornell University Press, 1985), p. 88; Claude Nicolet, *Space, Geography, and Politics in the Early Roman Empire,* trans. Hélène Leclerc (Ann Arbor: University of Michigan Press, 1991), p. 135.

35. ADBR 5G 112, found in a separate quire at the beginning of the register.

36. See ADBR B812, 819, 831, 836, 859, 1019, 1177, 1936, 1939–1942, 1948, 1952, and 1957. These registers date from the late thirteenth to the mid-sixteenth centuries, and the number of islands listed over this period of time ranges from twenty to fifty.

37. See Jacques Heers, *Family Clans in the Middle Ages: A Study of Political and Social Structures in Urban Areas*, trans. Barry Herbert (Amsterdam: North-Holland, 1977).

38. ADBR B831, fols. 44r, 45v.

39. Ibid., fol. 47r. Sites of memory are discussed in Pierre Nora, *Conflicts and Divisions*, vol. 1 of *Realms of Memory*, trans. Arthur Goldhammer (New York: Columbia University Press, 1996).

40. On the changing architectural space of islands, see Henri Broise, "Les Maisons d'habitation à Rome aux XVe et XVIe siècles," in *D'une ville à l'autre: Structures matérielles et organisation de l'espace dans les villes européennes (XIIIe–XVIe siècle)*, ed. Jean-Claude Maire Vigueur (Rome: Ecole Française de Rome, 1989), pp. 609–29.

41. It was, incidentally, around this time that the episcopal court began generating the first cadastral maps ever used in Marseille. In this, the court was following a cadastral trend that was transforming record keeping among ecclesiastical lords all over France; some good examples, beside those from Marseille, can be found in Paris and Arles from the seventeenth century onward.

42. Jacques Heers, *Espaces publics, espaces privés dans la ville: Le Liber terminorum de Bologne (1294)* (Paris: CNRS, 1984), pp. 33–45; Janet L. Abu-Lughod, "The Islamic City— Historic Myth, Islamic Essence, and Contemporary Relevance," *International Journal of Middle East Studies* 19 (1987): 167.

43. See Henri Broise and Jean-Claude Maire Vigueur, "Strutture famigliari, spazio domestico e architettura civile a Roma alla fine del medioevo," in *Storia dell'arte italiana*, ed. Giulio Bollati and Paolo Fossati (Turin: Einaudi, 1983), pt. 3, 5: 99–160.

44. Ferdinand Tönnies, *Community and Society (Gemeinschaft und Gesellschaft)*, trans. and ed. Charles P. Loomis (East Lansing: Michigan State University Press, 1957).

45. Derek Keene discusses some of the physical and social effects of the property market in his "The Property Market in English Towns A.D. 1100–1600," in *D'une ville à l'autre*, ed. Jean-Claude Maire Viguer (Rome: Ecole Française de Rome, 1989), pp. 201–26.

46. On the question of "dehumanizing," see John B. Harley, "Silences and Secrecy: The Hidden Agenda of Cartography in Early Modern Europe," *Imago Mundi* 40 (1988): 65–66.

47. Turnbull, "Cartography and Science in Early Modern Europe," p. 6.

48. Leon Battista Alberti was developing both theoretical and practical solutions to the problems of mapping urban spaces by the mid-fifteenth century. Assuming that Marseille's cartographic patterns mirrored those of Florence and Rome, where Alberti worked, this suggests that the elaboration of both notarial cartography and scientific surveying techniques may have been roughly contemporaneous. See John A. Pinto, "Origins and Development of the Ichnographic City Plan," *Society of Architectural Historians Journal* 35 (1976): 36–38.

49. Germane to this are the observations of Mary Douglas, *How Institutions Think* (Syracuse: Syracuse University Press, 1986), pp. 58–67.

3

SPACES OF ARBITRATION AND THE ORGANIZATION OF SPACE IN LATE MEDIEVAL ITALIAN CITIES

CHARLES BURROUGHS

The law shaped late medieval social space. Any discussion of medieval practices of space, therefore, must attend to the legal framework of such practices, especially those involving the physical or even conceptual redefinition of the setting of action. In medieval Italy, city statutes typically included detailed provisions regarding the maintenance and, to a degree, improvement of public space. Often these came under the purview of a magistracy, with its own statutes and institutional memory, expressly concerned with the physical condition of a city. Nevertheless, for all the appeals to abstract values, city statutes and related legal provisions were in general responsive to, rather than productive of, urban process and change.[1]

In any city, on the other hand, the protagonists in the development of its physical fabric and image included legal professionals. Among the corporate organizations dominant in the medieval city states, the lawyers' guild often enjoyed a lofty position.[2] In contrast, the shifts associated with the Renaissance gave at least a few individual lawyers the opportunity to exert enormous influence and, to a wider group, essential roles in an increasingly bureaucratic form of government. As Lauro Martines has demonstrated for Florence, the study of the legal profession provides an excellent vantage point for understanding the momentous transition from the medieval to the early modern state.[3] In contrast to Martines's focus on the elite, men of high birth and exhaustive university training, I am concerned here with a wider spectrum of legal professionals. Most, of course, were men of more modest means and qualifications, notaries rather than lawyers, whose sphere of activity was usually more restricted in social and topographical terms. In medieval cities, however, their profession was held in high esteem, in contrast to later assessments.[4] Indeed, the ubiquity and importance of notaries in the affairs of late medieval Italians is a crucial element in the history of mentalities, that is, in Peter Burke's felicitous phrase, in the production of a "notarial culture."[5]

Whatever the status of a lawyer, the city was more than a neutral background for his operations. We readily think of legal transactions as ritualized events performed according to a social script conferring authority and resulting in documents that guaranteed assent through familiar means, notably official language and format and the signatures or marks of protagonists and witnesses. The force of a legal transaction, however, might also derive from the setting of its enactment, which might confer, for example, prestige or charisma, or offer a symbolic testimonial function to a wider audience than the witnesses registered in the documents. Grander lawyers, no doubt, often conducted business in premises expressly designed to impress or even intimidate those who came before them. The city as a whole, however, served as a setting for jurisdiction, though the connotations and character even of its most conspicuous symbols of justice and social order might change with shifts of regime and political climate.[6]

The concern with civic order and harmony in medieval city states was expressed in statutory prescriptions and, to varying degrees, realized in their implementation. Ideally, a city's statutes regulated and guided the procedures through which, in individual cases, agreement was reached and given sanction through notarial writing and format.[7] In Florence, a competitive or, quite often, agonistic climate gave way in the course of the fifteenth century to an autocratic political regime and a courtly, celebratory humanism that elevated consensus, in a general sense, to a supreme value.[8] At the same time signs of social and cultural difference increasingly marked the urban fabric, notably the conspicuous private residences that appeared alongside and competed visually with the older monuments of corporate solidarity.

This shift had striking architectural implications that allow us to see legal practices as practices of space. Structures intermediate between domestic and public space—typically in the form of an open fronted portico or loggia (figure 3.1)—were prominent, if not indispensable, in the typical medieval Italian urban environment. In many (but by no means all) cases, these intermediate spaces subsequently disappeared or declined in a complex process that has not been systematically discussed.[9] On the basis of evidence from Florence and Rome, I will argue that such spaces, especially street porticoes, had served the late medieval notariate as appropriate, symbolically charged settings for certain kinds of transactions. While it is well known that the emergent autocratic political regimes of the Renaissance presided over profound transformations in the urban fabric, I draw attention to a reworking of spaces in accordance with tendencies within humanist culture and with changing attitudes toward legal texts and procedures. Porticoes and related infrastructural elements stand revealed as an architectural/spatial symptom of and factor in a momentous transformation both of the political order and of its legal armature and expressions.

SPACES OF ARBITRATION: ARCHITECTURE, RITUAL, AND THE REAFFIRMATION OF THE SOCIAL BODY

A crucial function of notaries in the late medieval Italian city was to conduct and register cases of arbitration, thus giving legal sanction to a reconciliation achieved between quarreling parties, often members of the same family or neighborhood.[10] Arbitration was a formalized process emblematic of the core ideology of any medieval corporate body, whether city, guild, or confraternity; it involved the restitution of unity and harmony when disturbed or damaged through actions often construed as unnatural because they seemed injurious to a divinely ordained state of the world.[11] The character of the ensuing legal act and the document resulting from it required attention not only to the text of the document, but also to two distinct spatial matrices, the space of the text and the space or setting of its production. A legal document is recognized at a glance as an array of signs within a formulaic spatial matrix, the material space of the text.[12] Any legal act also required a setting, a space of

Figure 3.1. The Rucellai Loggia, Via della Vigna Nuova, Florence.
Courtesy of Alinari/Art Resource, New York.

performance, that related transaction to polity. The loggia or portico was such a setting.

No ritual practice was more crucial in the reconciliation of cosmic or natural and social harmony than marriage, with its symbolic and physical investment of bodies in the regeneration of household and society. Among the elite the requisite ceremonies visibly positioned the couple concerned and their families at the center of widening circles of alliance and association. In a fractious medieval city, betrothal presupposed extensive and delicate negotiations conducted in large part to allay actual or potential issues of disagreement or conflict among the parties to the eventual agreements. The agreement was guaranteed and displayed in the wedding.[13]

A priest presided at a wedding, a notary at a betrothal. The involvement of legal expertise and authority in marriage, however, is less well documented than it is in making last wills and testaments. The contrast of the two practices is instructive. If a will was a device to secure diachronic harmony by binding a successive generation or generations to the testator's will and values, marriage both constituted and staged a synchronic alliance of households. In marriage, the wedding rituals dramatized the couple's position in physical and social topography. In Florentine elite circles, such rituals included conveying the bride's trousseau to the bridegroom's house, with pride of place given to the pair of richly ornamented chests (now usually called *cassoni;* the fifteenth-century term was *forzieri*), which were carried in triumph through the streets.[14]

Around 1470 a notable shift occurs in the imagery on marriage chests; scenes of romance yield to more erudite, classical themes. Christiane Klapisch-Zuber argues that the change arose from the transfer of the commission for the chests, once a responsibility of the bride and her family, to the bridegroom and his kin. It was also roughly contemporary with a striking change in the wedding ritual—the withdrawal of the chests from the traditional procession from the house of the bride's father to that of the groom. Instead, the chests were now simply delivered to the bridegroom's house by the workshop responsible for their manufacture.[15]

In a related study, Klapisch-Zuber has drawn attention to an early sixteenth-century treatise by a Roman patrician, Marcantonio Altieri, who attributed the decline of the traditional wedding rituals of his class to its loss of autonomy in the face of the papal usurpation of power. There is, therefore, a clear political urgency in his discussion of Roman wedding rituals that, as he describes them, served both to dramatize the potential for conflict and violence on social occasions and to engender and demonstrate solidarity among the Roman citizen aristocracy.[16] In this case, the restoration of a political world—a microcosmic order—is at stake in an unusually self-conscious consideration of marriage practices as central to the health of a society.

In a wider sense, then, medieval arbitration was a diffuse cultural practice involving diverse modes of implementation in various arenas of social interaction. Arbitration existed as a specific procedure, e.g., at Rome, where a particularly remarkable arbitration ritual is documented until the late fifteenth century.[17] Briefly, the Roman arbitration procedure was as follows: The disputing parties were brought together in the presence of a notary to present their cases before an individual of higher status. Those seeking arbitration were required to assent to this individual's judgment. The losing party was required to submit to a physical chastisement carried out, in public, by the victor, whose blows were apparently largely symbolic and not struck to cause real physical pain. The ritual was, accordingly, highly theatrical in character, involving not only the two disputants and the arbitrator, but also the audience who collectively bore witness.

Where did arbitrations take place? A recent study of the notarial records from a specific but representative district *(rione),* Parione, between 1471 and 1484, lists four main sites of notarial transactions, among them the portico.[18] The probable location was the facade portico that constituted a typical feature of late medieval houses in Rome, where interior porticoes were appearing in only a few, particularly grand houses by the late fifteenth century.[19] Documents specifically recording cases of arbitration refer to devices assuring the dignity of the ceremony and of the arbitrator himself, on which depended the success of the transaction.[20] A portico contained such devices, e.g., a raised seat, but it was itself such a device. Frame function and sign function coincided.

In Rome front porticoes of medieval type remained a standard element of houses throughout much of the fifteenth century. Some still exist, though they have generally been closed. The use of *spolia* (or at least carved *all'antica* ornaments) in such porticoes suggests that their construction or reconstruction extended into the period of the diffusion of humanist ideals.[21] The evidence for their use and cultural significance is scattered, but extensive evidence suggests that porticoes accommodated the display of family coats of arms and those of other families allied through marriage.[22] These intermediate spaces diagrammed, therefore, the network of legally constituted alliances that both manifested and guaranteed a family's place within the city's elite, and formed a highly charged and visible setting for the marriage ritual.

In his treatise on weddings, in particular, Altieri stresses a kind of staged kidnapping, reenacting the rape of the Sabine women. The bride was brusquely dragged into her new home, which then became the scene of elaborate dances of reconciliation and the restoration of social order.[23] Altieri does not mention the spatial or architectural requirements of such a ritual, which he perhaps took for granted; at the very least, however, the portico staged the entry sequence into a house as a

drama of the merging of alliance and lineage, grounded in the imagined
origins of the Roman citizen elite.

The theme of the facade portico provoked significant reflections on
the part of the greatest observer of the quattrocento city, Leon Battista Alberti, who composed his treatise on architecture during his extended period of residence in Rome, although he certainly knew such portico-rich
cities as Bologna and Padua. In his treatise Alberti commends the use
of facade porticoes, especially as sites for images of important events in
the life of a family or city, in other words, as a place for the registration
and mobilization of social memory.[24] His claim that in antiquity porticoes were often semicircular in plan is unfounded either in Vitruvian
prescription or, as far as I know, in extant architectural remains.[25] Alberti
perhaps conflated the ancient Roman theater, with its semicircular au-
ditorium, with the exedral motifs prominent in ancient building complexes. This association of the facade portico with theater, however, also
echoed practices in Roman humanist circles, in which porticoes or loggias—whether exterior or, more probably, interior—accommodated the
performance of ancient drama, becoming literally theatric spaces.[26]

For all Alberti's approval of facade porticoes, he also expresses a certain ambivalence about them. He notes a report that porticoes tend to
become the haunt of servants, a usage that would subvert the enclosed,
quasi-sacral character Alberti famously assigns to the individual house
as a self-contained little city.[27] In this passage, Alberti moves from the
consideration of porticoes as a stage, an object of the gaze of spectators
in the street, to a platform for viewing the street, though in this case
such viewing has negative connotations because it was done by unruly
servants.

Such a negative assessment echoes a celebrated passage in the
chronicle of the Roman citizen and lawyer Stefano Infessura, a fervent
champion of municipal resistance to the papal usurpation of municipal
privileges and rights in Rome, particularly under Pope Sixtus IV
(1471–1484). Soon after his accession, Sixtus received a state visit from
the king of Naples, who, after riding through an urban fabric still largely
of medieval aspect, observed that the pope would never truly be master
of a city in which porticoes provided potential mischief makers with hid-
ing places and vantage points.[28] In other words, in an era of the relative
centralization of authority, a city's ruler should make the physical space
of the city transparent to surveillance and accessible for disciplinary

action. Jural spaces alternative or external to those controlled by the regime were to be suppressed. The pope, writes Infessura, took the king's advice.[29]

Facade porticoes would indeed soon disappear from the Roman streetscape; only one of the countless palaces built in the later fifteenth and the sixteenth century has a facade portico.[30] No doubt Sixtus's administrative action was an important factor in a transformation that was perhaps far more gradual than Infessura suggests. As a committed Ghibelline, he had reasons for blaming papal tyranny for a complex phenomenon,[31] an element of which was the disappearance of the Roman tradition of arbitration, which is not documented after 1500.[32] The shifts in marriage ritual, noted above, belong in the same context.[33]

Specific action against porticoes, if it took place, occurred in the context of the elaboration of an all-encompassing legal environment by successive popes, not least Sixtus IV. Papal provisions favored the erection of large and magnificent houses, in part through the compulsory purchase of neighbors' property in the interest of the beauty of the city. A major step in the codification of this legislation occurred in the pontificate of the Florentine Leo X (1513–1521), son of Lorenzo de' Medici, who presided over a proliferation of palaces and even of palace streets, that is, linear enclaves of grand houses that would become characteristic of major Renaissance cities.[34] An important Roman example is the Via Giulia, which Leo's predecessor Julius II developed to set off a projected grand new palace of justice. It was designed to centralize a range of legal services and procedures by providing notaries' offices around a rectangular courtyard.[35] Leo abandoned Julius's plans, and the street reverted to a high-status residential artery ripe for investment on the part of Raphael and other courtiers.

The architectural and spatial paradigms emerging in Rome in the Renaissance had largely, of course, been developed elsewhere and imported by popes and other patrons interested in modernizing a city with whose local, i.e., medieval, traditions they had little patience. No city was more important in the establishment of new paradigms than Florence, where shifts in the urban environment were profoundly implicated not only with the history of the law, as we saw in Rome, but also with its public image.

FLORENCE:
FOUNTAIN OF THE NOTARIATE

In 1375 the humanist Coluccio Salutati, the most illustrious of Florentine notaries, was appointed chancellor of Florence. Famous for ethical
and political writings that reinforced and celebrated the resolve of the
Florentine people to resist the power and hegemonic ambitions of the
Milanese state, he also wrote in praise of his own profession.[36] In Salutati's
Florence the political system was republican in form, although quite
narrowly oligarchic in practice. The ubiquity of notarial training and of
access to legal counsel, however, were among the factors encouraging
wider identification with the Florentine state. Though many notaries
studied at major universities, they received their basic preparation at
grammar schools, which were instrumental in producing an unusually
cultured and extensive Florentine merchant class who had an almost
obsessive devotion to record keeping and to the preservation of civic
and familial memory. The culture conferred particular significance on
notaries and their skill in the authoritative registration of important
deeds and words. For leading notaries it was often the ability to write
clear and classically inspired Latin, rather than the technical legal knowledge of law, that ensured success.[37]

The notaries and "judges," i.e., lawyers with a doctoral degree, were the
two constituents of the lawyers' guild membership (Arte dei giudici e
notai). The government drew on its membership not only for men to
serve in state office, as was normal for members of the elite, but also for
crucial professional expertise. The prominence of the legal profession in
civic affairs was given visible expression on the occasion of public ceremonies, notably the funerals of eminent citizens, especially if members
of the Arte dei giudici e notai.[38] Of the two professional groups represented in the guild, the notaries were far more numerous than the doctors
of law and held an inferior position within the guild in the early years.
But notaries were especially prominent in medieval Florence because
the city did not boast a university famous for the study of canon and civil
law. Florentines made a virtue out of this lack; in the words of the chron-
icler Goro Dati, "just as Bologna is the fountain of the law, so Florence
is that of the notariate."[39]

The opening story of Boccaccio's *Decameron*, written about 1350,
shows the high prestige and position enjoyed by notaries in Florence.

Boccaccio presents a rogue notary, Ser Cappelletto, whose practices constitute the reversal of what would normally be expected and who feels thoroughly ashamed of himself if any of his notarial acts is discovered to be other than completely corrupt.[40] Boccaccio was himself a member of the lawyers' guild, but an important dimension of his book is the ironic capsizing of traditional hierarchies and distinctions, beginning with his mockery of the rather ideal conception of the notary current in Florence in his time. In the Florence of Boccaccio and Salutati, who was appointed chancellor in the year of Boccaccio's death, the prominence of notaries as an organized profession and as a reservoir of vital skills and experience must have seemed assured. The Medicean coup of 1434, however, brought with it realignments that inexorably marginalized notaries as a force in public life.

Changing practices of space marked this decline. One of the most important ceremonies in the Florentine ritual year was the feast of Corpus Domini with its great midsummer procession through the city. Until the middle of the fifteenth century the lawyers' guild controlled the cult and the procession, which then passed under the protection of the Dominican friars of S. Maria Novella.[41] As Martines notes, the position of notaries within the Arte dei giudici e notai strengthened at the same time as notaries lost ground to the lawyers in the city at large.[42] A telling instance concerns the qualifications for advancement to the office of chancellor. In the 1440s—not coincidentally, perhaps, at a time when the implications of the Medici ascendancy were becoming clear— portraits of great men of Florence were painted in the guild palace. Among those receiving this honor were the greatest of Florentine chancellors, the humanist and notary Leonardo Bruni, who died in 1444, and his successor Poggio Bracciolini, also a notary.[43] Poggio's successor, however, was Benedetto Accolti, the first chancellor with a doctorate in law.[44] This became, thereafter, a matter of course.

In the sixteenth century, neither individual notaries nor their guild played a role of any significance except as compliant and efficient instruments of a centralized princely state. Concomitant with the political transformation were vast changes in the physical appearance and spatial organization of the city, some of which are directly relevant to a consideration of legal practices of space.

FLORENCE AND THE
TOPOGRAPHY OF THE LAW

Since the thirteenth century, the main center of criminal jurisdiction in Florence had been the Palazzo del Podestà (now Bargello) in the Via del Proconsolo. The street took its name from the residence of the Proconsolo, the chief official of the guild of lawyers and notaries, who was also the honorary head of the whole guild apparatus. The guild itself oversaw and disciplined the activities of its members, jealously guarding their privileges. Many had premises in the dense neighborhood around the church of the Badia, the venerable Benedictine monastery whose campanile is still a conspicuous feature of the city's skyline. In republican Florence, therefore, this tower marked the lawyers' quarter, where stationers' shops and stalls clustered around the Badia and spilled into the Via del Proconsolo (figure 3.2).[45]

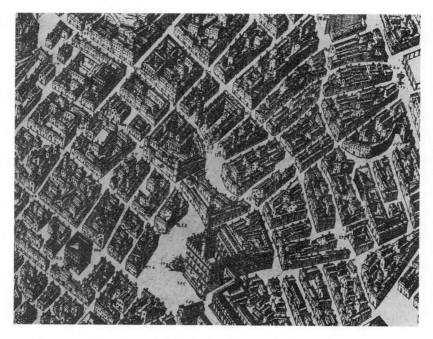

Figure 3.2. Stefano Bonsignori, bird's-eye view of Florence (detail), 1593: the Badia quarter. The Via del Proconsolo runs between the Badia and the Palazzo del Podestà (Bargello), also marked by a tower. Beneath (to the south of) the Badia appears the L-shaped Piazza della Signora, with the Palazzo Vecchio to the right, and the Loggia dei Lanzi at the bottom. Courtesy of Scala/Art Resource, New York.

Representations of notaries at work are infrequent. The frescoes depicting the activities of the prominent charitable confraternity of the Buonomini, therefore, are particularly significant for this study. These paintings, located in the church of the confraternity, illustrate various aspects of the latter's mission, involving charitable interventions in the lives of fellow citizens on the occasions of transitions typically requiring legal oversight, sanction, and registration. The frescoes show loggias— or at least loggia-like spaces—used as the site for exemplary legal acts, e.g., the provision of a dowry to an impecunious girl, with a notary present to orchestrate the action and record the details (figure 3.3).[46] Similar spaces also appear in the representations of betrothals or weddings in *cassone* panels.[47] The obvious imaginative, even fantastic aspect of much of this imagery clearly limits its usefulness as evidence, though in some cases the action is expressly localized in Florence. In the Adimari panel of the 1460s, for instance, the Baptistry characterizes the locale of an aristocratic wedding. The festivities take place in a public piazza or street under the shelter of a canopy (a kind of ephemeral loggia), while a portico,

Figure 3.3. Francesco Antonio del Cherico, fresco, church of S. Martino dei Buonomini, Florence. A notary registers the donation by the Buonomini di San Martino of a dowry to a poor young woman. Courtesy of Scala/Art Resource, New York.

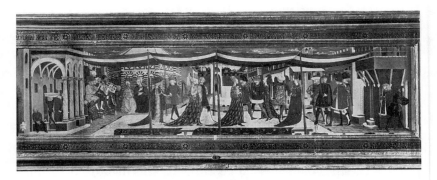

Figure 3.4. Anonymous, Adimari-Ricasoli wedding procession, 1440, Accademia, Florence.
Courtesy of Alinari/Art Resource, New York.

occupied by musicians, fronts the palace to the left (figure 3.4).[48] Such an image presupposes familiarity, at least on the part of the elite, with the employment on certain major ceremonial occasions of spaces intermediate between public and private domains.

Such intermediate spaces were by no means typical only of residential architecture. The loggias in the Buonomini frescoes reflect the association of such structures with institutional buildings, especially those dedicated to the physical and even moral well-being of their inmates or indeed of the citizen body in general. Facade porticoes, mostly of fifteenth-century date, still dignify a number of hospitals, though it is not clear exactly how they were used, apart from their obvious representative function.[49] The guilds also had loggias, some in the market area, some in the area where their members' premises were concentrated.[50] Indeed, a loggia adjoining the Palazzo del Proconsolo perhaps served the needs of the chief official of the lawyers' guild and/or the guild itself.[51]

Private loggias and porticoes facing the street were also a prominent feature of the late medieval environment, though they were less common than in Rome or, emphatically, in Bologna. The evidence suggests that in Florence only particularly populous and powerful families, or rather clans, maintained the relatively freestanding loggias that stood in conspicuous situations and were clearly charged with status. Such loggias surely carried far more cachet than the vaults that opened out in the basement stories of many houses and that no doubt usually accommodated commercial functions, though they could certainly be used for ceremonial purposes. Benedetto Varchi listed both types among the twenty-six still in existence in the mid-sixteenth century.[52]

Evidence for the diffusion and dating of private loggias and facade porticoes is at present scattered and incomplete. The house type favored by the city's elite underwent significant changes in the course of the century or so following the establishment of a republican regime and civic culture in the late thirteenth century.[53] Private loggias seem to be a phenomenon especially of the later stage of this process, i.e., the period of oligarchic restoration following the disruptions of the mid-fourteenth century.[54] The heyday of the private loggia, associated especially with the solemn ratification of contracts binding families and their relations to the social body, coincided with the early years of a public loggia, associated with the maintenance of the social body as a whole through the authority visibly vested in the chief magistrates of the city.

In the public loggia, the present Loggia dei Lanzi (figure 3.5), the city's government displayed itself to the assembled citizenry, giving visible form to the administrative, legislative, and judicial framework that encompassed the various constituencies within the city. As we have seen, notaries were prominent in both private and public affairs of late medieval Florence. In their distinctive and colorful dress, they were surely no less conspicuous among the notables who assembled on occasion in the public loggia than they were during transactions in private loggias and similar intermediate spaces.[55]

Though the erection of a public loggia had been planned for some time, the specific architectural character of the building, begun the year following the appointment of Salutati as chancellor, is very much a matter of its moment and of the promise of recovery from the multiple crises that had recently befallen the city.[56] In different ways, indeed, the late fourteenth-century loggia was associated with the two major civic buildings of the revolutionary republic. Spatially, it occupied a site syntagmatic with the adjacent city hall, while in formal architectural terms it alluded to or even cited a conspicuous and imposing paradigm, the interior elevation of the cathedral. The republican symbolism as well as function of the loggia was too emphatic to survive the passage to the subsequent autocratic regimes; I will return later to the sixteenth-century resignification that was emblematic of the transformed political environment.

We cannot fully understand the connotations of the public loggia and of its fate without giving due attention to its typological relationship with the private facade porticoes of the same general period. These clearly had an important civic aspect, drawing attention to a family's public status and governmental role, especially in its own district *(gonfalone)*.[57]

Figure 3.5. Loggia dei Lanzi (public loggia or Loggia della Signoria),
Piazza della Signoria, Florence. Courtesy of Alinari/Art Resource, New York.

In this context, it is useful to compare the Florentine patrician loggias with the *seggie* of Naples, one of which was located in each major district of the city and reserved for the gatherings of the nobles resident in that district.[58] Such an association of loggias with corporate aristocratic self-representation and civic status can be traced in Florence as well, for from the 1380s the Loggia or Tetto dei Pisani in the Piazza della Signoria accommodated meetings of the city's political and cultural elites.[59] Florentine private loggias were often located at a street crossing or other prominent position in public or at least neighborhood space, although close to the palace or palaces of the clan who enjoyed possession.[60]

Figure 3.6. Loggia degli Alberti, Via de' Benci, Florence.
Courtesy of Alinari/Art Resource, New York.

The most familiar such loggia, that of the Rucellai family, was constructed in the 1460s opposite the famous palace facade in an area inhabited by various branches of the family (see figure 3.1).[61] The Rucellai
were the leading family in their district around the Dominican convent
of S. Maria Novella; correspondingly, the Alberti dominated the district
in the vicinity of the Franciscan church of S. Croce until the end of the
fourteenth century. The Alberti loggia, markedly more primitive and
"medieval" than that of the Rucellai, is also still extant on the corner of
the Via de' Benci and the Borgo S. Croce (figure 3.6). We cannot judge
from appearances, however, because, as F. W. Kent has noted, the loggia

was reconstructed in the mid-fifteenth century following the family's return from exile.[62] From 1393 the Alberti clan suffered reverse after reverse, culminating in 1412 in a failed conspiracy against the Florentine
regime that led the latter to forbid even the women of the family, who
had been maintaining the Alberti presence in the city in the absence of
the men, to live in the ancestral houses. The loggia fell victim to the outrage and anger of the Florentine oligarchy at the same time.[63]

The Alberti and Rucellai loggias have in common not only their
functional similarity to the Neapolitan *seggie,* but also, as Kent notes, a
connection with a family's recovery from political calamity. In the case of
the Rucellai, Giovanni attributed his return to political favor to the operation of traditional networks of solidarity based in his district of the
city.[64] Therefore, clear ideological motives underlay the retention of these
venerable structures. The Alberti made no attempt to enhance or mod-
ernize their building through newfangled architectural ornament, and
even the Rucellai loggia, in its resemblance to the public loggia, may
well have seemed comfortingly traditional to the neighborhood men.
Both loggias were constructed or reconstructed in close relation to the
respective families' linked dynastic and political concerns, notably their
interest in prominent marriages as instruments and indicators of political recovery.[65]

BETWEEN HOUSE AND STREET:
CHANGING ARCHITECTURAL
BOUNDARIES

The decline of the loggia is generally dated to the fifteenth century,
although Florentine patricians such as the Alberti and Rucellai retained
their affection for these archaic structures.[66] In general, loggias were
never part of the novel palace type that emerged in the early fifteenth
century. The optimal form of the new design was a closed block surrounding a relatively geometrical, even cubic, courtyard with private porticoes on all four sides.[67] That this ideal type asserted itself gradually can
be seen in Cosimo de' Medici's own palace, erected in the late 1440s,
that incorporated a loggia, or at least a vault, within the building's enve-
lope (it occupied the southern corner on the Via Larga and was soon
closed up).[68]

The Medici palace was clearly a special case and many scholars have identified economic as well as stylistic concerns as factors for the persistence into the fifteenth century of a strong conservative tendency in palace architecture. Families stayed on their ancestral sites, using them to the full and expanding them if they could. Rather than constructing a new palace, they often remodeled existing buildings. Such remodeling tended to give at least the exterior a unified and up-to-date appearance, providing an effect of enclosure and impenetrability, even if, in some cases, this had little to do with the architectural character of the house as a whole.

Both fashion and economy militated, therefore, against the erection of loggias, but toward the end of the century concerns with economy were less important for those involved in the so-called "palace boom," exemplified strikingly by the mighty Strozzi palace.[69] By the late fifteenth century exterior loggias or porticos were entirely unthinkable for a fashionable palace facade; porticoes belonged in the courtyard, not in the street. This shift from a medieval to an early modern palace type represented a profound transformation of the urban fabric as a whole, involving, we may suppose, a corresponding change in how the "man in the street" experienced his environment. In Franchetti-Pardo's felicitous phrase, citizens now became spectators of, rather than protagonists or at least collaborators in the processes of urban change.[70]

In Florence and Rome the disappearance of facade porticoes or other spaces intermediate between the domestic realm of a house and the public realm of streets and piazzas is one of the most striking factors in the emergence of the early modern urban environment. A corollary was the establishment of a sharp separation of interior and public space, and the constitution of the latter as a kind of stage increasingly framed and defined by architectural compositions of varying formal, iconographical, and rhetorical charge.[71] The Renaissance was, in practice if not in theory, the era of the palace facade, which came to constitute an impressive and often semiotically dense but potentially dissimulative screen. The palace facade was an architectural analog to the metaphorical masks and screens required in the courtly culture of self-fashioning and display so widely diffused in sixteenth-century Italy; what Peter Burke has summarily characterized as a "land of façades."[72]

This claim may at first seem excessive. Anyone who has visited Bologna is aware of the continued existence of facade porticoes that in Bologna have become a distinguishing feature of the urban environment.

The houses of the Bolognese patriciate, however, were exempted from the general requirement to front houses with a portico: the *absence*, rather than *presence*, of a portico connoted status.[73] The otherwise ubiquitous porticoes threaded through the streets of Bologna gave particular emphasis to the relatively few new-style facades that appeared among them, including that of the mid-sixteenth-century residence and private academy of the emblematist Achille Bocchi (1488–1562). Various designs for this facade were published as engravings, apparently on single sheets.[74] It was a momentous innovation, for by means of the medium of print Bocchi's emblematically loaded facade floated free from the physical building to enter a theater, not of confronted built surfaces, but of complex configurations of imagery and text, such as appears, along with views of his palace, in Bocchi's famous and widely disseminated emblem book.[75]

LAW AND ITS REPRESENTATIONS IN POST-REPUBLICAN FLORENCE

In 1513 the celebration of Carnival in Florence included a magnificent but thoroughly uncarnivalesque procession. The procession celebrated the profound political change that had befallen Florence in the previous year. The republic had collapsed and the power of the Medici was reasserted, mainly in the person of Cardinal Giovanni, elder son of Lorenzo the Magnificent, who was about to be elected to the papal see as Leo X. Giorgio Vasari, that great partisan of the Medici, gives an extended description of the procession in the biography of one of the major artists concerned, Jacopo Pontormo.[76] A line of elaborate floats pulled by huge oxen rumbled through the streets, each accompanied by outriders on horseback. The floats carried, in order, Saturn and Janus, both evocative of the Age of Gold; Numa Pompilius, the founder of ancient Roman state religion; Caesar and Cleopatra, in a hardly subtle linking of sexual and political subjugation; Augustus Caesar, flanked by six pairs of poets proclaiming him a model of munificent patronage of the arts; Trajan, as the familiar paragon of the rule of law. Last of all appeared a float celebrating the return of the golden age.

The message was clear: the 1513 procession represented religion, literary culture, observance of social and gender hierarchies, and jurisprudence as equally serving an emerging political order, an "age of gold" predicated on the abandonment of the forms and style of the medieval corporate republic. Vasari's account of the procession is prominent in Manfredo Tafuri's discussion of Leo's deployment of ceremony and of triumphal imagery and architecture in both Rome and Florence for political ends.[77] Tafuri presents a general, all-encompassing ritual economy under Leo that leads him to overlook significant details both of the 1513 procession and of the pope's visit to his native city in 1515.

The attendants of Trajan in 1513 included ominous figures. Six pairs of doctors of law, *dottori legisti,* wearing ankle-length togas and capes of ermine rode surrounded by a large group of torchbearers, identified by Vasari as representatives of humbler trades associated with the practice of law: scribes, copyists, and notaries carrying papers and ledgers.[78] Vasari further distinguished the lawyers as dressed in antique garb, though this outfit doubtless resembled the robes of modern doctors of law (or judges). We can assume that the notaries and others wore familiar dress without any allusion to antiquity. The hierarchic separation of doctors of law and notaries was presented in 1513, then, as absolute, founded in humanist constructions of ancient institutions and practices.

Such a pageant of the legal professions was by no means a traditional motif of Carnival, but the 1515 triumphal entry of Pope Leo X into Florence indicates its significance.[79] At this lavish public ceremony, the main square, the Piazza della Signoria in front of city hall, was transformed by a huge quadruple triumphal arch representing Justice, located adjacent to, but also in implicit critique of, traditional sites of legal and judicial practice, notably the Badia district and the palace of justice (now the Bargello).

The details of the Arch of Justice in the Piazza della Signoria were evidently unknown to Vasari in the 1560s, when as court artist to the Medici archduke, he painted a representation of Leo's 1515 entry in the old city hall that was by now transformed into a ducal residence and architectural emblem of centralized monarchic rule (figure 3.7). The painting shows Leo's triumphal progress across the square with city hall in the left background; the pope receives the acclaim not only of the populace but also of the realm of nature, in the form of embracing figures representing the major local river and mountain range.

Centered in the background is the Loggia dei Lanzi, that took its current name from the lances of the guard stationed here by the Medici

Figure 3.7. Giorgio Vasari, *Entry of Pope Leo X into Florence*, 1515, fresco, Palazzo Vecchio, Florence. The procession traverses the Piazza della Signoria. Courtesy of Alinari/Art Resource, New York.

following their seizure of power in 1512. The republican associations of the building, noted above, had been intensified under the restored, anti-Medicean republic of 1494–1512. The republican government established as its defining constitutional innovation a Venetian-style deliberative body and the loggia became known as the Loggia del Consiglio Maggiore after this assembly.[80]

The resignification of this evocative structure was clearly vital to the Medici after 1512. They achieved this by displaying within it statues of compelling rhetorical force and symbolism. In the 1515 entry, for example, a stucco statue of Hercules, clearly visible in Vasari's painting, served as a heroic comrade for the soldiers stationed in the loggia. Later Cellini's *Perseus and Medusa,* still in the loggia, conceptualized Medici control and its civilizing outcomes in terms of the defeat and dismemberment of a female "monster"—a mingling of gender and political discourse already present in the 1513 procession.[81]

The symbolic representation of "justice" on the piazza was spatially and, in terms of the progress of the procession, temporally adjacent to the lawyers' district at the Badia. On exiting the square past the Palazzo della Mercanzia, where disputes involving the Florentine trades were adjudicated, the procession turned into the Via del Proconsolo and encountered an elaborate *apparato*. The exact design is not clear, but it certainly framed the facade of the Badia, now rendered symmetrical through the addition of a second, fictive portal to match the existing, off-center one. (This facade, one of Arnolfo di Cambio's buildings for the revolutionary commune of the late thirteenth century, was not the church front, but rather a masonry screen bringing order to the exterior of the choir and transept).[82] In line with the emphasis on the abbey church, the *apparato* represented Faith.

Both contemporary and modern accounts of Leo's entry emphasize the magnificent ephemeral decorations, such as the Arches of Justice and Faith. For many citizens, notably the local notaries and practitioners of ancillary trades, the ephemeral decorations were perhaps less impressive than certain permanent changes in the urban fabric. Contemporary observers note that preparations for the pope's entry included the removal of structures jutting into the streets. This provision echoed longstanding concerns enunciated in the city's statutes, but was perhaps also motivated by recent urbanistic measures in Rome, in whose image Florence was temporarily remade for this occasion. A focus of demolition was the lawyers' district around the Badia, where the removal of stationers' shops and similar structures freed the view of the church from the palace of justice.[83] In the place of a busy and intense scene of writing, especially of notaries who made up by far the majority of the guild's membership, there now appeared a transfigured city embodying transcendent values through a scenographic combination of word, image, and architecture.[84]

The representation of the law and its practitioners in the Carnival procession of 1513, then, had been in full accordance both with historical circumstance and with the concern of the new Florentine rulers to inscribe a static image of the law in the consciousness and even fabric of the city. The particular emphasis on robed *doctores* proclaimed an ideal conception of the law as an academic discipline at home in the rarified atmosphere of the schools of Bologna or Padua. The homology, staged in the 1513 procession, of the law with other disciplines and domains of knowledge situated it in a reformist model of encyclopedic ordering instituted by intellectuals, notably Poliziano, working in close collaboration with innovative early modern rulers.[85] The visual association with Trajan, as an authoritative, princely source of jurisdiction, echoed the humanist tendency to discount the medieval tradition of commentary on the classical legal codes in favor of a return to authentic, ancient texts.[86] Notaries, on the other hand, for all their deep involvement in every aspect of the life of the city, appeared in a subaltern and diminished position as copyists and mere executors of the determinations of others.

CODA: LEGAL CULTURES AND ARCHITECTURAL LANGUAGES

The elimination of such intermediate spaces as loggias or porticoes in the Renaissance urban environment, at least as an ideal, clarified and emphasized the articulation between the space of the house itself and that of the street or piazza, what we have come to call the distinction between public and private.[87] The architectural corollary was the emergence of the palace facade, a masonry screen conceptually and even, as in the Rucellai palace (figure 3.8), physically distinct from the body of the house and designed, as we saw in Rome, primarily as part of a scenographic streetscape.

The precocious facade of the Rucellai palace is emblematic of the shifts concerned, for it is no more than an ennobling, classical skin added in the 1450s to a remodeled group of disparate older buildings (see figure 3.4); it conceals, in other words, a traditional family compound.[88] The resulting illusion of a unified palace expresses the supremacy within the extended clan of a particular individual, the merchant Giovanni Rucellai, setting individual emblems associated with Giovanni alongside more traditional heraldic insignia of the clan. In addition, the facade also celebrates the marriage alliance Rucellai made with the Medici, to whom he had long been suspect as a relative of Palla Strozzi, Cosimo de' Medici's great rival and victim.[89]

Giovanni's expansionism within the family compound met with determined resistance from within the family and the jagged edge of the facade indicates the unfulfilled ambition to expand even further. Perhaps the loggia, which is unique in the history of palace building of the latter half of the fifteenth century in Florence, once had a conciliatory resonance, recognizing the support Giovanni had received from relatives and neighbors during his years of political marginality.[90] The tensions between traditional and more nuclear family structures in Florence still

Figure 3.8. Leon Battista Alberti, Rucellai Palace facade, Florence.
Courtesy of Foto Marburg/Art Resource, New York.

underlay conflicting contemporary scholarly hypotheses about the predominance of one or the other.[91]

The changing physical and social environment of late medieval
Florence constituted a veritable incubator for architectural experimentation. Of the two preeminent and sharply contrasted architects of the period, Filippo Brunelleschi and Leon Battista Alberti, neither was much
concerned with residential architecture. It has become something of an
orthodoxy to see Brunelleschi—the practitioner and professional—as
working within medieval traditions, while Alberti—the humanist, theorist, and courtier—is seen as establishing new protocols and paradigms,

especially through his critical absorption of classicism.[92] I argue that this underestimates the radicalism of Brunelleschi and his break with late medieval architectural method and principle, though he certainly operated in large part in situations and with expectations marked by continuity with long-established patterns of action and thought. Because he was the son of a successful notary, the question arises about the extent and significance of his exposure to certain kinds of legal knowledge and practice and to a particular legal culture.

The question becomes more acute in respect to the contrast with Alberti, who was a doctor of canon law trained at the university of Bologna. I must leave to another occasion a consideration of a link between the two men's conceptions of architecture, not as a technical process but as a mode of codifying human action and principle and projecting values and desires, and their specific knowledge and experience of the operation of law in human affairs.[93] Much remains to be done in the cultural history of law and legal practices in general in the Renaissance. Such a history would clearly have direct relevance for the history of urbanism, if not also for that of the emergence of new paradigms anticipating and even informing modernism (Brunelleschi) or postmodernism (Alberti).[94]

NOTES

Thanks are due to Barbara Hanawalt and Michal Kobialka for providing the impetus for the development of this essay. Daniel Smail, Thomas Cohen, and Sam Kinser read drafts and offered sage advice, which I was not always able or sufficiently prudent to follow.

1. The classic discussion of Italian city statutes in relation to the built environment is Wolfgang Braunfels, *Mittelalterliche Stadtbaukunst in der Toskana*, rev. ed. (Berlin: Gebrüder Mann, 1979); see also Giuseppina C. Romby, "Norme e consuetudini per costruire nella Firenze del Quattrocento," in *La città del Brunelleschi*, ed. Francesco Gurrieri (Florence: Vallecchi, 1979), pp. 93–99, illustrating the activities of the *ufficiali della torre*, the Florentine magistracy concerned with urban space. For their Roman counterpart, the *maestri di strada*, see Carroll William Westfall, *In This Most Perfect Paradise: Alberti, Nicholas V, and the Invention of Conscious Urban Planning in Rome, 1447–1455* (University Park: Pennsylvania State University Press, 1974), pp. 81–84.

2. See, e.g., Antonio I. Pini, *Città, comuni e corporazioni nel Medioevo italiano* (Bologna: Edizioni CLUEB, 1986), p. 280. A remarkable symptom of the growing prestige of lawyers in Italy was the development of funerary observances of particular dignity,

involving the emphasis on a particularly impressive tomb and the restriction of women's weeping; see Diane Owen Hughes, "Mourning Rites, Memory, and Civilization in Premodern Italy," in *Riti e rituali nelle società medievali*, ed. Jacques Chiffoleau, et al. (Spoleto: Centro italiano di studi sull'alto medioevo, 1994), p. 35.

3. This chapter is greatly indebted to Lauro Martines, *Lawyers and Statecraft in Renaissance Florence* (Princeton: Princeton University Press, 1968); on notaries see Arnaldo D'Addario, ed., *Il notaio nella civiltà fiorentina* (Florence: Vallecchi, 1985). An excellent wider account of the law and legal culture is Paolo Grossi, *L'ordine giuridico medievale* (Bari and Rome: Laterza, 1995). See also Aldo Mazzacane, "Law and Jurists in the Formation of the Modern State in Italy," in *The Origins of the State in Italy, 1300–1600*, ed. Julius Kirshner (Chicago: Chicago University Press, 1996), pp. 62–73.

4. Pini, *Città, comuni e corporazioni*, p. 280; Grossi, *L'ordine giuridico medievale*, p. 104; Denys Hay and John Law, *Italy in the age of the Renaissance* (New York: Longman, 1989), p. 289.

5. Peter Burke, *The Historical Anthropology of Early Modern Italy: Essays on Perception and Communication* (Cambridge and New York: Cambridge University Press, 1987), p. 113.

6. It is useful to think of notaries as engaged in "civic liturgies" constituting documentary modes as symbolic acts; see Brigitte Bedos-Rezak, "Civic Liturgies and Urban Records in Northern France, 1100–1400," in *City and Spectacle in Medieval Europe*, ed. Barbara A. Hanawalt and Kathryn L. Reyerson (Minneapolis: University of Minnesota Press, 1991), pp. 34–55, esp. p. 34.

7. The term "agonistic" is central in Ronald Weissman's account of Florentine social relations within their multiple, topographically defined communities (*gonfalone*, parish); in his view, Florentines sought release from such tense interactions in confraternities and other institutions that brought together residents of different parts of the city. See Ronald F. E. Weissman, *Ritual Brotherhood in Renaissance Florence* (New York: Academic Press, 1982). Weissman's thesis is accepted, though tempered, in the most thorough study of one of Florence's sixteen administrative districts (*gonfaloni*), Dale V. and Francis W. Kent, *Neighbours and Neighbourhood in Renaissance Florence: The District of the Red Lion in the Fifteenth Century*, Villa I Tatti 6 (Locust Valley, N.Y.: J. J. Augustin, 1982).

8. Grossi, *L'ordine giuridico medievale*, p. 251, notes the slow movement toward a "consensualismo" fully attained only in the era of humanism. On the prevalence of consensualist ideology in Renaissance Florence and the radical critique of it made by Machiavelli, see Victoria A. Kahn, *Machiavellian Rhetoric: From the Counter-Reformation to Milton* (Princeton: Princeton University Press, 1994), pp. 48–50. This change in ideology had much to do with the emergence of a new kind of elite of technically trained personnel involved in administration; on the "great grey phalanx of bureaucrats in Florence, see Howard Saalman, "The Transformation of the City in the Renaissance: Florence as Model," *Annali di Architettura: Rivista del CISA* 2 (1991): 73–82, esp. p. 75. Alvise Zorzi, "The Judicial System in Florence in the Fourteenth and Fifteenth Centuries," in *Crime, Society, and the Law in Renaissance Italy*, ed. Trevor Dean and K. J. P. Lowe (New York: Cambridge University Press, 1994), pp. 43, 51, 56–57, while noting the general emergence of a penal attitude toward criminal behavior, has emphasized the mediatory and conciliatory stance, even in

the later fifteenth century, of the Otto di Guardia and of Lorenzo de' Medici himself in relation to a concern to bring about "consensual composition of conflicts on the part of the new ruling oligarchy."

9. An exemplary discussion of this process, though with specific reference only to one city, is Henri Broise and Jean Claude Maire-Vigueur, "Strutture famigliari, spazio domestico e architettura civile a Roma alla fine del medioevo," in *Storia dell'arte italiana* (Turin: Einaudi, 1983), pt. 3, 5: 99–160. See also Charles Burroughs, *From Signs to Design: Environmental Process and Reform in Early Renaissance Rome* (Cambridge: MIT Press, 1990), pp. 29–44. On Florence see Gottlieb Leinz, *Die Loggia Rucellai: ein Beitrag zur Typologie der Familienloggia* (Bonn: Rheinische Friedrich-Wilhelms Universität, 1977).

10. On Florentine notaries and their culture, see Martines, *Lawyers and Statecraft* and, especially, D'Addario, ed., *Il notaio nella civiltà fiorentina*. Arbitration itself is exhaustively discussed by Thomas Kuehn, "Law and Arbitration in Renaissance Florence," chapter 1 of his *Law, Family, and Women: Toward a Legal Anthropology of Renaissance Italy* (Chicago: Chicago University Press, 1991), pp. 19–34, see also pp. 69–74. Kuehn argues persuasively that arbitration (or "composition," pacification) coexisted with litigation and penal procedures throughout the Renaissance, even finding a new space of operation with the consolidation of legal prosecution and punishment. Similar views are independently voiced by Zorzi, "Judicial System in Florence."

11. See Ronald F. E. Weissman, "From Brotherhood to Congregation: Confraternal Ritual between Renaissance and Counter Reformation," in *Riti e rituali nelle società medievali*, ed. Chiffoleau et al., pp. 77–81: confraternities, closely modeled organizationally on the commune itself, contributed to the maintenance and/or restoration of social harmony through various practices. In particular (p. 80), confraternities were called on "to perform quasi-municipal functions," including the pacification of quarrels, i.e., arbitration in a wider sense.

12. I have in mind here the conception of the page on which text appears, especially in manuscripts, as a composite material object, rather than a neutral carrier. For a manifesto of the "new philology," see Marina S. Brownlee, Kevin Brownlee, and Stephen G. Nichols, eds., *The New Medievalism* (Baltimore: Johns Hopkins University Press, 1991).

13. This aspect of marriage alliances is emphasized by Gene A. Brucker, *Renaissance Florence* (Berkeley: University of California Press, 1983), pp. 92–93. Francesco Guicciardini's opinion was doubtless widely shared: "There is nothing more difficult *(nel vivere civile)* than arranging marriages for one's daughters." See Marvin B. Becker, *Civility and Society in Western Europe, 1300–1600* (Bloomington: Indiana University Press, 1988), p. xxii.

14. There is considerable recent scholarship on marriage chests; my account here is heavily dependent on Christiane Klapisch-Zuber, "Les Femmes dans les rituels de l'alliance et de la naissance à Florence," in *Riti e rituali nelle società medievali*, ed. Chiffoleau et al., pp. 3–22.

15. Klapisch-Zuber, "Les Femmes dans les rituels," esp. pp. 7–10. For an insightful and nuanced reading of shifts, specifically in the representation of Lucretia in *cassone* paintings, involving ultimately a "hierarchy ordering male speech over female chatter and the image of woman over the feminine word," see Cristelle L. Baskins, "Corporeal Authority in the Speaking Picture: The Representation of Lucretia in Tuscan Domestic Painting," in *Gender Rhetorics: Postures of Dominance and Submission in History*, ed. Richard C. Trexler

(Binghamton, N.Y.: Medieval and Renaissance Texts and Studies, 1994), pp. 187–200 (esp. p. 199). This article belongs to an impressive number of recent feminist studies, by Baskins and others, of Florentine domestic imagery.

16. Christiane Klapisch-Zuber, "Une Ethnologie du mariage au temps de l'humanisme," in her *La Maison et le nom: Stratégies et rituels dans l'Italie de la Renaissance* (Paris: Editions de l'école des hautes études en sciences sociales, 1989), pp. 137–49. Altieri's work, *Li Nuptiali*, composed between 1506 and 1509, was never published but circulated in manuscript in the sixteenth century. Altieri assembles material both from ancient sources and from memories, current in his day, of Roman practices before the imposition of papal authority. Noting his emphasis on the rape of the Sabine women, the violent episode at the origin of the Roman polity and population, Klapisch-Zuber comments (pp. 142–43) that this "ritual is the enactment of the symbolic resolution of a real situation, a conflictual relationship of forces. By reading the story of the first wives of the Romans behind the marriage rituals of his day, Altieri reminds the Roman aristocracy that the shortest route from disorder to order . . ., from political blindness [*aveuglement*, perhaps "shortsightedness"] to social harmony, is the ritual of alliance" (my translation). For Altieri, the rape of the Sabines is represented in every "apto nuptiale," but especially the brusque reception given a new bride by her father-in-law at the entrance of his palace, into which he drags her. Subsequently, the unity and internal order of the social elite is celebrated and displayed through the complex maneuvers of a special dance (p. 144).

17. Anna Maria Corbo, "Relazione descrittive degli archivi notarili Romani dei secoli XIV–XV nell'Archivio di Stato e nell'Archivio Capitolino," in *Sources of Social History: Private Acts of the Late Middle Ages*, ed. Paolo Brezzi and Egmont Lee (Toronto: Pontifical Institute of Mediaeval Studies, 1984), pp. 61–62. According to Corbo, "arbitration is the most interesting institution that appears in Rome in this period" (p. 61). Further, "arbitration seems to assume the role of popular drama, in which the arbiters are directors who regulate the conduct of the offending and offended parties" (p. 62). Corbo does not compare the Roman practice with that of other cities, nor does she seek to explain its decline. A clue might be her observation that the arbiter himself, often a man learned in the law, "becomes, through those he judges, a source of law *(fonte di diritto)*" (p. 62). By the end of the fifteenth century, only the classical law code or the prince could serve as authoritative sources of law. Corbo's comments are echoed by Maria Luisa Lombardo, "Nobili, mercanti e popolo minuto negli atti dei notai romani del XIV a XV secolo," in *Sources of Social History: Private Acts of the Late Middle Ages*, ed. Brezzi and Lee, pp. 308–9, noting that arbitration "is still completely unstudied." Indeed it is not even mentioned by any of the authors in Massimo Miglio, ed., *Un pontificato e una città: Sisto IV (1471–1484)*, Littera antiqua 5 (Vatican City: Scuola Vaticana di paleografia, diplomatica e archivistica, 1986). Though many of the essays in this useful volume draw on notarial records, none discusses the notariate (see esp. Anna Modigliani et al., "Il Rione Parione durante il pontificato Sistino: Analisi di un'area campione," in ibid., pp. 663–740, who uses notarial records to study several trades, but not the notariate). It may be that a district, marked by foreign residents and influences as much as Parione was, was relatively quick to abandon Roman-style arbitration as a local practice likely to meet derision from outsiders. Laurie Nussdorfer, "Writing and the Power of Speech: Notaries and Artisans in Baroque Rome,"

in *Culture and Identity in Early Modern Europe (1500–1800): Essays in Honor of Natalie Zemon Davis,* ed. Barbara Diefendorf and Carla Hesse (Ann Arbor: University of Michigan Press, 1993), pp. 103–18, dealing with a later period, does not mention arbitration.

18. Anna Modigliani, "Il Rione Parione," p. 663. It is not clear how many of these cases involved arbitration.

19. On the occurrence of porticoes, see especially Giovanna Curcio, "I processi di trasformazione edilizia," in *Un pontificato e una città,* ed. Miglio, pp. 706–22, esp. p. 709: "In 40% of the documents, the front of a house opens in a portico; in half the cases with columns *[colum(p)natus]."*

20. Burroughs, *From Signs to Design,* pp. 38–39, 251.

21. This seems to be true of the Casa Bonadies in the Via del Banco di Sto Spirito (oral communication, Ronald Malmstrom). On the issue in general see Burroughs, *From Signs to Design,* pp. 29–44.

22. Domenico Gnoli, *La Roma di Leone X; Quadri e studi originali* (Milan: Editore Ulrico Hoepli, 1938), p. 16; Burroughs, *Signs to Design,* p. 41. In a letter, Thomas Cohen has pointed out to me the importance of the decline of the vendetta: with the waning of urban warfare, the nobility took to easier coexistence in a broadly pacific context in which highly public truces between adversaries, involving many witnesses, were no longer necessary. He also notes the statutory existence of *pacieri* (peacemakers) among municipal officials in the later sixteenth century, though he finds no evidence of their activity. It is likely, he thinks, that *pacieri* had previously played a significant role in the affairs of the city.

23. Altieri, *Li Nuptiali,* p. 144, insists that the rape of the Sabines is represented in every "apto nupiale." He describes the brusquely conducted entry of a bride into her new home. But this violent episode at the threshold is succeeded by a complex dance in which the unity and internal order of the social elite is recognized and celebrated.

24. Leon Battista Alberti, *De re aedificatoria,* ed. Giovanni Orlandi and Paolo Portoghesi, 2 vols. (Milan: Polifilo, 1966), 2: 803 (IX.iv): "Indeed, it would be appropriate to display painted and sculpted images of the brave and memorable deeds of citizens, along with their portraits, both in porticoes and dining rooms" (my translation); cf. *On the Art of Building in Ten Books,* trans. Joseph Rykwert (Cambridge: MIT Press, 1989), p. 299. The ancient examples cited by Alberti clearly involve interior porticoes, but in contemporary Rome, porticoes mainly occurred, if at all, on the house fronts.

25. Alberti, *De re aedificatoria,* 2: 795 (X.iii); *On the Art of Building,* trans. Rykwert, p. 296: "The ancients used to add either a portico or a hall onto their houses; not always composed of straight lines, but sometimes of curved ones, like a theater. Off the portico they would add a vestibule, almost always a round one." The association here of the portico with the vestibule indicates that Alberti has a facade feature in mind.

26. On the use of the loggia in fifteenth-century contexts as a space for dramatic representations see Westfall, *In This Most Perfect Paradise,* pp. 52–53.

27. Alberti, *De re aedificatoria,* 1: 339 (V.ii): "porticum quidem et vestibulum non servorum magis, uti Diodorus putat, quam universorum civium gratia positum arbitramur"; *On the Art of Building,* trans. Rykwert, p. 119: "The portico and the vestibule were not reserved for servants, as Diodorus thinks, but are for citizens of all ranks, as we would like to suggest." In the Latin text, the portico and vestibule are not simply juxtaposed, as Rykwert's translation suggests; rather the latter situates the former. In the previous passage (V.i), Alberti had referred to the portico—but not the vestibule—as one of a number of elements that are considered necessities, even though they began as enhancements for the sake of convenience *(commoda)*; the sentence on the portico expands on this generalization.

28. Stefano Infessura, *Diario della città di Roma di Stefano Infessura scribasenato*, ed. Oreste Tommasini (Rome: Forzani, 1890), pp. 79–80: "and in conversation [the king] told the pope he wasn't master of this city *(terra)*, and that he could not be master of it because of the porticoes *(porticali)* and narrow streets and the projecting structures *(mignani)* . . . and he advised him to throw down the *mignani* and porticoes, and to widen the streets." It is not clear from this if the porticoes, like the *mignani*, projected from the buildings, or were incorporated within them, like those of Bologna that stood on private property, though made accessible by statute to public use. See Francesca Bocchi, "Un simbolo di Bologna: i portici e l'edilizia civile medievale," in *Simbolo e realtà della vita urbana nel tardo medioevo*, ed. Massimo Miglio and Giuseppe Lombardi (Manziana [Rome]: Vecchiarelli, 1993), p. 121.

29. In this passage, however, there is no specific mention of porticoes. See Infessura, *Diario*, p. 85: "On January 8, 1480, Pope Sixtus began to put into effect the advice that King Ferrante gave him when he stayed in Rome in January 1475; that is, he began to demolish projecting structures *(mignani)* and to widen streets, and he began in the district of the weapons dealers *(armaroli)* in Ponte."

30. On the Palazzo Massimo alle Colonne, see Charles Burroughs, "The Building's Face and the Herculean Paradigm: Agendas and Agency in Roman Renaissance Architecture," *Res: Aesthetics and Anthropology* 23 (1993): 7–30.

31. For Infessura's political sympathies see his *Diario*, pp. xiii, xx, xxii, 51 n. 2. Infessura (ca. 1440–ca. 1500), a lawyer and professor of law at the Roman university, served as *scribasenato* (chancellor) of the municipal government of Rome.

32. Corbo, "Relazione descrittiva," p. 61. For Infessura's lament about Sixtus's sale of notarial offices, including many in the municipal domain, thus making them less accessible to Roman citizens, see Paola Pavan, "Permanenza di schemi e modelli del passato in una societa in mutamento," in *Un pontificato e una città*, ed. Miglio, p. 311.

33. In general, see the comments of Becker, *Civility and Society*, p. 21: "beginning with the Italian humanists of the fifteenth century . . ., dissatisfaction mounted . . . with ideas of atonement, reparation, and restitution." And: "The conception of rendering visible satisfaction as an essential for the pacification of one's neighbors and their ultimate reconciliation with God was considered entirely remote from the true meaning and spirit of the Gospels."

34. The term is used by Saalman, "Transformation," p. 79. On the type see George L. Gorse, "A Classical Stage for the Old Nobility: The Strada Nuova and Sixteenth-Century Genoa," *Art Bulletin* 79, 2 (1997): 301–27.

35. Suzanne B. Butters and Pier Nicola Pagliara, "Il Palazzo dei Tribunali e Via Giulia a Roma," *Zodiac* 14 (1997): 14–29; I am grateful to Linda Pellecchia for this reference. The new building was not planned to accommodate all the city's notaries, but only those involved

in ecclesiastical business of various kinds. On the city guild of notaries, headquartered on the Capitoline Hill, see Antonio Martini, *Arti, mestieri e fede nella Roma dei papi*, Roma cristiana 13 (Bologna: Cappelli, 1965), pp. 108–9, 250.

36. See Eugenio Garin, "Coluccio Salutati e il *De nobilitate legum et medicinae*," in *Atti del Convegno su Coluccio Salutati* (Buggiano: Edito dal Comune di Buggiano, 1981), pp. 17–25. Garin notes that by the late fifteenth century, Salutati's reputation had gone into decline and that the *De nobilitate* was the only work of his to be printed in the Renaissance (Venice, 1542). Se also Brucker, *Renaissance Florence*, p. 292; D'Addario, *Notaio nella civiltà fiorentina*, pp. 116–17, n. 114.

37. Paul F. Grendler, *Schooling in Renaissance Italy: Literacy and Learning, 1300–1600* (Baltimore: Johns Hopkins University Press, 1989), pp. 169–70.

38. D'Addario, ed., *Notaio nella civiltà fiorentina*, p. 251, n. 275.

39. D'Addario, ed., *Notaio nella civiltà fiorentina*, p. 26, n. 7; reviewing the city's guilds in the early fifteenth century, Dati writes: "the foremost guild is that of the Judges and Notaries, and this has a proconsul above its consuls and enjoys great authority, and can be said to be the origin of the notarial discipline as practised throughout Christendom; there arose the great masters and authorities in the field. *La fonte de' dottori delle leggi è Bolongnia, e la fonte de' dottori della noteria è Firenze*" (my italics). For Florence's reputation as a center of notarial training, see Brucker, *Renaissance Florence*, p. 289; for statistical analysis, see David Herlihy and Christiane Klapisch-Zuber, *Tuscans and their Families: A Study of the Florentine Catasto of 1427* (New Haven: Yale University Press, 1985), pp. 261–98.

40. D'Addario, ed., *Notaio nella civiltà fiorentina*, pp. 21–22, n. 1. Alfred Doren, *Das Florentiner Zunftwesen*, vol. 2 of *Studien aus der Florentiner Wirtschaftsgeschichte* (Stuttgart: J. G. Cotta'sche, 1908), p. 266, takes Boccaccio at his word, and sees this novella as evidence for public discontent with the malfeasance of notaries. On the pervasive, not undeserved suspicion of notaries in Florence, culminating in antinotary legislation of the end of the fifteenth century, see Martines, *Lawyers and Statecraft*, pp. 46–49.

41. D'Addario, ed., *Notaio nella civiltà fiorentina*, pp. 241–42, n. 269, n. 270. The notaries' guild was in charge of the cult from 1317 at latest. The high point of the procession seems to have been in the years shortly before the Medicean coup of 1434, perhaps significantly in view of the date of its transfer out of the guild's hands.

42. Martines, *Lawyers and Statecraft*, p. 50; cf. D'Addario, ed., *Notaio nella civiltà fiorentina*, p. 28, n. 8.

43. D'Addario, ed., *Notaio nella cultura fiorentina*, p. 239, n. 267; Martin Wackernagel, *The World of the Florentine Renaissance Artist: Projects and Patrons, Workshop and Art Market*, trans. Alison Luchs (Princeton: Princeton University Press, 1981), p. 148, n. 93. No trace remains.

44. Hay and Law, *Italy in the Age of the Renaissance*, pp. 293–94.

45. A famous example of such a business in this area in the fifteenth century was the shop of Vespasiano da Bisticci, located across the street from the Badia in the Via del Proconsolo. See Giuseppe M. Cagni, *Vespasiano da Bisticci e il suo epistolario* (Rome: Edizioni di storia e letteratura, 1969), p. 47.

46. D'Addario, ed., *Notaio nella civiltà fiorentina*, p. 252, n. 276.

47. See, e.g., the Esther *cassone* from the Apollonio di Giovanni shop discussed by Cristelle Baskins, with frequent reference to the role of a loggia in the depicted wedding ceremony: Cristelle L. Baskins, "Typology, Sexuality, and the Renaissance Esther," in *Sexuality and Gender in Early Modern Europe: Institutions, Texts, Images*, ed. James G. Turner (Cambridge and New York: Cambridge University Press, 1993), pp. 47, 49.

48. Anne B. Barriault, *Spalliera Paintings of Renaissance Tuscany: Fables of Poets for Patrician Houses* (University Park: Pennsylvania State University Press, 1994), pp. 66–67, noting the possibility that the panel is from a wall decoration, rather than a chest.

49. The Ospedale S. Paolo, erected in the later fifteenth century, had links with the lawyers' guild, whose arms appear in a portal in the portico facing the Piazza S. Maria Novella; see D'Addario, ed., *Notaio nella civiltà fiorentina*, p. 243, n. 270. Other hospitals with loggias include the Ospedale San Matteo (now the Accademia), the Bigallo, the Spedale degli Innocenti, and the Ospedale S. Maria Nuova. The two latter porticoes, like that of S. Paolo, are fifteenth century. See Giovanni Fanelli, *Firenze: architettura e città*, 2 vols. (Florence: Vallecchi, 1973), 2: 246.

50. Edgcumbe Staley, *The Guilds of Florence* (1906; reprint, New York: Methuen, 1967), p. 325.

51. Gurrieri, *Città del Brunelleschi*, p. 13. A map of the stretch of the Via del Proconsolo between the Via San Procolo and the Canto de' Pazzi shows a loggia on the Via San Procolo behind the Casa del Proconsolo. On two sides it is surrounded by Pandolfini property.

52. For a distinction between the two types in formal terms, without comment on differences of status or function, see Attilio Schiaparelli, *La casa fiorentina e i suoi arredi nei secoli XIV e XV*, ed. Maria Sframeli and Laura Pagnotta, 2 vols. (1908; reprint, Florence: Casa editrice le Lettere, 1983), 1: 68. Fanelli, *Firenze: architettura e città*, p. 40, lists thirty-four private loggias documented in medieval Florence.

53. Giovanni Fanelli, *Firenze* (Bari: Laterza, 1980), pp. 37, 45.

54. Fanelli, *Firenze*, pp. 37, 45, associates loggias with a late fourteenth-century change in residential typology. For a map and list illustrating the distribution of both private and institutional loggias in central Florence, see Gurrieri, *La città del Brunelleschi*, appendix 14 (np). The map is at too small a scale to be of much use (it was presumably made for display at the exhibition that the book accompanied). Fanelli, *Firenze: architettura e città*, p. 40, lists and, in some cases, maps thirty-four medieval private loggias, some destroyed already in the medieval period. Fanelli quotes the sixteenth-century intellectual Benedetto Varchi's assertion that twenty-six private loggias existed in his time. Elsewhere (*Firenze*, pp. 37, 45), Fanelli associates loggias with a change in the typology both of public and private buildings in the late fourteenth century.

55. D'Addario, ed., *Notaio nella civiltà fiorentina*, pp. 248, 250, 252. A hood and cloak, usually in *pavonazzo* blue, made up the typical costume of notaries.

56. See Nicolai Rubinstein, *The Palazzo Vecchio, 1298–1532: Government, Architecture, and Imagery in the Civic Palace of the Florentine Republic* (Oxford: Clarendon Press, 1995), pp. 86–87; the loggia was built from 1374, with major construction from 1380 and the inauguration in 1382, which marked the repression of the Ciompi uprising. It was used, e.g., for the inauguration of the Signoria.

57. Francis W. Kent, "The Rucellai Family and its Loggia," *Journal of the Warburg and Courtauld Institutes* 35 (1972): 397–401, emphasizes the persistence of loggias in relation to the author's conviction of the persistence of the *gonfalone* as a unit of local government dominated by major patrician families. For the association of loggias, at least in the Trecento, with magnate values, see Rubinstein, *Palazzo Vecchio*, p. 86. Rubinstein suggests that certain Florentines had a Visconti loggia in Milan in mind. In Urbino, the medieval cathedral adjoined a public square overlooked by a loggia belonging to the Montefeltro family; the loggia allowed activities and persons of distinct status to coexist and interact in the same space. See Andreas Tönnesmann, "Le Palais ducal d'Urbino: Humanisme et realité sociale," in *Architecture et vie sociale*, ed. Jean Guillaume (Paris: Picard, 1994), p. 138, noting that with the construction of the new residence, the piazza lost its popular character and became effectively a "cour d'honneur."

58. Cesare Foucard, "Descrizione della città di Napoli e statistica del Regno nel 1444," *Archivio storico per le provincie napoletane* 2 (1872): 732. Loggias also identified divisions of Milan, though apparently on a smaller topographical scale than in Naples; see M. Gazzini, "Solidarietà vicinale e parentele a Milano: Le scole di S. Giovanni sul Muro a Porta Vercellina," in *L'Età dei Visconti: Il dominio di Milano fra XIII e XV secolo*, ed. Luisa Chiappa Mauri, Laura De Angelis Cappabianca, and Patrizia Mainoni (Milan: La Storia, 1993), pp. 303–30.

59. Rubinstein, *Palazzo Vecchio*, p. 86, n. 76. The building was called a loggia in early modern sources, which date its construction to 1364, i.e., after the Florentine victory over Pisa that supposedly supplied prisoners that built and gave their name to the structure. Recent investigations indicate a date in the 1380s, as part of a general remodeling of the west side of the piazza. However, this does not rule out the existence of an earlier loggia-like structure in the same area.

60. This situation of loggias as neighborhood centers perhaps was usurped or came to be discredited by the somewhat similar use of street intersections by more plebeian groups. Francis W. Kent has drawn attention to the use in this way of *canti*, notably the Canto alla Macigna, a meeting place of a group of local lads who gained a political role at latest in the aftermath of the Pazzi conspiracy when they hunted down the enemies of Lorenzo de' Medici. See Francis W. Kent, "Il ceto dirigente fiorentina e i vincoli di vicinanza nel quattrocento," in *I ceti dirigenti nella Toscana del Quattrocento*, ed. Riccardo Fubini (Monte Oriolo, Impruneta: Papafava, 1987), p. 77.

61. Francis W. Kent, "The Making of a Renaissance Patron of the Arts," in *Giovanni Rucellai e il suo Zibaldone*, ed. Alessandro Perosa and Francis W. Kent, 2 vols. (London: Warburg Institute, 1981), 2: 60–62; Brenda Preyer, "The Rucellai Palace," in ibid., 2: 163, 2: 205–6.

62. Kent, "The Rucellai Family," p. 401; see also Marco Tasso, "Il 'canto' degli Alberti di Firenze," *Antichità Viva* 10/4 (1971): 20–36. Under the term "loggia" I refer to Tasso's "tettoia," which he dates to the late fourteenth century and distinguishes from the largely walled-up "loggia" within the bulk of the early fourteenth-century palace. On the fortunes of the Alberti family see Susannah F. Baxendale, "Exile in Practice: The Alberti Family in and out of Florence," *Renaissance Quarterly* 44 (1991): 720–56. The loggia was probably built around the time of the funeral of Messer Nicolaio Alberti, celebrated in 1377 with particular magnificence (Baxendale, p. 725) and the foundation at the end of the Ponte

Rubaconte of the Oratory of the Madonna della Grazia by Messer Jacopo Alberti in 1374 (Leonardo Ginori Lisci, *The Palazzi of Florence: Their History and Art*, 2 vols. [Florence: Giunti Barbera, 1985], 2: 617). The loggia was on the corner of the Via de' Benci, which led down to the bridge in an area developed by the Alberti following an extensive land purchase in 1358. Probably then, the Alberti loggia and the public loggia were constructed around the same time.

63. Kent, "The Rucellai Family," p. 401; on the occasion of the final expunging of the Alberti presence in Florence see Baxendale, "Exile in Practice," pp. 730, 737.

64. Kent, "The Making of a Renaissance Patron," p. 28.

65. Baxendale, "Exile in Practice," pp. 729–33, notes that the men of the Alberti family delayed entering into legal marriages until the return from exile, i.e., at the time the loggia was rebuilt. For the well-known link between Giovanni Rucellai's marriage plans for his sons and the interests involved in the construction of the loggia see Kent, "The Making of a Renaissance Patron of the Arts," pp. 66–70.

66. For an argument that loggias continued to be maintained and used well into the sixteenth century, see Francis W. Kent, "The Rucellai Family," and Francis W. Kent, *Household and Lineage in Renaissance Florence: The Family Life of the Capponi, Ginori, and Rucellai* (Princeton: Princeton University Press, 1977), p. 244, n. 57. Apart from the perhaps unusual case of the Rucellai, Kent cites mainly literary references. In his article, "Palaces, Politics, and Society in Fifteenth-Century Florence," *I Tatti Studies* 2 (1987): 45, Kent mentions in passing that certain loggias, along with towers and other rather outmoded architectural elements, remained the joint property of clans who were otherwise divided into more nuclear households. Possibly legal complexities contributed to architectural and spatial immobility!

67. Vittorio Franchetti-Pardo, "Cultura brunelleschiana e trasformazioni urbanistiche nella Firenze del Quattrocento," in *La città del Brunelleschi*, ed. Gurrieri, pp. 79–92, fails to discuss loggias as such, but otherwise characterizes very well the spatial and architectural shifts occurring in the fifteenth century.

68. Franchetti-Pardo, "Ceti dirigenti e scelte architettonicho-urbanistiche," in *I ceti dirigenti nella Toscana del Quattrocento*, ed. Fubini, refers to the loggia set by Michelozzo in the facade of the Medici palace as a motif frequent in the previous century but now going out of style.

69. Franchetti-Pardo, "Ceti dirigenti," pp. 230–31.

70. Franchetti-Pardo, "Cultura Brunelleschiana," p. 80.

71. For a discussion of the conceptual as well as architectural character of the early modern facade, see Burroughs, "The Building's Face and the Herculean Paradigm." I am grateful to Thomas Cohen for discussing with me his work on the use and marking of different kinds of urban and domestic space in Renaissance Rome.

72. Burke, *Historical Anthropology*, p. 12.

73. Bocchi, "Simbolo di Bologna," pp. 119–32. The requirement to build a portico is expressed trenchantly in the statutes of 1288 (p. 127), issued by a popular regime triumphant over its aristocratic adversaries. Bocchi cites a case of a fourteenth-century house constructed without a portico, but notes that after 1506 the lack of a portico became de rigueur as a status symbol of the new elite allied with the papal government (p. 132). For a

well-documented example, see Domenico Lenzi, "Palazzo Fantuzzi: un problema aperto e nuovi dati sulla residenza del Serlio a Bologna," in *Sebastiano Serlio: Sesto Seminario Internazionale di Storia dell'Architettura, Vicenza 31 agosto–4 settembre 1987*, ed. Christof Thoenes (Milan: Electa, 1989), p. 33; in 1517 the patron received a license to rebuild his palace, along with a special permit allowing him to demolish the existing portico. The new building was closely based on Roman models.

74. Two versions were published, in prints of 1545 and 1555.

75. Among important recent contributions see Elizabeth S. Watson, *Achille Bocchi and the Emblem Book as Symbolic Form* (Cambridge and New York: Cambridge University Press, 1993), pp. 63–66; Karen Pinkus, *Picturing Silence: Emblem, Language, Counter-Reformation Materiality* (Ann Arbor: University of Michigan Press, 1996). Neither Pinkus nor Watson is an architectural historian; the best discussion of the facade as such remains Johann K. Schmidt, "Zu Vignolas Palazzo Bocchi in Bologna," *Mitteilungen des Kunsthistorischen Instituts in Florenz* 13 (1967): 83–94. Bocchi's emblem book appeared in 1555, with a second, vastly transformed, edition in 1574.

76. Giorgio Vasari, *Le vite de' più eccellenti pittori, scultori e architetti: nelle redazioni del 1550 e 1568*, ed. Rosanna Bettarini and Paola Barocchi, 6 vols. (Florence: Sansoni, 1966–1987), 5: 310–13.

77. Manfredo Tafuri, *"Jugum meum suave est:* mito e architettura nell'età di Leone X," in his *Ricerca del Rinascimento: Principi, città, architetti* (Turin: Einaudi, 1992), pp. 141–222, esp. pp. 141–44. On the Medicean mobilization of public ceremony, see also Volker Breidecker, *Florenz, oder "Die Rede, die zum Auge spricht": Kunst, Fest, und Macht im Ambiente der Stadt* (Munich: Fink, 1990), pp. 292–309.

78. Vasari, *Vite*, 5: 312: "On the sixth float . . . was Trajan, most just emperor, in front of whom, as he sat on the float, advanced, on fine and beautifully equipped horses, six pairs of doctors of law, in togas to their feet and hoods of fur, according to the ancient dress code for those of doctoral status; their outriders, carrying torches in great number, were scribes, copyists, and notaries with books and writings in their hands."

79. Contemporary descriptions and other relevant texts are collected and discussed in Ilaria Ciseri, *L'ingresso trionfale di Leone X in Firenze nel 1515* (Florence: Olschki, 1990). The ceremony has attracted much scholarly attention; see especially the now classic article by John K. G. Shearman, "The Florentine *Entrata* of Leo X, 1515." *Journal of the Warburg and Courtauld Institutes* 38 (1975): 136–54; also Tafuri, "Mito e architettura," pp. 143–44.

80. Tafuri, "Mito e architettura," p. 141.

81. Yael Even, "The Loggia dei Lanzi: a Showcase of Female Subjugation," *Women's Art Journal* 12 (1991): 10–14.

82. On the Badia see Walter and Elizabeth Paatz, *Die Kirchen von Florenz, ein kunstgeschichtliches Handbuch*, 6 vols. (Frankfurt am Main: Klostermann, 1940–1955), 1: 264–80; Fanelli, *Firenze: architettura e città*, 2: 13–15. The facade of the church visible from the adjacent major street, the Via del Proconsolo, was not the west front, but rather a screen erected in the late thirteenth century to regularize the rear of the church and to create, no doubt, an appropriate pendant for the exterior of the Bargello, across the street.

83. For the general program of street improvement, see Ciseri, *Ingresso trionfale*, pp. 37–38. On the demolitions around the Badia, see pp. 99–100. A contemporary observer,

quoted by Ciseri, reports that "the government had seen to the demolition of all those roofs that shelter the shops of the stationers around the Badia" (la Signioria aveva fatto levare via tutti que' tetti che sono sopra quelle botteghe di quegli cartolai che sono intorno alla Badia di Firenze).

84. On the *apparato* around the Badia facade and the inscription appearing over the second, fake door of the church (LEONI X PONT MAX FIDEI CULTORI), see Ciseri, *Ingresso trionfale*, pp. 100–101. The proximity of the Bargello, containing the city's major criminal courts, had certain resonances specific to this period; as noted by Laura Ikins Stern, *The Criminal Law System of Medieval and Renaissance Florence* (Baltimore: Johns Hopkins University Press, 1994), p. 230, "In contrast [with the fourteenth and early fifteenth centuries], in the later fifteenth century, interclass crimes predominated, showing greater class conflict and a philosophy of persecution that benefited the rich."

85. Jean Céard, "Encyclopédie et encyclopédisme à la Renaissance," in *L'Encyclopédisme,* ed. Annie Becq (Paris: Klincksieck, 1991), p. 61, noting the roles of Poliziano in Laurentian Florence and Guillaume Budé in the France of Francis I.

86. This was an important concern in the intellectual circle around Lorenzo il Magnifico; on Poliziano's studies of legal texts, see Giovannangiola Tarugi, "Le *Pandette* del Poliziano e Lodovico il Moro," in *Interrogativi dell'umanesimo,* ed. Giovannangiola Tarugi, 3 vols. (Florence: Olschki, 1976), I: 1–10; Ian Maclean, *Interpretation and Meaning in the Renaissance: The Case of Law* (Cambridge and New York: Cambridge University Press, 1992), pp. 15, 50, on the Renaissance interest in Justinian's ban on interpretation, which had been neglected in the Middle Ages; also Michael D. Reeve, "Classical Scholarship," in *The Cambridge Companion to Renaissance Humanism,* ed. Jill Kraye (New York: Cambridge University Press, 1996), p. 30.

87. For a historicization of the notion of the private sphere, as a product and characteristic feature of early modern culture, see Roger Chartier, ed., *A History of Private Life. Part 3: Passions of the Renaissance* (Cambridge Mass.: Belknap Press, 1989), pp. 15–19, 399–403.

88. Brenda Preyer, "The Rucellai palace," pp. 155–228. On the facade, see Burroughs, *From Signs to Design,* p. 41.

89. The marriage took place in 1466; the wedding feast was held in and around the recently completed loggia, as we learn from Giovanni's extended account of the festivities. See Alessandro Perosa and Francis W. Kent, eds., *Giovanni Rucellai e il suo Zibaldone,* 2 vols. (London: Warburg Institute, 1960): I: 28–34, 146.

90. Kent, "Making of a Renaissance patron," pp. 27–30.

91. In a now classic essay, Richard Goldthwaite, "The Florentine Palace as Domestic Architecture," *American Historical Review* 77 (1972): 977–1012, argues for the emergence of nuclear family structure. The opposing case has been made especially by Francis W. Kent; relevant recent contributions include "Palaces, Politics, and Society in Fifteenth-Century Florence," *I Tatti Studies* 2 (1987): 41–70, and "Il palazzo, la famiglia, il contesto politico," *Annali di architettura* (1991): 59–72.

92. The bibliography is too vast to be given here. A key contribution in returning Brunelleschi to a medieval frame of reference was that of Howard Burns, "Quattrocento Architecture and the Antique: Some Problems," in *Classical Influences on European Culture*

A.D. 500–1500, ed. R. R. Bolgar (Cambridge: Cambridge University Press, 1971), pp. 269–87. Burns emphasizes the architect's recourse to medieval volumetric types. In a recent, monumental monograph, Howard Saalman (*Filippo Brunelleschi: The Buildings* [University Park: Pennsylvania State University Press, 1993]) sharply contrasts Brunelleschi, whom he sees as an all-around traditionalist, with the radical innovativeness of Alberti. For the radical Brunelleschi, founder of tendencies anticipating aspects of Modernism, see the various formulations of Manfredo Tafuri, e.g., his *Theories and History of Architecture* (New York: Harper and Row, 1980), pp. 16–17. Tafuri, no less than Burns, distances Brunelleschi from the imitation of classicism, seeing him rather as engaged in "dehistoricization," with "classic antiquity as . . . only a prop" (p. 16).

93. Charles Burroughs, "Grammar and Expression in Early Renaissance Architecture: Alberti and Brunelleschi," *Res: Anthropology and Aesthetics*, 33 (1997): 9–40.

94. A postmodern Alberti *(avant la lettre)* is emerging from various recent discussions; see, e.g., Anthony Grafton, "Panofsky, Alberti, and the Ancient World," in *Meaning in the Visual Arts: Views from the Outside,* ed. Irving Lavin (Princeton: Princeton University Press, 1995), pp. 123–30.

4

ARCHITECTURE AND THE
ICONOCLASTIC CONTROVERSY

ANDRZEJ PIOTROWSKI

*Establishing discontinuities is not an easy task even for history in
general. And it is even less so for the history of thought. . . . Generally
speaking, what does it mean, no longer being able to think a certain
thought? . . . Ultimately, the problem that presents itself [in this
question] is that of the relationship between thought and culture.*

MICHEL FOUCAULT, *THE ORDER OF THINGS*

If one takes into account the number of publications on the topic, it is possible to suggest that architectural historians usually consider the Gothic
style the highest achievement of European architecture in the Middle
Ages. Byzantium, although politically powerful and culturally rich, is seen
as a secondary influence in the development of European architectural
styles. To put it another way, the Great Schism of 1054 is implicitly built
into the taxonomies of the history of architecture. This understanding of
the architecture of the Middle Ages, I would argue, exists largely because
Gothic or Romanesque styles seem to have been "better explained" than
has the Byzantine. Erwin Panofsky's *Gothic Architecture and Scholasticism*
is a good example of how this clarity and consistency in our knowledge of
medieval architecture has been constituted.[1]

Moving beyond this traditional scholarly approach to medieval architecture, I suggest that the representational functioning of sacral

Byzantine architecture is more symbolically powerful and complex than has been recognized by earlier scholarly studies on this subject. I will examine some attributes of architecture that do not fit into the traditional taxonomies of style and their focus upon the ritual-based functionality of churches and suggest that the representational functioning of Byzantine architecture is grounded in the theological and philosophical issues of the Iconoclastic controversy. More specifically, I believe the Byzantine paradox associated with the representation of the divine, on the one hand, became the theological and philosophical issue and, on the other hand, found its fullest manifestation in Byzantine architecture. Moreover, in contrast to the Scholastic mode of thought and Gothic architecture, I suggest that Byzantine churches reached their highest development not when they resolved, but rather when they gave a material form to contradictory but coexistent ideas. This essay will explore how this paradox was possible and what space of representation emerged in this process.[2]

The controversy concerning truth in representation of the divine led to its political outcome, Iconoclasm.[3] Between 726 and 843, the Byzantine Empire prohibited the representational depiction of the divine as a violation of the spirituality of worship, thus banning all figurative imagery in churches. In 754, the so-called Iconoclastic Council in Hiereia, proclaiming that the divine nature is completely uncircumscribable and cannot be depicted or represented by artists in any medium whatsoever, caused the rampant destruction of art that has given the Iconoclastic controversy its negative place in history. The theological and philosophical ideas surrounding the Iconoclastic controversy, however, were much more complex than this political outcome would suggest.

In *Icon: Studies in the History of an Idea*, Moshe Barasch traces certain aspects of the Iconoclastic controversy to the neoplatonic thought of Plotinus (204–270) that gave symbolic prominence to visual experience and to its early Christian counterparts in the writings of Tertullian (150–225) and Origen (182–251), who also argued against visual religious representation.[4] It was, however, an anonymous writer of the early sixth century who has become known as Pseudo-Dionysius who turned the representation of the divine into a philosophical issue that, I believe, exerted a tremendous influence on the development of sacral architecture.

It can be said that the writing of Pseudo-Dionysius is concerned with ambiguity and contradiction in theology. Central to his thinking was the idea of the negative theology, that is, the notion that God is known in all things and as distinct from all things. *He is known through knowledge and through unknowing* [emphasis mine]. Of him there is conception, reason, understanding, touch, perception, opinion, imagination, name, and many other things. On the other hand he cannot be understood, words cannot contain him, and no name can lay hold of him. He is not one of the things that are and he cannot be known in any of them. He is all things in all things and he is no thing among things. He is known to all from all things and he is known to no one from anything.[5]

This apparent set of contradictions raises questions about the possibility of representational naming, of giving a corporeal representational shape to the divine: "just as the senses can neither grasp nor perceive the things of the mind, just as representation and shape cannot lay hold of the intangible and incorporeal, by the same standard of truth beings are surpassed by the infinity beyond being, intelligences by that oneness which is beyond intelligence."[6] And yet, in the following passage, Pseudo-Dionysius holds that "God is not absolutely incommunicable to everything. By itself it generously reveals a firm, transcendent beam, granting enlightenments proportionate to each being, and thereby draws sacred minds upward to its permitted contemplation, to participation and to the state of becoming like it." The sacred minds, therefore, "are raised firmly and unswervingly upward in the direction of the ray which enlightens them."[7] Thus, Pseudo-Dionysius asserts, knowing and representing the divine go beyond the capabilities of human thought and of material means. At the same time, divine benevolence offers the possibility of narrowing the gap separating the two domains and of allowing some limited human understanding. In his efforts to reach this state, Pseudo-Dionysius pointed out the divine presence in the complexity of thought and in thought's interaction with the world ("of him there is conception, reason, understanding, touch, perception, opinion, imagination, name"). Pseudo-Dionysius also accepted paradox as his mode of inquiry. The exploration of how conflicting themes or statements coexist was for him the way to study divinity, and this is reflected in his theological discourse. On the one hand, Pseudo-Dionysius disturbs the sense of closure within rational thought by juxtaposing seemingly contradictory logocentric meanings—"knowing through unknowing," for example. On the other hand, Pseudo-Dionysius resorts to the language of metaphor when he implies a divine intervention into the human world, evoking analogies of spatial or visual phenomena—for example, "drawing upward" and "the ray which enlightens."[8]

Pseudo-Dionysius extensively discusses two other issues that have particular application to my analysis of Byzantine architecture. The first is the issue of hierarchy. In his writing, hierarchy is the expression of a gradual transition, of the graded passing from the domain of the divine to the domain of the mortals.[9] The theological importance of such a concept cannot be overstated. In a deeply divided universe, hierarchy allows the possibility of bridging the two contradictory realities, acting as a site for God's symbolic descent and for symbolic ascent of the human mind.[10] This process is accomplished not through the reconciliation of opposites, but through revealing the symbolic value in the contradictions. Without losing the power of its symbolic tension, the coexistence of two contradictory realities was presented as a relationship that could be structured by its intermediate conditions, by the sites that negotiated the paradox.

The second topic of special interest is Pseudo-Dionysius' doctrine of symbols. His writing makes multiple references to *The Symbolic Theology,* his lost comprehensive treatment of the subject. Pseudo-Dionysius used the term *symbolon,* the meaning of which, as Barasch points out, is similar to the contemporary meaning of the French or English word "symbol," but it differs in a way that is important for this study. Barasch, after studying many scattered and fragmentary observations concerning this doctrine, asserts that "in the context of Dionysian theology the function of the symbol is to overcome the contrast between God's transcendence and the hierarchy that links God to the material world."[11] It is possible because, as Barasch suggests, unlike the contemporary meaning of the word *symbol* that tends to

> emphasize the gap between the object (or form) that serves as symbol and the idea (or other content) that is to be symbolized, . . . in Dionysian thought, the symbolon, while never negating the difference between symbol and symbolized, represents mainly what they have in common. Symbolon, in his view, is not only a sign but is actually the thing itself.[12]

Dionysian thoughts on contemplation as enlightenment—bringing divine light to the human mind—are an especially important example of this symbolon.[13] The divine light is referred to in terms of familiar characteristics—as a physical phenomenon—and as a powerful and multi-faceted symbol. Light symbolizes divine benevolence and wisdom for Pseudo-Dionysius, as in his claim that God "pours out on everyone the shining beams of his inspired teaching."[14] Such light is presented as capable of a symbolic guidance. Seeing that which is revealed, therefore, goes beyond the literal act of looking. Intelligence, thinking itself, is defined metaphorically as the eye, as a receptacle of divine signs.[15]

In contrast, during the time of Iconoclasm, the Iconoclastic doctrine that was used to justify the Iconoclastic law was constructed to present the representation of the divine as a univocal issue, bringing to the fore the easiest to control aspect of representation, the figurative depiction of the divine. After all, it is the very nature of figurative depiction to secure certainty, to allow a depicted figure to be easily recognized and univocally interpreted.[16] Rather than exploring Dionysian thoughts about how or whether it was possible to think the unthinkable, theologians and politicians attempted to reduce the problem of depicting the divine to a set of elemental symbolic categories about which they could argue in terms of whether or not a representation of the divine can be justified. The defenders of images developed the so-called Christological argument, in which they interpreted the Incarnation as a precedent for the representation of the divine prototype, that is, Christ was a representation of God the Father. Another example of an explanation for the rectitude of using images was based on their symbolic usefulness. Following the teachings of Pope Gregory the Great that images are like books for illiterate believers, the defenders of images argued that the value of an image was in its didactic function.[17] Because the major issue became not modes of thinking but correctness of interpretation, theologians and politicians attempted to ground their arguments on a stronger authority than their opponents. These attempts became so numerous that Edward James Martin devotes an entire chapter of his *A History of the Iconoclastic Controversy* to recording the various authorities and reasons given.[18] Consequently, at the time, the Iconoclastic controversy was shifted away from what it meant to represent and instead became focused on whether or not to represent the divine. When simplified in this way, the questions concerning truth or value in representation became, in Martin's words, "a political weapon rather than a debatable problem."[19]

One thinker of the time whose writing did reflect some of the earlier complexity of Dionysian discourse was Saint John of Damascus

(675–749). As Peter Brown points out, John of Damascus had studied two different symbolic ideologies, the Christian and the Muslim, which may account for his ability to deal with contradictions and complexities of thought and meaning without resorting to reductive processes.[20] In his *On the Divine Images: Three Apologies against Those Who Attack the Divine Images*, John of Damascus redefines Dionysian paradoxes in direct reference to the material world. On multiple occasions, he glorifies the symbolic function of matter, giving as examples the material dimension of holy signs described in the New Testament as well as to the materiality of the Gospel-book itself.[21] Most intriguing for our understanding of Byzantine architecture are his observations concerning matter and light. For instance, he discusses shadows cast by objects as the extensions of these objects; this is why, he argues, that shadows cast by the bodies of saints possess special powers.[22] Elsewhere, following the Christological argument, he argues that the materiality of the human body is a "fleshy veil" that covers the soul. Consequently, although thoughts are immaterial, this means that "it is impossible to think without using physical images."[23] Moreover, he treats looking itself as a major symbolic issue. Metaphorically equating an icon with a dark glass, he draws an analogy between looking directly into the light of sun through a dark glass and viewing the icon's representation of the divine; in both cases, a limited physical or symbolic transparency mediates unreconcilable differences.[24] In this way, bodily sight gains a new signifi-cance for John of Damascus who argues that it is only "by using bodily sight [that] we reach spiritual contemplation."[25]

Although many buildings of the time manifest these ideological concerns, they cannot be read like literary texts. Buildings do not make arguments. Rather, they represent by structuring experiences in order to imply thoughts. In Byzantine churches, the relationships between figurative mosaics and architectural form have long been acknowledged as being especially important for the symbolic functioning of these buildings. In one of the most important studies of these relationships, *Byzantine Mosaic Decoration: Aspects of Monumental Art in Byzantium*, Otto Demus asserts that "the [classical] Byzantine church itself is the 'picture-space' of the icons"; thus, "it is the ideal iconostasis."[26] Later, other scholars argued that the symbolic program—that is, the reasoning behind choice of subject and placement of images in the space of a Byzantine church—served as the basis for an icon in general.[27] Demus proposes three systems of symbolic meaning operating within a Byzantine church. First, a church is "an image of the Kosmos, symbolizing heaven, paradise . . . and the terrestrial world in an ordered hierarchy."[28] Second, "the building is conceived as the image of . . . the places sanctified by Christ's earthly life."[29] Third, the building becomes the symbolic "Calendar of the Christian year" in which "icons are arranged in accordance with liturgical sequence of the ecclesiastical festivals."[30]

Demus's approach to the symbolic functioning of Byzantine art and the structure of his inquiry overlook many attributes of architecture that are important for my discussion.[31] Take, for example, the issue of light that Demus discusses in terms of its "economy," that is, economy of architectural means used to produce rich coloristic effects.[32] This equation of the richness of visual effects, high degree of visibility, or correctness of perceived shapes with their symbolic value, seems to be an obvious oversimplification of the problem of representation. In order to avoid such limitations in my own discussion of how post-Iconoclastic Byzantine sacral architecture is the expression of the ideas surrounding the Iconoclastic controversy, I need to distinguish between *figurative* and *nonfigurative representation*. Figurative representation assures that a depicted form is recognizable as an appearance of something known from physical reality or as a figural form commonly associated with a particular interpretation.[33] The concept of nonfigurative representation, which I would like to introduce, refers to the mode of representation that establishes the relationships between given material forms or visual phenomena and symbolic reality without resorting to specific figures and familiar appearances. It is this underexplored nonfigurative representation that is related to the Dionysian ideas.[34]

I will demonstrate how architecture represented symbolic reality by discussing two Byzantine churches, one built before and one after Iconoclasm. The first one I will examine is the Katholikon in the Monastery of Hosios Loukas, built in Greece around the third quarter of the tenth or the first quarter of the eleventh century.[35] The Katholikon was an important center of a healing cult associated with Saint Luke and his material remains preserved in the crypt.[36] The Katholikon is also the only Middle Byzantine church in which both the building and the interior decoration are well preserved.[37] But it is more than its completeness that, according to Byzantine scholars, makes Hosios Loukas "the most important Byzantine monument to have survived in Greece."[38]

In *Byzantine Mosaic Decoration: Aspects of Monumental Art in Byzantium,* Demus points out a very specific aspect of the relationship between architecture and mosaics. To substantiate his observations of how physical space symbolically interacts with a depicted space, he refers to Hosios Loukas as well as to another church, the Katholikon, built in Daphni, Greece, around 1180–1100. While discussing oriental influences, Demus associates what he calls "magical presence" with the relationship between figurative mosaics and empty physical space. He stresses the symbolic importance of the hieratic frontality of depicted figures while also noting that "the fact that the frontal figures surround the room on all sides makes the empty space in the middle seem their real domain."[39] In the second zone of church decorations, the one dedicated to the Life of Christ, the pictures depict holy events in a nonhieratic manner but are positioned in the squinches of the naos in such a way that the depicted symbolic space doubles the physical space.[40]

Figure 4.1 shows the Nativity, a mosaic located in the squinch in Hosios Loukas. According to Demus, "in the Nativity, the concave landscape with the open cave in the center is adequately fitted to the physical cavity of the niche in which it is placed. The adoring Angels bow in the most actual sense to the Child who, in the center of the composition,

Figure 4.1. Nativity, southeast squinch in the Katholikon in the Monastery of Hosios Loukas. Photograph courtesy of the author.

is sheltered and surrounded by all the other forms and figures."[41] Not only the Nativity but all other mosaics (the Annunciation, Baptism, Presentation, and Transfiguration) placed in the squinches in both churches use the squinch to double the depicted space that was the site of a holy event. Demus sees this manipulation of space as creation of "the 'spatial' icon" that allows depicted scenes to "take on an air of spatial reality."[42]

I suggest, however, that the void space in front of the mosaic—the space in the center of the Nativity, for example, or the void space in the Annunciation through which the Angel crosses to approach Mary located on the other side of a squinch—has a quality that I have called nonfigurative representation. That is to say, while remaining empty and amorphous, the physical void space of a squinch acquires a degree of concreteness, materiality, and tactility. And this very process of solidifying the physical void space allows this space to represent a holy site in a nonfigurative manner. Squinches or domes make this symbolic process more perceivable by heightening the interactions between a figurative depiction and the void space. The same space and the same symbolic process, however, extend into the whole interior of the church. By simply being present in the church, a believer becomes a part of this different spatial reality.

This symbolic transformation of the void space is only one of many aspects of how a Byzantine church establishes the space of representation. Light is another one. Even though the pictures showing the unusual quality of daylight in Hosios Loukas have appeared on a cover of several books devoted to the history of Byzantine architecture, the relationship between the light and the building's form has not yet been adequately analyzed.[43] The interior of Hosios Loukas is filled with light that can best be described as emanating from both the windows and the walls. Figure 4.2 shows an unusual reversal of visual phenomena. In the center of the picture, where the material form of the building would seem to be the deepest, bright light unexpectedly emanates from a small arched opening located in the corner on the second level. Usually daylight comes through the thinnest or perforated elements on the outermost edge of a building. In Hosios Loukas, this reversal of what is expected draws one's attention.

This visual phenomenon is a consequence of the particular design of this building. As can be seen on the plan of the second floor (figure

Figure 4.2. The southeast corner of the naos in Hosios Loukas, the same corner where the mosaic of the Nativity is located. Photograph courtesy of the author.

4.3), the naos is surrounded by a border of complex structures forming what I would call a porous shell. There are two kinds of spaces within this shell. First, there are the volumes extending the central space of the naos, such as the two transepts and the bema.[44] These spaces are widely open to the core of the naos and reveal the exterior wall on the other side. They can be seen as the volumes filled with light on the left and right sides of figure 4.2. Second, there are the volumes within the shell. These spaces are much more enclosed, like rooms, and are open to the core of the naos only through small arched openings. One such opening is the unusual source of light in the center of figure 4.2. Both kinds of these spaces within the shell have windows that open to the outside. The upper parts of the window openings are filled with ceramic screens perforated by small but multiple round apertures. The lower parts of the window openings are filled with thin slabs made of white marble. Some windows, almost exclusively those on the second floor, also have larger rectangular openings between the stone slabs and the ceramic screens.[45] Some of these rectangular openings can be seen in figure 4.8 showing the exterior view of the whole building. These larger openings are placed in such a way that they are not visible from the floor of the naos.[46] It is this set of hidden rectangular openings that allows more daylight into

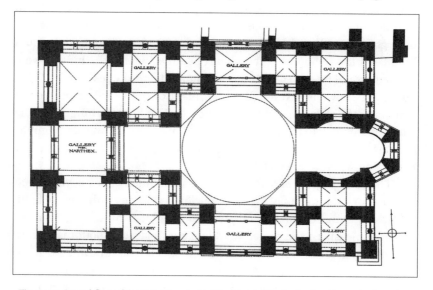

Figure 4.3. Second floor of the Katholikon in the Monastery of Hosios Loukas. Drawn by the author from a plan published by Schultz and Barnsley in 1901.

the enclosed spaces within the shell and make them appear as if they were unexpectedly glowing from within.

Windows are among the many elements Robert Schultz and Sidney Barnsley described in their comprehensive 1901 study of the Monastery of Hosios Loukas. Based on the condition of Hosios Loukas at that time, before a more recent restoration, they suggest that the rectangular openings might have been operable by a set of shutters made of very thin slabs of marble.[47] Moreover, Schultz and Barnsley describe a few remaining "pieces of strongly coloured glass . . . such as blue, red, and orange" that had been used to fill apertures in the perforated screens.[48] Although they treat these window screens as merely primitive predecessors of Gothic stained glass windows, they note that such a composition could resemble "a semitransparent colour mosaic."[49]

In the context of my reading of the symbolic functioning of this church, this information about the original construction of windows is important. When the small apertures of the window screens were glazed with coarse pieces of dark colored glass and the larger rectangular openings were either completely opened or closed by thin slabs of stone, the interior would have been darker than in figure 4.2, as today all these openings are glazed with colorless and fully transparent glass. Like mosaics, the screens with the colored glass must have glittered with sparkles of intense color. The intensity of light transmitted by the colored glass or reflected by the gilded background of the mosaics would have been low. Only the rectangular openings, when the shutters were opened, would have created bright though hidden sources of light. What figure 4.2 shows is just a delicate remnant of the visual phenomenon that was originally created in this church. The light coming from the small openings like the one in the center of figure 4.2 was as bright as or maybe even brighter than the light coming directly from the visible perforated window screens.[50]

The construction of symbolic visual phenomena goes beyond even the paradoxical infusion of the deep, enclosed volumes with intense light. In Hosios Loukas, walls literally emanate light. Schultz and Barnsley carefully measured the carved marble panels placed at bottoms of window openings and concluded that these panels are, on average, about one and three quarter inches thick. In some places, however, they are carved out to only half an inch thick. The white marble is semitranslucent and even today, despite the artificially high intensity of the light in the interior, it is possible to observe that these panels transmit daylight. This is why, as Schultz and Barnsby noted, the Greeks call these translucent slabs Phengites, "the Gleaming Stone."[51] These panels are treated differently on each side: symbolic signs and decorative motifs are precisely carved into the exterior surfaces, while the surfaces exposed to the interior of the church are flat and roughly finished. On sunny days, when seen from the interior, these stone panels reveal compositions made of warm, earth-colored spots of transmitted light. As in the Dionysian concept of dissimilar similarity, these images made of transmitted light are both similar to and different from the symbolic signs carved on the exterior surfaces. One can only imagine how much more visible and symbolically engaging these gleaming images were when the interior was much darker.

Phengites, the semitranslucent slabs of marble, can be found in other places inside this building as well. While Phengites built into windows mark the exterior edge, the Phengites inside the church mark the interior edge of what I have called the porous shell. These interior panels are easily visible from the floor of the core of naos. For example, the balustrades of the second floor gallery (figure 4.4) are constructed from them, and they are built into the base of the iconostasis. Some of these slabs can be seen in figure 4.2. Figure 4.4 shows how one of the gallery balustrades looks on a sunny day. The translucent slabs transmit daylight and delicately glow with the same warm, earth-colored light described earlier. This time the sculpted side of each panel faces the interior and resembles all the other decorated stone surfaces. The visibility of the carving on these slabs shows that it is the thickness that makes some areas more and other areas less translucent. In this way, one's awareness of continuity of solid matter is heightened at the same time as a paradoxical impression is created that any slab made of stone could transmit this inner light if it were thin enough. Because this phenomenon happens on the inner edge of the porous shell, the visual impression resonates with the visual phenomenon of bright light in the small opening in the center of figure 4.2 discussed earlier. Intense light seems to be captured within the parameters of the porous shell, almost as if the inner part were made of an unusual mixture of physical matter and bright light.[52]

There are other instances of the use of light and of the optical characteristics of physical matter in this church that could be discussed here. The visual quality of airiness created by the light reflected in surfaces

Figure 4.4. Gallery balustrade made of semitranslucent slabs of marble in Hosios Loukas.
Photograph courtesy of the author.

covered with gilded mosaics and polished stone is the most immediate and has been referred to in many studies.[53] However, I want to point to one other previously overlooked example that shows that the relationship between light and solid matter was explicitly related to the symbolic function of the church. In the bema, symbolically the most important place in a Byzantine church, the building was designed to create an unusual phenomenon of light, solid matter, and time. As can be seen on the plan of the second floor (see figure 4.3), the space of the bema is defined by two shallow cylindrical niches on the southern and northern sides of the altar. Figure 4.2 shows one of these shallow niches on the left as it can be seen across the core of the naos from the second floor. The niche seems to thin out the wall. Although the whole surface of the niche has been covered with stone panels, one of these panels is lighter than the others and is surrounded by a darker stone frame. The plan shows that this panel, located in the center of the shallow niche, closes what would be an opening connecting the space of the bema with a room on the gallery level. An identical opening with a closing panel exists in the other shallow niche. Although today these lighter panels almost blend visually with the stone veneer covering the shallow cylindrical niches, they looked different in the past. For the reasons discussed earlier, in the past there was a strong difference in the light intensity between the darker bema and the bright light captured within the gallery room. The lighter panels are made of thin semitranslucent slabs of white marble and were the only places where the bright light behind the wall was revealed to the bema. Especially during morning prayers, when the eastern light flooded the spaces of the gallery rooms on each side, the thinner panels would glow in the darker space of the bema. Although the Phengites I discussed earlier also transmitted light, their symbolic functioning was different. Phengites mounted in windows or balustrades still allowed for the transmission of light to be understood as a physical phenomenon because, in each case, the source of daylight was simultaneously revealed. In comparison, the light phenomenon created by the panels in the bema seemed physically less real or rationally explainable. Figure 4.2 shows a fragment of one of the two arched openings on the ground floor that lead from the bema to adjacent spaces, the Diaconicon and Prothesis. These openings are located directly below the lighter panels and they reveal what in the past was the dark interior of the building continuing behind the wall. Imagine how paradoxical it must have appeared that, right above these arched openings, in the middle of a large solid stone wall, a stone panel transmitted mysterious light from within.

I believe that these visual phenomena played a fundamental role in the symbolic functioning of Hosios Loukas.[54] Because light glows from within its most solid parts, solid matter is presented as filled with this unusual light. This phenomenon can be seen as a physical analogue to John of Damascus' idea that a material body can veil the soul. I believe that this interpretation, the possibility that the material form of a church could embody a sense of spiritual reality, was explicitly prompted by the designers of this church.

Ernst Diez and Otto Demus in 1931 and Demus in 1976 published both color and black-and-white photographs of a particular mosaic that would guide a believer toward its analogue to the Christological argument.[55] Figure 4.5 shows this mosaic, which was an unusual depiction of Christ. The deepest recesses of Christ's face, instead of being dark, are bright. Although Demus explained this "mysterious and even 'magical'" effect of the mosaic as an almost accidental result of counteracting the "blinding radiance" of the golden background and high contrast of light within that vault, he also observed that it appeared "as if light were breaking through the features, as if it radiated through the relief at its seemingly lowest points."[56] This description is reminiscent of the way Phengites transmit light and of the unusual light phenomenon shown in figure 4.2. Simultaneously, the mosaic suggests a particular theological interpretation—the Christological argument. The resemblance between the light phenomena in the depicted face of Christ and the light coming from the deepest recesses and solid matter of this building is of great symbolic significance. I contend that this depiction of Christ represented figuratively what the building and light represent in a nonfigurative way: that a material form is a veil of the immaterial. Christ's face provided a figurative representation, a recognizable figure that illustrates the symbolic narrative of the Christological argument.[57] The whole building, with the light phenomena of its porous shell and Phengites, does not resemble any familiar appearance. It is exactly the way all these architectural phenomena contradict what is familiar about physical solid matter that transforms the space of this church into the nonfigurative representation of a sacred site.

The symbolic function of the relationship between matter and light can be observed in Byzantium much earlier than the time when Hosios Loukas was built. Translucent stones were used for eucharistic cups and in buildings; as early as the fifth and sixth centuries, for example, translucent stone was used in Byzantine Ravenna to glaze church windows. These thin slabs survived in some windows of the Mausoleum of Galla Placidia (ca. 425–450). Windows in San Vitale (546–548) are now filled with glass treated to resemble translucent stone.

Because San Vitale was built before the Iconoclasm, I will use it to expand the time frame of my discussion. During the time separating construction of San Vitale and Hosios Loukas, the overall scheme of the Byzantine church was changed. The octagonal double shell scheme of San Vitale was replaced by the Greek cross scheme of Hosios Loukas (see figure 4.3). Although the geometry is different, the symbolic objective of material form remained the same—to transform earthly materials into a place for the contemplation of the divine.[58]

Figure 4.6 shows that, in San Vitale, a person looking at the walls from the center of the interior can perceive the building's shell as made of several intricate layers. Especially on the side from which the sunlight is coming, these layers are differently lit—the closer a layer is to the center of the interior of the building, the darker it appears. The volume of

Figure 4.5. Mosaic in the south transept in Hosios Loukas, before restoration. Photograph courtesy of Harvard University Press and the American School of Classical Studies, Athens, Greece.

the material shell seems to be filled with light and the depth of space is made perceivable by the changes of light intensity. Paradoxically, the layers resemble woven fabric, instead of looking like walls made of solid building materials. They look like screens made of various arched openings and seen against the light. In this process, the walls of San Vitale lose their perceptual solidity. The symbolic function of the infusion of light into the material structure of a building may be seen as similar to that in Hosios Loukas.[59] Further comparison between Hosios Loukas and San Vitale reveals profound symbolic differences. Consider the relationship between the interior and exterior in these two churches. Seen from the outside, Byzantine churches present themselves as spatial compositions of parts organized around a central vertical volume. Despite the complexity of such a composition, the visibility of the vertical core transforms them into figural singularities. Although Hosios Loukas and San Vitale are organized around central volumes, figures 4.7 and 4.8 show that they look very different. The treatment of the exterior of Byzantine churches changed during the time period between them. Figure 4.7 shows how the builders of San Vitale emphasized the precise geometry

Figure 4.6. Interior of San Vitale, Ravenna. Photograph courtesy of the author.

of the exterior and the uniformity of materials. The bricks that were used
to construct this exterior are flat and manufactured with great precision.
The surfaces produced by these bricks are smooth, and the resulting
geometry is perfectly controlled. Figure 4.8 shows that the exterior of
Hosios Loukas, in contrast, was made of rough, earthy materials. Its construction technique was much less systematic, almost as if random
pieces of stone and brick were brought together. While the exterior of San
Vitale presented a perfectly constructed object, the exterior of Hosios
Loukas blends with or grows out of the randomness of the surrounding
landscape. The exterior of Hosios Loukas thus acquires a great degree of
tactility through this interrelationship between the land and the building.

During the same time interval separating construction of San Vitale and Hosios Loukas, the interiors of the churches, specifically the way the central volume was spatially defined, also changed. As described earlier, at the time San Vitale was built, the walls surrounding the central space were transformed into layers of screens saturated with light (see figure 4.6). Similar to the exterior, this interior is homogeneous in its own character, as if made of a delicate but uniformly woven material. In comparison, the porous shell surrounding the core of the naos in Hosios Loukas is much less uniform. This interior reveals a tension between the physicality of the building and the unreal character of visual phenomena. On the one hand, the interior is made of large slabs of stone polished to show its grain, especially in places where surfaces can be touched. As can be seen in figure 4.2, parts of this building appear large and solid, as if independent buildings were placed inside a church.[60] In places that are meant to be seen from a distance, on the other hand, the same building reveals what is physically impossible—stones are filled with light or have surfaces made of reflected light. The material form of this building, while solid at the bottom, becomes a play of visual phenomena at the top. This tension is not between different lighting effects but between two different modes of thinking. What seems familiar and easy to comprehend about physical reality is juxtaposed with phenomena that must be acknowledged without easy explanation. Both aspects of reality are heightened and, because these phenomena exist within immediate spatial proximity, the juxtaposition of these two modes of thinking becomes unavoidable.

I believe that this double quality of the interior of Hosios Loukas—being physically real and physically impossible—is a nonfigurative representation of the symbolic reality that Pseudo-Dionysius discussed. At the same time, this symbolic reality is contained in the explicitly corporeal exterior. In Hosios Loukas, more explicitly than in San Vitale, the spiritual reality of a sacred place has been metaphorically circumscribed by the material form of a building.

In conclusion, the space of representation of churches like Hosios Loukas gave form to ideas grounded in Dionysian thought. In their use of the void space, light, and material form, the constructed perceptual phenomena strongly prompted a symbolic interpretation. At the same time, these phenomena did not attempt to resemble anything familiar. The void space in front of a mosaic acquired a degree of concreteness in

Figure 4.7. Exterior of San Vitale, Ravenna. Photograph courtesy of the author.

the interplay between the mosaic and this void space. The stones, of which the interior of the church is made, lost their concreteness by being infused with light. The more corporeal the exterior of the church, the more spiritual the interior. Consequently, in Hosios Loukas physical reality is what we know it to be and, at the same time, like nothing we know. It is this set of paradoxical reversals that represents a symbolic reality. These qualities of perception produce an unusual sense of place. By making a paradox perceivable, this space of representation provided a sense of a site suspended between two contradictory realities. It is this intermediate condition between the domain of God and the domain of the mortals that Dionysian hierarchy had implied.

This nonfigurative representation played a crucial role in the constitution of the space of representation during the Middle Byzantine period. It was also this symbolic function of nonfigurative representation that transgressed the limitations of figurative depiction and thus escaped the closure of the Iconoclasm. Both the representational function of Byzantine architecture and its influence remain underexplored. Though it goes beyond the scope of this essay, I suggest that it was exactly the paradoxical and poetic nature of nonfigurative representation

Figure 4.8. Exterior of the Katholikon in the Monastery of Hosios Loukas.
Photograph courtesy of the author.

that can be traced as Byzantine imports in the architecture of Eastern Europe, Italy, Spain, and France.

This discussion of Byzantine architecture as a space of representation also highlights a broader issue: not only the architectural construction of symbolic interactions between thought and experiential phenomena, but also the limitations built into the practices of constructing architectural knowledge. The knowledge of Byzantine architecture can be seen here as emblematic for all these epistemological practices that erase our ability to see how concepts of reality different than our own are represented. The notion of practice and the notion of space in this collection of essays encourages going beyond these traditional epistemological boundaries. Both words, *practice* and *space,* refer to the act of doing or the possibility of shaping something rather than to a resulting construct. Although the material form of architecture is always fixed in physical space and matter, the way it implies thoughts is anything but systematic and stable. The relationship between what may be experienced and what may be thought never acquires a degree of certainty that could support a totally stable explanation. Buildings, unlike studies of architecture, do not communicate and are not literally persuasive. Buildings represent. The interaction between a building and thought is a unique, architecture-specific, symbolic practice. Because of its complexity, our understanding of this practice does not fit into nineteenth-century disciplinary paradigms. Consequently, when buildings are approached as spaces of representation, they became epistemologically vulnerable. As I showed, the specificity of the symbolic functioning of a building can be easily dismissed by a particular mode of knowing, or its essential attributes can even be altered in the name of epistemological clarity and consistency. The architecture of the Middle Byzantine period shows that the complex mode of thought that a building represents makes it beautiful and fascinating even as it turns the building into an extremely vulnerable object of knowledge.

NOTES

This research of Byzantine architecture was supported by the University of Minnesota Graduate School and by the McKnight Arts and Humanities Summer Fellowship. I would also like to thank Professor Nikos Zias, Director of the Directorate of Byzantine and Postbyzantine Monuments at the Hellenic Ministry of Culture, for permitting me to study on-site and document Hosios Loukas and for helping me investigate the changes made in this church. I am grateful to Father George for his help and hospitality during my visit to Hosios Loukas. Collecting the photographic documentation of San Vitale in Ravenna was possible thanks to permission granted to my assistant and me by Don Giuliano Trevisan, Opera di Religione della Diocesi di Ravenna.

1. Erwin Panofsky, *Gothic Architecture and Scholasticism* (New York: NAL Penguin, 1951). Since the appearance of Panofsky's influential study in 1951, Gothic architecture has frequently been interpreted as the material reflection of Scholasticism. The scholarly method that Panofsky uses itself follows the Scholastic mode of thought he discusses. The way Panofsky constructs his argument parallels the two principles of Scholasticism, *manifestatio* and *concordantia*. Manifestatio, according to Panofsky, was aimed at the "elucidation or clarification" of thought as it manifests itself within "the completeness, self-sufficiency, and limitedness of a system of thought," while concordantia was aimed at finding a concordance or solution to any conflict of symbolic meaning through the "acceptance and ultimate reconciliation of contradictory possibilities" (pp. 31–32, 64). Although Panofsky recognizes the importance of different ideas in the formation of Gothic architecture, he discusses them only to show how they were reconciled; see, for example, his treatment of the relationships between mysticism and nominalism in the late Middle Ages (pp. 14–15). I would argue, then, that the logocentric construct of Scholasticism, systematically formed (manifestatio) and freed of contradictions (concordantia), guided both the development of

the Gothic style and of Panofsky's argument. As a result, how Panofsky studies his object of inquiry predetermines his conclusions. In such inquiry, Gothic architecture will always appear superior to the other kinds of architecture of the time.

2. Similar to Stephen Nichols, I see the understanding of representational functioning as the central issue in the new explorations of medieval architecture. See Stephen G. Nichols, "The New Medievalism: Tradition and Discontinuity in Medieval Culture," in *The New Medievalism*, ed. Marina S. Brownlee, Kevin Brownlee, and Stephen G. Nichols (Baltimore: Johns Hopkins University Press), pp. 1–2, 22.

3. It is noteworthy that the issue of the symbolic value of an icon has been discussed as an essential for understanding Western civilization from antiquity to our times. See, for example, Gilles Deleuze, "The Simulacrum and Ancient Philosophy," in *The Logic of Sense*, trans. Mark Lester with Charles Stivale, ed. Constantin V. Voundas (New York: Columbia University Press, 1990), pp. 253–79; Jean Baudrillard, "Simulacra and Simulations," in *Selected Writings*, ed. Mark Poster (Stanford: Stanford University Press, 1988), p. 170.

4. Moshe Barasch, *Icon: Studies in the History of an Idea* (New York: New York University Press, 1992).

5. Pseudo-Dionysius the Areopagite, "The Divine Names," in *Pseudo-Dionysius: The Complete Works*, trans. Colm Luibheid (New York: Paulist Press, 1987), 7.3, col. 872A, pp. 108–9.

6. Pseudo-Dionysius, "The Divine Names," 1.1, col. 588B, p. 49.

7. Pseudo-Dionysius, "The Divine Names," 1.1, col. 588C–D, 589A, p. 50.

8. See the discussion of "poetic imagery" in Pseudo-Dionysius the Areopagite, "The Celestial Hierarchy," in *Pseudo-Dionysius: The Complete Works*, trans. Colm Luibheid (New York: Paulist Press, 1987), 2.1, col. 137B, p.148; see also the discussion of light, p. 205.

9. Barasch, *Icon*, p. 163; and Pseudo-Dionysius, "The Celestial Hierarchy," 2.1, col. 373A–C, p. 197.

10. Pseudo-Dionysius, "The Celestial Hierarchy," 2.5, col. 401A, p. 206.

11. Barasch, *Icon*, p. 167; Pseudo-Dionysius, "The Celestial Hierarchy," 2.3, col. 397C; 2.1, col. 376B, C, pp. 198–99; also, 1108A, B, p. 284.

12. Barasch, *Icon*, p. 167.

13. Pseudo-Dionysius, "The Celestial Hierarchy," 2.3, col. 397C, pp. 204–5.

14. Pseudo-Dionysius, "The Celestial Hierarchy," 2.3, col. 400B, p. 205.

15. Pseudo-Dionysius says that God "grant[s] the beneficent rays of its own light to whoever views it with the eyes of the intelligence" (Pseudo-Dionysius, "The Celestial Hierarchy," 2.3, col. 400B, p. 205).

16. The political dimension of visual certainty during Iconoclasm was discussed by Peter Brown, *The Rise of Western Christendom: Triumph and Diversity A.D. 200–1000* (Cambridge, Mass.: Blackwell, 1996), p. 248.

17. Pope Gregory the Great on didactic function of images in Wladyslaw Tatarkiewicz, *Estetyka Sredniowieczna*, vol. 2 of *Historia Estetyki* (Warsaw: Arkady, 1988), p. 99. Greek and Latin with English translation in Wladyslaw Tatarkiewicz, *History of Aesthetics*, 3 vols., ed. Cyril Barrett (The Hague: Mouton, 1970–74), p. 105.

18. Edward James Martin, *A History of the Iconoclastic Controversy* (New York: AMS Press, 1978), pp. 130–45.

19. Martin, *Iconoclastic Controversy*, p. 78. This political shift is not that different from how contemporary knowledge of the Iconoclastic controversy is constituted. Though the visual form and its meanings were central to this controversy, the way we know it is mostly based on information that survived in writing and is almost exclusively about theological, political, or military issues. Neither Edward James Martin's text of 1930 nor Moshe Barasch's of 1992 present any images that could illustrate the cultural and ideological phenomenon of the Iconoclastic controversy. As Anne Middleton noted, medieval discourses are primarily based on literary studies and even contemporary poststructural critical methods tend to "reduce all historical phenomena [of the Middle Ages] to purely linguistic events" (Anne Middleton, "Medieval Studies," in *Redrawing the Boundaries: The Transformation of English and American Literary Studies*, ed. Stephen Greenblatt and Giles Gunn [New York: MLA Publication, 1992], pp. 20–21). Indeed, current epistemological concepts privilege verbal explorations and underestimate the specificity of significatory practices built into material forms, architecture in particular. Even if nonverbal records are discussed, figurative depictions are much more likely to be studied than architectural form and phenomena of perception.

20. Brown, *Western Christendom*, p. 247. It seems also noteworthy that Pseudo-Dionysius was a part of a similar cross-cultural environment.

21. St. John of Damascus, *On the Divine Images, Three Apologies against Those Who Attack the Divine Images* (Crestwood, N.Y.: St. Vladimir's Seminary Press, 1980), Apology I.16, pp. 23–24; II.14, p. 61.

22. St. John of Damascus, *On the Divine Images*, Apology I.22, p. 31.

23. St. John of Damascus, *On the Divine Images*, Apology III.12, p. 72; I.8, p. 18.

24. St. John of Damascus, *On the Divine Images*, Apology II.5, p. 53.

25. St. John of Damascus, *On the Divine Images*, Apology III.12, p. 72.

26. Otto Demus, *Byzantine Mosaic Decoration: Aspects of Monumental Art in Byzantium* (New Rochelle, N.Y.: Caratzas Brothers, 1976), p. 13.

27. This interpretation has been used in the history of Byzantine art. See, for example, James Snyder, *Medieval Art: Painting, Sculpture, Architecture, 4th–14th Century* (New York: Harry N. Abrams, 1989), pp. 150–51.

28. Demus, *Mosaic Decoration*, p. 15.

29. Demus, *Mosaic Decoration*, p. 15.

30. Demus, *Mosaic Decoration*, pp. 15–16.

31. As in the case of Panofsky's studies of Gothic architecture, Demus' conclusions are consistent with the epistemological structure he introduces. His study is as much about interpreting signs as it is about establishing a system of interpretation. The movement of a beholder and consistency in the way mosaics are viewed are essential for understanding how these symbolic systems work. Demus discusses figurative mosaics almost exclusively and explains their placement and size as being consistent for a practical reason—to ensure that the distance and the angle of view within the physical space of a church will provide the correct proportions and good visibility of the figures.

32. Demus, *Mosaic Decoration*, p. 35.

33. Figurative representation can be seen as grounded in the Aristotelian concept of

imitation of nature and Plato's process of doubling. See Aristotle, *"Physics," The Complete Works of Aristotle,* (Princeton: Princeton University Press, 1984), 1: 194a, 199a. Plato, "The Phaedo," *The Dialogues of Plato,* (Oxford: Oxford University Press, 1926), 2: 214–15.

34. The nonfigurative representation can be seen as related to the Dionysian concept of dissimilar similarity. Pseudo-Dionysius, "The Divine Names," 1.9, col. 916A, p. 118.

35. Although many historians believe that the Katholikon was built in 1025, Carolyn Connor, in her study of the crypt at Hosios Loukas, suggests that it was built earlier—between 956 and 970; Carolyn Loessel Connor, *Art and Miracles in Medieval Byzantium: The Crypt at Hosios Loukas and Its Frescos* (Princeton: Princeton University Press, 1991), p. 82.
There are two churches in the Monastery of Hosios Loukas, Panagia church and the Katholikon. In this essay I will refer exclusively to the Katholikon.

36. The symbolic function of the material remains of Saint Luke can be seen as related to the teachings of Saint John of Damascus. The emergence of this cult was discussed in Connor, *Art and Miracles,* p. 96.

37. As Otto Demus notes, we unfortunately have no complete and homogeneous decorations of the ninth or even tenth century. Many church decorations were destroyed or altered at the time of Iconoclasm. Demus, *Mosaic Decoration,* p. 54. See also a similar comment in Connor, *Art and Miracles,* p. 68.

38. Cyril Mango, *Byzantine Architecture* (Milan: Electa Editrice, 1978), p. 124.

39. Demus, *Mosaic Decoration,* p. 44. It seems important to note that, by associating what he calls "magical realism" with oriental influences, Demus effectively placed this "exotic" symbolic phenomenon outside of his system of interpretation (pp. 43–44).

40. A squinch is an architectural term that signifies a transition between a dome and two intersecting walls. Its material form is in the shape of a niche consisting of two vertical perpendicular surfaces merging into a small half-dome at the top. (It should be noted that the transition between two different geometries, a square [cube] and a circle [sphere], has been acknowledged as symbolically important in various examples of the history of architecture).
The naos, in the tradition of Byzantine sacral architecture, was the place of liturgy combining the centrally located large volume of space and the sanctuary.

41. Demus, *Mosaic Decoration,* p. 23. Although Demus' observations were made about mosaics in Daphni, they apply to the similar mosaic in Hosios Loukas shown in the illustration.

42. Demus, *Mosaic Decoration,* pp. 23–44.

43. See, for example, the cover of Richard Krautheimer, *Early Christian and Byzantine Architecture* (New York: Penguin Books, 1979).

44. The bema, in the tradition of Byzantine sacral architecture, was the slightly raised part of a church containing the altar.

45. The only rectangular opening on the ground floor is located in the treasury, the room that has always been closed.

46. I believe that in some cases the top part of the gallery balustrades now might be missing. These elements would have hidden small fragments of the rectangular openings that can be seen from the floor of the naos today.

47. Robert Weir Schultz and Sidney Howard Barnsley, *The Monastery of Saint Luke of Stiris, in Phocis* (London: Macmillan, 1901), pp. 25–26. They referred to a similar solution existing in the cathedral of Torcello, near Venice.

48. Schultz and Barnsley, *Monastery of St. Luke*, p. 25. According to information given to me by the employees of the Archeological Museum of the Hosios Lucas Monastery, no samples of any original glass used in the screens survived to our times.

49. Schultz and Barnsley, *Monastery of St. Luke*, p. 25.

50. I am currently in the process of developing a method that would allow studying the original light phenomena in this church.

51. Schultz and Barnsley, *Monastery of St. Luke*, p. 25.

52. The unusual quality of this inner space filled with light was even more vivid when the whole interior was darker.

53. See, for example, Snyder, *Medieval Art*, p. 149, or Nano Chatzidakis, *Hosios Loukas: Byzantine Art in Greece*, Manolis Chatzidakis, gen. ed. (Athens, Greece: Melissa Publishing House, 1997), p. 18.

54. References to the symbolic function of light and matter can be found in the story of the life of Saint Luke. In one instance, the vision of the Saint's body "gleaming wondrously" and "seen entirely as light" is juxtaposed to the limitedness of judgment based on appearances of things; Carolyn Loessel Connor and Walter Robert Connor, *The Life and Miracles of Saint Luke of Steiris: Text, Translation, and Commentary* (Brookline, Mass.: Hellenic College Orthodox Press, 1994), ch. 63, pp. 103–5.

55. Ernst Diez and Otto Demus, *Byzantine Mosaics in Greece: Hosios Lucas and Daphni* (Cambridge, Mass.: Harvard University Press, 1931), plate II, and fig. 18; Demus, *Mosaic Decoration*, figs. 26 and 27A (pages unnumbered). Some other mosaics on the vault of the southern transept were treated in a similar manner.

56. Demus, *Mosaic Decoration*, p. 36.

57. The mosaic shown in figure 4.5 no longer looks this way. The photograph of the current appearance of this mosaic was published in Chatzidakis, *Hosios Loukas*, fig. 35, p. 44. After restoration, all the mosaics in the southern transept ended up looking similar to the other mosaics in the church. All the unusual reversals of light disappeared. Because whatever was producing this unusual image has been removed, it is difficult to investigate this problem. I would like to offer a possible explanation, however. In *Byzantine Mosaics in Greece*, Diez and Demus suggested that the mosaic depicting this "unreal" face of Christ might have been a small copy of the medallion on the dome that was destroyed during an earthquake (p. 32). If true, this would even more strongly support my contention. When larger and placed above the center of the naos, this unusual image might have even more explicitly prompted viewers to interpret the visual phenomena of Hosios Loukas as analogues to the Christological argument. It would also mean that in order to make the small image in the transept look like the lost medallion, somebody had to cover the pieces of existing mosaic with layers of paint. Possibly, this later alteration was found inappropriate during the restoration work. This also seems probable in light of information given to me by Professor Nikos Zias, Director of the Directorate of Byzantine and Postbyzantine Monuments at the Hellenic Ministry of Culture. In response to my question concerning the reason for the changes in appearance of this mosaic, Professor Zias suggested that it is possible that "additional colors were added to the figures, especially to the faces, to heighten their effect at some time in the past after the construction of the mosaics" (Letter of September 8, 1997).

58. SS. Sergius and Bacchus (527–536) and even Hagia Sophia (532–537) in Istanbul can be seen as other double-shell spatial arrangements dealing with the same symbolic issue.

59. In San Vitale, the mosaic that survived in the apse shows that figurative representation engages physical space in a way similar to that discussed regarding the mosaics in the apses of Hosios Loukas.

60. This can be observed even better in bigger churches built in that time, as, for example, in San Marco in Venice (1063–1094) or in the later St. Front in Périgueux (mid-twelfth century).

5

STAGING PLACE/SPACE

IN THE ELEVENTH-CENTURY

MONASTIC PRACTICES

MICHAL KOBIALKA

The notions of place and space are associated in our minds with concepts defined by geometry and axonometry. Above and beyond their scientific attributes, however, they also express a mode of thinking that uses these two notions to describe the process of representing what is thinkable and doable under a specific set of dispositions and conditions. As Michel de Certeau noted in *The Practice of Everyday Life*:

A place *(lieu)* is the order (of whatever kind) in accord with which elements are distributed in relationships of coexistence. It thus excludes the possibility of two things being in the same location *(place)*. The law of the "proper" rules in the place: the elements taken into consideration are *beside* one another, each situated in its own "proper" and distinct location, a location it defines. A place is thus an instantaneous configuration of positions. It implies an indication of stability.

A *space* exists when one takes into consideration vectors of direction, velocities, and time variables. Thus space is composed of intersections of mobile elements. It is in a sense actuated by the ensemble of movements deployed within it. Space occurs as the effect produced by the operations that orient it, situate it, temporalize it, and make it function in a polyvalent unity of conflictual programs or contractual proximities.[1]

Two things are worth noting. First, the notion of place is connected with the order as well as exclusion; the notion of space is connected with mobility and the ensemble of movements. Second, the distinction between place and space suggests that space is a practiced place—"thus the street geometrically defined by urban planning (a place) is transformed into a space by walkers. In the same way, an act of reading is the space produced by the practice of a particular place: a written text, that is, a place constituted by a system of signs."[2] Since they are defined by the order, places can be identified. Since they are composed of the intersections of mobile elements, spaces can be actualized. This identification and actualization happens, as Michel Foucault reminds us, in "an open field of specifiable and describable relationships" wherein the doer of action and her or his representational practices occupy diverse positions defined by orientations, references, and linkages that are in a continuous variation. "It is a simultaneous play of specific remanences."[3]

Taking a cue from postmodern treatment of place and space, which views them as discursive formations consisting of material as well as immaterial components, I will explore how these two notions were defined by medieval representational practices and how they functioned in the second half of the eleventh century. What prompted this inquiry was my current project, which investigates the past and present rationalizations used to construct what is to be made visible and material in the Middle Ages. Whereas our notion of representation is grounded in the Aristotelian process of imitation of nature or in Platonic doubling of the "one" that becomes "two," both modified by Leon Battista Alberti's rules of perspective (1435), I believe that the medieval concept of representation had little to do with the prevailing tradition in Western culture that considers representation in terms of optical geometry (and its ideological, cultural, political, and social consequences) or in terms of today's taxonomies that express the typology of Christ's passion as drama and theater. Rather, it embraced the ever-shifting relationship between theological, historical, and spiritual formulations that defined the conditions of existence in a place and in a space. To substantiate this point, I will discuss (1) the processes that led to the institutionalization of representation in the second half of the eleventh century and (2) the eleventh-century copy of the *Regularis concordia,* used to explain the emergence of medieval liturgical drama and theater.

Consider the following text:

> On Easter Sunday . . ., at Nocturns . . .: While the third lesson is being read, four of the brethren shall vest, one of whom, wearing an alb as though for some different purpose, shall enter and go stealthily to the place of the "sepulchre" and sit there quietly, holding a palm in his hand. Then, while the third respond is being sung, the other three brethren, vested in copes and holding thuribles [censers] in their hands, shall enter in their turn and go to the place of the "sepulchre," step by step, as though searching for something. Now these things are done in imitation of the angel seated on the tomb and of the women coming with perfumes to anoint the body of Jesus. When, therefore, he that is seated shall see these three draw nigh, wandering about as it were and seeking something, he shall begin to sing softly and sweetly, *Quem quaeritis.* [Whom do you seek?] As soon as this has been sung right through, the three shall answer together, *Ihesum Nazarenum.* [Jesus of Nazareth.] Then he that is seated shall say *Non est hic. Surrexit sicut praedixerat. Ite, nuntiate quia surrexit a mortuis.* [He is not here. He has risen just as it was predicted. Go, tell this because he has risen from the dead.] At this command the three shall turn to the choir saying *Alleluia. Resurrexit Dominus.* [Alleluia. The Lord is risen.][4]

This passage is quoted to explain the "origins" of medieval drama and theater. The argument is made that, in the tenth century, the signs of drama can be found in the antiphonal dialogue of the Easter *Quem quaeritis* chant that describes the visit of the three Marys to the sepulchre where the body of the crucified Christ was buried. The *Regularis concordia,* where this text is found, is treated as the earliest medieval record of a theatrical representation in which a merger between some form of mimetic action, dialogue, and setting unequivocally takes place.[5]

I do not intend to argue for or against this narrative. I would like, however, to draw attention to an event that took place in the second half of the eleventh century, that is, the writing/copying of another *Regularis concordia.* Traditionally, the temporal gap between the 970–973 *Regularis concordia* and the eleventh-century *Regularis concordia* has not been taken into consideration by scholars, even though it was duly acknowledged. Consequently, the document, seen as an unproblematic or problematic record of the past, acquired an abstract status of a material cipher used to establish the credibility of a discourse or the emergence of liturgical drama.

As in its tenth-century equivalent, the *Regularis concordia* from the second half of the eleventh century was associated with Christ Church in Canterbury.[6] The manuscript is written in medieval Latin. Unlike its tenth-century counterpart, it has Anglo-Saxon glosses above the descriptive texts or the prayers that were added to the monastic or liturgical observances, such as, for example, the prayers for the king and the benefactors. The names and prayers that constitute the legitimate part of the Christian worship are in Latin only, however. This manuscript contains a full-page illustration that depicts three figures seated under a canopy with three arches. In the center, there is the image of King Edgar. Under the arch on the right, there is an archbishop with pallium, possibly Dunstan, and, under the left arch, a bishop, possibly Aethelwold. The three figures hold a long scroll. Below the scroll, there is a monk looking upwards, apparently in the act of genuflecting.[7] The manuscript begins with the *Proem* and is followed by a list of chapters and then by the twelve chapters themselves. There is also an epilogue, which ends in the middle of folio 27b. The remaining portion of this folio page is filled by a new text written in red ink, which does not belong to the body of the *Regularis concordia*. The *Quem quaeritis* can be found in this manuscript on folio page 21b.

Unlike its tenth-century equivalent, the eleventh-century *Regularis concordia* comes from the time of the establishment of Norman monasticism, which was influenced by the Cluniac model. William the Conqueror attempted to reorganize the English church with the help of Norman monks. He appointed a number of them to vacant abbacies. As a corollary of this action, two separate traditions began to coexist in England: English monasticism shaped by modified versions of the tenth-century *Regularis concordia,* the *Rule* of Saint Benedict, or the individual customs of monastic houses, and Norman monasticism shaped by Cluniac consuetudinaries.

If, as Michel de Certeau proposes, the text is inscribed because of what has already been inscribed "by the law," "which makes itself believed and practiced," the tenth-century and the eleventh-century copies of the *Regularis concordia* should not be seen as the same or reduced to being a singular record of a monastic history.[8] To corroborate this point, I will focus on the representational practices that delimited how it was possible to think about, record, and make visible objects in the second half of the eleventh century.

My argument is that the events in the second half of the eleventh century, that is, the Berengar-Lanfranc Eucharist controversy, Saint Anselm's prayers, Lanfranc's *Constitutions,* and the eleventh-century *Regularis concordia,* disclose an epistemic break in the concept of representation in a monastic place, exposing for a brief moment a space of instability in a society based, at least theoretically, upon an ideological stability. By taking leave of their "authorities" (both theological/scriptural and ecclesiastical), these events not only altered the convention, which had operated until now to realign the different traditions and daily practices to control gnosiologic self's most imperceptible movements of thought, as the tenth-century *Regularis concordia* may suggest, but also produced a space where the tension between the different positions destabilized the approved convention.[9] By so doing, they partook in the process of proliferation of the new practices whose "attributes and properties" were embodied in the texts and the images produced. This momentary instability is the object of study here. I am interested in investigating the remanences of a movement within a discursive formation before this movement was classified or let itself be classified in the name of an ideological stability as an immobile place (de Certeau's order and the practice of exclusion) by an authorized representational practice.

The Berengar-Lanfranc controversy started in the summer of 1049 when Berengar put forth that the body and blood of Christ were not in the Eucharist and that baptism and marriage were mere ceremonies of no importance. Throughout the 1050s, Berengar's ideas were both criticized (the theologians of the monasteries of Chartres and Fécamp, the Council of Rome, 1050; the Council of Vercelli, 1050; the Council of Tours, 1054) and approved (the theologians from Metz and Rome). In 1059, Berengar was summoned by Pope Nicholas II to attend the Easter Council in Nicea. Berengar's writings were burnt and he himself was forced to accept a Eucharistic confession drawn up by Cardinal Humbert. The text was a confession of belief in physical Eucharistic change. It emphasized the fact this change occurred in the realm of the five senses, that is, the body of Christ which was broken during the Mass was not a symbol but the actuality.[10]

Berengar reluctantly accepted Humbert's statement of a physical presence. The verbal acceptance was not enough, however. He was made to sign the oath acknowledging his acceptance of the change during consecration. Only now, when it was embodied in the text, did the verbal acceptance become a physical and material sign of the confession within a highly textual, theological framework. A copy of the oath, incorporated into the canon collections under the opening words "Ego Berengarius," was sent by the pope to the churches in Italy, Gaul, and Germany.[11]

This statement of reality in the sacrament was undeniably an extreme case of the identification of the Eucharistic with the physical and historical presence of Christ. On the other hand, its political or ideological, rather than theological, character invited diverse reinterpretations and rationalizations ever since it had been promulgated. As it is argued, Humbert's treatment of Berengar had been shaped by Humbert's involvement in the controversy with the East over the use of leavened or unleavened bread in the Eucharist.[12] This argument notwithstanding, H. Chadwick observes that "even those who thought Berengar dangerously mistaken to emphasize the nonliteral, nonphysical understanding of the sacrament of the altar, had deep reservations about Humbert's formula that Pope Nicholas II had blessed."[13] Berengar went almost immediately back on his oath by proving that the formula was internally self-contradictory. He asked: How can a material object represent an invisible object or a spiritual truth? Upon his return to France, Berengar repudiated his oath and returned to his previous teaching.

In 1063 Lanfranc's *Liber de corpore et sanguine Domini* expressly supported the 1059 settlement against Berengar.[14] Lanfranc defended the formula that the Body of Christ was present in the Eucharist *sensualiter* (sensually) and that "the bread and wine which are laid on the altar are after consecration not only a sacrament but also the true body and blood of our Lord Jesus Christ, and they are physically taken up and broken in the hands of the priest and crushed by the teeth of the faithful, not only sacramentally but in truth." [15] The emphasis on the physical nature of this change reflected the theological discussion stimulated by Aristotle's *Categories*.[16] According to Aristotle, the visible universe of individual things *(topos idios)* was juxtaposed to a substratum of invisible primary substances floating in general space *(topos koinos)* conceived as the outer-most celestial sphere. The visible "accidents" or dimensions of height, width, and length of things were the sensible evidence of the primary substances.[17] Using the Aristotelian doctrine of substance, scholastics tried to clarify the meaning and the identity of physical events that accompanied spiritual or theological changes. This formula implied that the presence of a new substance on the altar meant the destruction of the bread, because two substances of this kind could not occupy the same area simultaneously. In the light of this shift, Lanfranc's position was clear: if the body of Christ became *sensualiter* present on the altar, its substance must have replaced the substance and the earthly material of the bread. The fact that the bread was visible to the faithful was a sign of divine mercy to spare them the horror of the act, though "occasionally the mask dropped and pious eyes saw the very flesh itself." [18]

Berengar questioned the use of Aristotle's doctrine by asking how could a material object represent an invisible object or a spiritual truth. He thus appealed to the old tradition of Ambrose, Saint Augustine, and Gregory the Great and its clear distinction between "enacted in an image" and "received in truth." This tradition must be interpreted, preferably with the aid of reason, to illuminate mysteries like the sacraments. Reason cannot be used in a haphazard way, but according to preestablished rules. Berengar claimed that the material bread and wine could coexist with, though they were directly opposed to, the spiritual body and blood. His argument was grounded in the interpretation of the sentence *Hoc est corpus meum, quod pro vobis tradetur* [This is my body, which is given for you] (1 Cor. 11:24). According to Berengar, this sentence could only make sense if *hoc* referred to the bread and the subject of the sentence was preserved intact till the end of the sentence. This argument was further supported by the grammatical doctrine that pronouns replacing nouns signified substance. Thus, in the sentence, the subject was the substance of the bread, and the change of/in the substance would make the sentence meaningless. Unlike Lanfranc, who could explain how one substance was replaced by another in the Eucharist during the Mass, Berengar believed that the reality existed in a manner that was only known to God and that could be perceived and affirmed by senses/grammar. Thus, he suggested that there existed the sacrament that was visible *(sacramentum)* and that to which the sacrament referred (*res sacramenti*—the Body of Christ), which was invisible.

The Berengar-Lanfranc controversy is not only an example of an institutional sanctioning of a new practice, but also discloses a change in the position and the identity of a seeing or speaking subject. Within the Western theological/monastic tradition, this process of establishing the identity involved God and the self.[19] As the Supreme Being, God is the source of all that is. He exists everywhere, in all things, and through all things. The fact that He neither began to exist nor will cease to exist entails that He always was, is, and will be forever. This is what all patristic texts say. In the second half of the eleventh century, these statements are given an elaborate interpretation guided by reason—*Fides quaerens intellectum* [Faith seeking reason]. Following this principle, Saint Anselm makes an argument that, in a rational manner, reveals the truth of the writings of Church Fathers. That is, to the extent that His Being is interpreted spatially, God exists as a whole, as absolutely present in every place and in no place. To the extent that His Being is viewed temporally, God is present at all times and at no time.[20] His magnitude, as Saint Anselm would assert in *Proslogion*, is that which a greater cannot be thought.[21] In other words,

> if our ordinary way of speaking were to permit, the [Supreme Being] would seem more suitably said to be *with* a place or *with* a time than to be *in* or *at* a time. For when something is said to be *in* something else, it is signified to be contained—more than [it is thus signified] when it is said to be *with* something else. Therefore, [the Supreme Being] is not properly said to be *in* any place or time, because [the Supreme Being] is not at all contained by anything else. And yet, in its own way, it can be said to be in every place and time, inasmuch as all other existing things are sustained by its presence in order that they not fall away into nothing. [The Supreme Being] is in every place and time because it is absent from none; and it is in no [place or time] because it has no place or time.[22]

All things, including human beings, come from nonbeing into being through something other than themselves, that is, the Supreme Being,

> since whatever exists exists through the Supreme Being, and since all things other [than the Supreme Being] can exist

through it only if it either [efficiently] causes them or else in the
material [out of which they are made], necessarily nothing be-
sides it exists except by its [efficient] causing. And since there
neither is nor was anything except this Being and the things
made by it, [this Being] was not able to make anything at all
through anything else than through itself.[23]

The self was thus made not as a copy of anything that existed prior to
it being begotten, but as a representation defined by a similitude to
divinity. All things, including the self, living in the space provided by the
creator, that is, in a homogeneous space of the divine hermeneutics,
affirmed his magnitude.[24] The Supreme Being, who exists in all existing
things as well as in all places, conferred upon the self an identity that
resided in the transmitted *logos.* The self's task was to uncover, rather
than to create, order, correct, or command, the language (the Word) with
which God had endowed the earth. New words did not describe the
self's reality, but it was enunciated through the expression of the sacred
already present in everything created, though not entirely visible. It is
not entirely visible because this "Word, by which [Supreme Wisdom]
speaks of creatures, is not at all likewise a word [or an image] of creatures—because this Word is not the likeness of creatures but is rather
the principal Existence."[25] Even though this Word is coeternal with the
Supreme Being, whereas the creation is not, when the Supreme
Being/Spirit speaks of itself, it speaks of all created things.[26] The *imago
dei,* thus, turned the self into a theological self whose identity could only
be fulfilled through the practice of the divine structure defined by the
logos, perceived by a rational mind, and presented as a visible affirmation
of the Supreme Truth.

The question of how to represent the Eucharist, as the Berengar-
Lanfranc controversy suggests, was no longer a matter of a patristic interpretation. Biblical and patristic writings on the Eucharist, in which
the concrete stands for the abstract, the particular for the universal, were
consulted but modified by an official ecclesiastical sanction applied to
establish the coherence of the believing community. This sanction privileged Lanfranc's view of the universe of substances made visible over
Berengar's reality known only to God and made according to reason in
the image of God. This being the case, medieval monastic practices of
the second half of the eleventh century were a special instance of the

cognitio Dei, the process of and the desire to apprehend God, presented as elaborate cross-references that multiplied different affirmations between divine substances and their verbal as well as visual signs embodied in, rather than recorded by, the text, in this case, in the interpretation of *Hoc est corpus meum.*[27]

On the other hand, the theological self needed to realize his/her presence in the homogenous space of the transcendent God. This involved the process of remembering or recollection that happened beyond the confines of material time and space—a merger between *cogo* (to collect, bring together, assemble) and *cogito* (to know). Augustine argued that to know was to recollect. In the act of knowing, the subject remembered or recollected what previously had been dispersed.[28] Recollection, thus, involved interiorization of "empty places" *(topoi)* into the space of memory. During this process of recollection, the sequential successions of interiorization of images or unclassified and unarranged abstract notions already contained in memory were transformed into coherent propositions *(logoi),* and as such "images of images" were referred to verbal and nonverbal signs and images.

The interplay between interiorized experience and exteriorized verbal and nonverbal signs acquired a different reading in Saint Anselm's 1072 collection of prayers. One of the forms of the prayer was meditation, which was required in monastic houses by the Benedictine *Rule.* By the time of Anselm, meditation was perceived as a complex exercise in the tradition of private devotion *(preces privatae).* Its purpose was to help a monk achieve an understanding of an ordered life of dedication to God through the process of interiorization and inwardization of divine truth.[29] This understanding signified the process of being able to recall the images in various ways and degrees of intensity and to relate them to the particular needs of the present situation.

For Anselm, as for Augustine, meditation was the mental activity whose function was to bridge the gap between knowledge of earthly things and knowledge of the attributes of God. That knowledge was acquired in the process of a mental movement from images to cognition *(cogitatio),* from cognition to meditation *(intellectus),* and from meditation to contemplation *(sapientia).* For Anselm, thus, there were two ways of obtaining knowledge: first, knowledge that came from the senses in the form of images (material substances) that, when stored in memory, were available for examination by rational faculty of cognition and meditation;

and, second, knowledge that came from the mind's introspective knowledge of itself that, in turn, led from the intuitive self-knowledge of the
mind to knowledge of immaterial substances such as truth, beauty, love,
virtue, etc. It was only through the combination of these two kinds of
knowledge that the mind could reach toward the knowledge of God.
Fides quaerens intellectum expressed the belief that nothing in faith was
contrary to reason.

A prayer to Saint Peter is a good example here. Even though the
prayer followed the traditional Carolingian pattern of using one of the
incidents from the life of the saint to reach the light of truth, Anselm
strengthened the message by using the immediate images of emotional
states that existed in life here and now or that were stored in and committed to the memory, the pattern that he would elaborate in his seminal
Cur Deus Homo in a few years' time. Traditionally, the suppliant approaching Saint Peter would recall Saint Peter's denial of Christ and his role as
shepherd of the sheep. Note the difference between the Carolingian and
Anselmian prayers. First, the Carolingian prayer:

> Most holy Peter, prince of the Apostles, my shepherd and
> provider, to whom power to bind and to loose has been given by
> your Master, loose me, I pray, from all the bonds of my iniqui-
> ties, and intercede for me, that the Lord, your Master, may look
> on me, as he looked on you.[30]

And, now, Anselm's prayer:

> The sheep is sickening to death: his ulcers swell, his wounds
> are reopened and grow putrid. The wolves have tasted his blood.
> They are waiting for him to be cast away. Faithful shepherd,
> turn your eyes on him: see that he is one of yours. If he is
> strayed, nevertheless, he has not denied his Lord and shepherd.
> If, through the filth, you cannot recognize the face of one
> washed white in the fountain of Christ, at least you see that he
> confesses the name of Christ, who had thrice to ask you 'Lovest
> thou me?' before he said 'Feed my sheep.'[31]

The difference between these two prayers is evident. It could be suggested that Anselm's prayer describes the desire of the self (a faithful),

who is engaged in the process of recalling verbal and nonverbal signs to erase the distinction between earthly things and spiritual knowledge and to present him/herself to the mediating other (an image of a saint) in order to affirm the existence of God. These three states, "in the mind," "in the mind and outside the mind," "in the mind and necessarily outside the mind," corresponding to the cognition-meditation-contemplation triad were, for Anselm, indispensable for the religious experience of the self. This religious experience of the Self no longer existed only in verbal form, which depended on scriptural authority, but on reason alone *(sola ratione).*[32] While the prayers retained their quality as interior reflections, Anselm wrote them down not only to interrelate faith and reason, but also because what they signified was what was really taking place during the act of meditation. In writing out the prayers, he created a model for theological investigation in which oral and written models were inseparable and produced a new text. This text acted as an intermediary between the words in the mind, which constituted a mental text, and the images in and outside the mind, which gave rise to contemplation. Through his commitment to reason without scriptural authority, Anselm succeeded in connecting abstractions of the highest order of reality and the existence of a superior nature forming a material expression of things in the mind either through an image of corporeal things or their conception.[33]

This expression, unlike the expression of God, which does not need a model, depended on the prior existence of something else. This something else is not only the process of establishing the likeness to other things, but also the reality of their being, which is embodied, rather than recorded, in the text of a prayer and sustained through "the conserving presence" of the Supreme Being.[34] When a rational mind, states Anselm, conceives of itself in meditation, the thought is its own image as it is formed by impression (faith). The rational mind brings forth this image, but it cannot separate itself from it since faith is a received text.[35] Consequently, it establishes one that is an exploration of faith by reason. During this exploration, statements are made about reality.

The Berengar-Lanfranc controversy and Saint Anselm's 1072 meditations are two examples of the shifts in the mode of thinking that took place in the second half of the eleventh century. The written words marked the traces of the movement of these ideas that explained the relationship between the theological/monastic self and real essences.

They did so by multiplying affirmations within the space of the mind and necessarily outside the mind.[36]

This being the case, what are the implications of this process for theater studies? If the Berengar-Lanfranc controversy and Saint Anselm's *Prayers* and *Meditations* exemplify the transformations in the spiritual and theological service to God, does the *Quem quaeritis* partake in elucidating the epistemological and representational shift in the second half of the eleventh century? To answer these questions, consider Lanfranc's monastic and political activities in England.

Before Lanfranc, a Norman abbot, became the archbishop of Canterbury (on August 29, 1070) and started his program of rebuilding the English cathedral church and other monastic buildings, he had visited Canterbury. Lanfranc's silence about the existing practices has been interpreted as a sign that older traditions had disappeared or had fallen into complete neglect. However, a record found in Eadmer's *Miracula Sancti Dunstani* indicated that some form of the celebration of the Easter resurrection existed. The passage describing the healing of a cripple contains a statement that he was cured when the priests, under the guise of three women, approached the sepulchre looking for the body of Christ.[37]

Is this allusion to the three Marys who are looking for the body of Jesus Christ, a reference to a monastic custom celebrated on Easter Sunday? If this is a possible scenario, then this Easter ceremony belonged to a discursive formation that included the Berengar-Lanfranc controversy, the shift in the mode of meditation as exemplified by Saint Anselm's prayers and meditations, and the *Regularis concordia* written/copied after 1066. Thus, unlike the tenth-century *Quem quaeritis*, which was an act of elaboration on the services of Holy Week that were prescribed by the secular *Ordo Romanus primus*, this eleventh-century *Quem quaeritis* can be said to express a new mode of the functioning of physical representations accompanying spiritual changes.

Whether the *Quem quaeritis* successfully performed this function is open for discussion. The *Regularis concordia* from the second half of the eleventh century could be seen as a code that attempted to collate on the same textual plane the practices that were binding in England before the Conquest. This line of reasoning would then explain why scholars have interchangeably used the tenth- and eleventh-century versions of the *Regularis concordia* to explain their theories of the emergence of liturgical drama in the early Middle Ages. However, such a practice obliterates an event that took place at that time and may disturb the language of intelligibility that promoted current historical investigations. Sometime between 1070 and 1075, Lanfranc compiled a collection of customs that would govern monastic life in England. He might have heard of the *Regularis concordia*, but no mention of it appears in his consuetudinary. Even though the manner of liturgical celebration was in its essentials that described by Dunstan, Aethelwold, and Oswald, the local usage was questioned. For example, two great feasts of Dunstan and Elphege were removed from the calendar; the reliquaries of the saints, who had been canonized by local acclamation, were opened, though the authenticity of the remains was never challenged.[38] More importantly, while putting together a monastic code, Lanfranc decided to circumvent the local custom. In his statement to prior Henry, Lanfranc stated that his constitutions were

> compiled from the customs of those monasteries which in our day have the greatest prestige in the monastic order. We have added a few details and have made certain changes, particularly in the ceremonies of certain feasts, considering that they should be kept with greater solemnity in our churches.[39]

In order to achieve this, certain observances were altered. I draw attention to the changes in the ceremonial character of Easter Sunday. Recall the description of the celebration of the Night Office on Easter Sunday recorded in the *Regularis concordia,* and quoted in this essay, before reading Lanfranc's recommendation. According to the *Constitutions:*

> On Easter Day, before the night choirs, all the bells shall be rung for Matins, then by two and two as usual. At the invitatory there shall be four in copes, and the psalms as in the Rule, that is, *Domine in virtute tua,* etc. During the lessons thuribles shall be borne around, as laid down for Christmas. All the rest of the Office shall be according to the monastic rite.[40]

Thus, the celebrations on Easter Sunday did not follow a modified canonical Roman code as was suggested by the *Regularis concordia,* but a far more elaborate and meditative observance as specified in the Benedictine *Rule.* The monastic Office for Easter Day described in the Rule gave the following directions for the Night Office: the brethren were to rise at about 1:00 A.M. and go to church where they would chant six psalms. Then they would read four lessons with their responses. Afterward six other psalms with Antiphons would be sung. Four more lessons with their responsories, three canticles, and the *Alleluia* would follow. Then another four lessons from the New Testament and responsories would be read, and when the fourth responsory was finished, *Te Deum laudamus* would be chanted. When completed, the abbot would read the Gospel. After the Gospel, the hymn, *Te decet laus* would be chanted, and the blessing would be given. Then, Matins would begin.[41]

This being the case, it can be argued that the eleventh-century copy of the *Regularis concordia* functioned in the space that produced and was produced by the representational practices positioned in the dynamic landscape of ecclesiastical conflicts, *preces privatae*, and new monastic regulations. The physical layout of the manuscript expressed this complex new mode of functioning of representational practices. Although in medieval Latin, the text, and especially the descriptive parts and prayers added to the standard monastic or liturgical observances, was to be deciphered with the help of the Anglo-Saxon glosses running above it to perform functions that had been designed for it a century later.

Whether or not the *Regularis concordia* did so is not entirely clear. It is possible to suggest, however, that Lanfranc's collection of monastic customs, which showed little resemblance to the customs in the tenth-century consuetudinary, altered the earlier practices. They were either superseded or coexisted with other practices as indicated in *Miracula Sancti Dunstani*. The tenth-century *Regularis concordia*, copied in the eleventh-century post–Norman conquest England, was thus to perform functions that were foreign to its initial design. One the one hand, the *Regularis concordia* was used to express the strength of the Anglo-Saxon tradition that had been established by Dunstan, Aethelwold, and Oswald and was now eradicated by Norman abbots in various ways, including the removal of the feast of Dunstan from the calendar. One the other hand, the celebrations described in the consuetudinary were to accommodate the theological changes which redefined not only the Eucharist, but also the function of a written text.

Is it possible that the *Quem quaeritis* from the eleventh-century *Regularis concordia*, executed by the monks during the Night Office on Easter

Day, was no longer a practice of verification of the most imperceptible movements of thought? When used at all, did the post–Norman conquest *Quem quaeritis* function alongside other narratives within the historiographic field? Like the Eucharist viewed in terms of Lanfranc's real and substantial presence, the three Marys and the Angel, when allowed to appear, could not perform the function initially designed for them to express the obligation of truth contained in the *Qui facit veritatem venit ad lucem* statement and were now used to embody, clarify, and affirm the theological *logos:*

> Quem quaeritis?
> Ihesum Nazarenum.
> Non est hic. Surrexit sicut praedixerat.

Positioned within an enclosed monastic discourse and place, the *Quem quaeritis* was defined by the monastic experience of the self, be it meditation or the Chapter, which was executed "in the mind," "in the mind and outside the mind," and "in the mind and necessarily outside the mind"—*Fides quaerens intellectum.*

To use a metaphor, Lanfranc, like Berengar and Anselm, was a foreigner in the land. The name of the land was different. In Berengar's case, it was ecclesiastical politics. In Anselm's case, it was private devotion *(preces privatae).* In Lanfranc's case, it was monasticism in England. The three of them constructed and brought new representational practices into a place that had been designed by and for someone else. The Berengar-Lanfranc controversy, Anselm's meditation practices, and the *Constitutions* destabilized the authorized or accepted practice. In this moment of instability, the interplay between representational places and spaces became visible before its traces were washed away by the mechanism of a classificatory grid, or, to paraphrase de Certeau, in the place of the traces, there appeared facts that were recorded and are today assumed to be historically valid and that are shaped from conflicting imaginations, at once past and present.[42]

What was left were the real and visual representation of the Eucharist, the real and visual representation of prayers, and the real and visual representation of the resurrection of Christ. The Berengar-Lanfranc controversy sanctioned a singular interpretation of *Hoc est corpus meum* that camouflaged the political practice that had determined it and defended the notion of real presence in the Eucharist. Its function was to affirm the real presence of Christ. Saint Anselm altered the mode of operation of prayers along the trajectory of cognition, meditation, and contemplation. Now, meditation, rather than being an unrestrained process, was embodied in the text. It function was to affirm the *logos* through finding the connection between thoughts and words. Lanfranc designed the monastic practice in England while "virtually ignorant as yet of English practices." His constitutions established not only new monastic practices in England, but also a grid of control in order not to diminish the real presence of Christ. Whereas the tenth-century *Regularis concordia* presented a labor to compose practices which would reveal the most imperceptible movements of monk's thoughts, the *Constitutions* was a text which embodied the relationship between faith and reason. Its function was to affirm the monastic practices of the most prestigious monastic orders of the time.

Hoc est corpus meum. "This is my body," said Christ during the Last Supper. The words were assigned spiritual value by the apostles. This central *logos* to Christian worship calls back the memory of the one that has disappeared. It constitutes the point of departure for incarnating the discourse. This practice happens in a space where the movement of theological thought can produce unexpected tensions, new connections, and new alignments. In the eleventh century, these new positions destabilized the approved convention. This momentary instability was as ephemeral as the thought that conceived it. By identifying a place and a practice where the *logos* can manifest itself and become effectual, this movement was classified in the name of ideological stability. Unlike in the tenth century (970–973) or the twelfth century (the ternary discourse on the Eucharist), in the eleventh century, monastic practices embodied the body of Christ as *substantialiter* in the real presence, the interconnections between thoughts, written words, and things, the theological coherence, and the material representation of the Scriptural *logos*: the Berengar-Lanfranc Eucharist controversy, Saint Anselm's prayers, Lanfranc's *Constitutions,* and the eleventh-century *Quem quaeritis.*

NOTES

1. Michel de Certeau, *The Practice of Everyday Life* (Berkeley: University of California Press, 1988), p. 117.

2. De Certeau, *The Practice of Everyday Life*, p. 117.

3. Michel Foucault, "Politics and the Study of Discourse," *The Foucault Effect*, ed. Graham Burchell, Colin Gordon, and Peter Miller (London: Harvester Wheatsheaf, 1991), p. 55.

4. *The Monastic Agreement of the Monks and Nuns of the English Nation*, translated from the Latin and with introduction and notes by Dom Thomas Symons (London: Thomas Nelson, 1953), pp. 49–50; and *Consuetudinum saeculi X/XI/XII monumenta non-Cluniacensia*, ed. Kassio Hallinger, *Corpus Consuetudinum Monasticarum* 7.3 (Siegburg: Schmitt, 1984), pp. 124–27.

5. See, for example, Edmund K. Chambers, *The Mediaeval Stage*, 2 vols. (London: Oxford University Press, 1903); Karl Young, *The Drama of the Medieval Church*, 2 vols. (London: Oxford University Press, 1933); O. B. Hardison, *Christian Rite and Christian Drama in the Middle Ages* (Baltimore: Johns Hopkins University Press, 1965); Jody Enders, *Rhetoric and the Origins of Medieval Drama* (Ithaca, N.Y.: Cornell University Press, 1992).

6. British Library, Cotton MS Tiberius A3, fols. 3r–27v.

7. British Library, Cotton MS Tiberius A3, fol. 2v.

8. De Certeau, *The Practice of Everyday Life*, pp. 148–49.

9. For further discussion of this problem, see "Holy Space and Representational Place in the Tenth Century," in *Theatre and Holy Script*, ed. Shimon Levy (Brighton, England: Sussex Academic Press, 1999), pp. 11–21; and *This Is My Body: Representational Practices in the Early Middle Ages* (Ann Arbor: University of Michigan Press, 1999), chapter 1.

10. "I, Berengar, . . . believe that the bread and wine which are laid on the altar are after consecration not only a sacrament but also the true body and blood of our lord Jesus Christ, and they are physically taken up and broken in the hands of the priest and crushed by the teeth of the faithful, not only sacramentally but in truth." [Ego Berengarius, . . . mihi que firmavit; scilicet panem et vinum quae in altari ponuntur, post consecrationem non solum sacramentum, sed etiam verum corpus et sanguinem Domini nostri Jesu Christi esse, et sensualiter non solum sacramento, sed in veritate manibus sacerdotum tractari, frangi et fidelium dentibus atteri.] Lanfranc, *De corpore et sanguine Domini, Patrologiae Cursus Completus. Series Latina*, ed. Jacque Paul Migne, 221 vols. (Paris: Garnier Fratres, 1884), 150: 410 D–11 A. (Cited hereafter as *Patrologiae*.) The English text is quoted in Gary Macy, *The Theologies of the Eucharist* (Oxford: Clarendon Press, 1984), p. 36. See also H. Chadwick, "Ego Berengarius," *The Journal of Theological Studies* 40 (October 1989): 414–45.

11. See *Patrologiae*, 150: 411 BC for the text of the oath that is a slightly modified version of the already quoted statement regarding physical presence in the Eucharist; and *Patrologiae*, 150: 411 D–412 A for the description of the actions undertaken by Pope Nicholas II.

12. "The Greeks defended their use of unleavened bread by claiming that it symbolized the Trinity, the Spirit represented by the leaven, while the unleavened bread of the West would be a *corpus imperfectum et inanimatum*. In reply, Humbert and others insisted that only the salvific body and blood of Christ were present here. Further to speak of the bread *symbolizing* anything would be a deep error. Firstly, because after the consecration,

there would be no true bread present and, secondly, somehow to think that there would be a presence of the Lord in the bread different from that of the incarnate, risen Lord, would split the unity of Christ." Macy, *The Theologies of the Eucharist*, p. 38.

13. Chadwick, "Ego Berengarius," p. 416.

14. Richard Southern notes that the controversy and this oath were not, as it is traditionally maintained, about the real presence of the body and blood of Christ in the Eucharist, but whether the presence was real and substantial in the Aristotelian sense of substance (Lanfranc and the Council), or real but *not* substantial in the Aristotelian sense of substance (Berengar). In both statements, the term "substance" was critical in describing the mode of presence in the sacrament of the Eucharist. However, the very definition of "substance" was ambiguous enough to be used by the opposing parties to support their views. If Lanfranc's alternative were to be accepted, the presence of a new substance on the altar would mean the destruction of the substance of the bread, because, in this linear transfer, two substances of this kind could not occupy the same space. If Berengar's alternative were to be accepted, the material bread and wine would coexist with the spiritual body and blood, thus conveying the simultaneity of sign and *res*. Both alternatives claimed a representation of a reality in terms of objective actuality. See Richard W. Southern, *Saint Anselm* (Cambridge: Cambridge University Press, 1990), p. 44.

15. "Corpus et sanguinem . . . non solum sacramento, sed in veritate manibus sacerdotum tractari, frangi et fidelium dentibus atteri." *Patrologiae*, 150: 411.

16. See John Marenbon, *Early Medieval Philosophy* (London: Routledge and Kegan Paul, 1983), ch. 8.

17. Aristotle, "Categories," *The Complete Works of Aristotle*, ed. Jonathan Barnes (Princeton: Princeton University Press, 1984), ch. 5.

18. Southern, *Saint Anselm*, p. 48. In *De corpore et sanguine Domini*, Lanfranc describes an incident from his boyhood when a priest had found real flesh and blood on the altar during Mass, and the visibly converted elements had been sealed as relics within the altar.

19. See Mark C. Poster, *Erring* (Chicago: University of Chicago Press, 1984), for a discussion of representational functions in theology.

20. See Saint Anselm, *Monologion* in *Patrologiae*, 158: 169 CD–173 C. See also Saint Anselm, *A New, Interpretative Translation of St. Anselm's Monologion and Proslogion*, ed. and trans. by Jasper Hopkins (Minneapolis: Arthur J. Banning Press, 1986), chs. 20–21.

21. "Ergo domine, non solum es quo maius cogitari nequit, sed es quiddam maius quam cogitari possit." [Therefore, O God, not only are You that than which a greater cannot be thought, but You are also something greater than can be thought.] Saint Anselm, *Proslogion* in *Patrologiae*, 158: 235 C. See also *St. Anselm's Proslogion*, translated with an introduction and philosophical commentary by M. J. Charlesworth (Oxford: Clarendon Press, 1965), pp. 136–37; Saint Anselm, *A New, Interpretative Translation*, p. 245.

22. Saint Anselm, *A New, Interpretative Translation*, p. 121; *Monologion* in *Patrologiae*, 158: 176 AB.

23. Saint Anselm, *A New, Interpretative Translation*, p. 79; *Monologion* in *Patrologiae*, 158: 154 C.

24. See Michel Foucault, *The Order of Things: An Archaeology of the Human Sciences* (New York: Random House, 1973), ch. 3.

25. Saint Anselm, *A New, Interpretative Translation*, p. 145; *Monologion* in *Patrologiae*, 158: 188 B.

26. Saint Anselm, *A New, Interpretative Translation*, pp. 145–46; *Monologion* in *Patrologiae*, 158: 189 AB.

27. In the twelfth century, the concept of the *cognitio Dei* was further transformed to accommodate the heightened interest in divine creation. Philosophy, biblical study, and the visual arts recorded a shift of emphasis from the universality of *Logos* to the reciprocal dialectic of *theosis* (a mystical conjunction of the ascending individual with the descending god). See R. W. Hanning, "'Ut enim faber . . . sic creator:' Divine Creation as the Context for Human Creativity in the Twelfth Century," *Word, Picture, and Spectacle*, ed. Clifford Davidson (Kalamazoo, Mich.: Medieval Institute Publications, 1984), pp. 95–149.

28. Saint Augustine, *The Confessions of Saint Augustine*, trans. E. M. Blaiklock (Nashville, Tenn.: Thomas Nelson, 1983), bk. 10, ch. 11, pp. 250–51.

29. Anselm's definition of meditation is closely related to the concept of memory. According to Mary Carruthers, medieval memory advice stressed synesthesia in making a memory-image. That is to say, the images were supposed to be seen, felt, and to have taste or tactile qualities. The process of recollection was a process of remembering the places where each "bit" of knowledge was stored. These places *(loci, sedes)* were to be properly lighted, moderate in size, different from one another in shape, and not too crowded. See Mary Carruthers, *The Book of Memory: A Study of Memory in Medieval Culture* (Cambridge: Cambridge University Press, 1990), chs. 1–2.

30. Quoted in Southern, *Saint Anselm*, p. 97.

31. Southern, *Saint Anselm*, p. 102. See also *The Prayers and Meditations of Saint Anselm with the Proslogion*, translated and with an introduction by Sister Benedicta Ward, foreword by R. W. Southern (London: Penguin Books, 1973).

32. *Monologion* in *Patrologiae*, 158: 145 A. See also Brian Stock, *The Implications of Literacy: Written Language and Models of Interpretation in the Eleventh and Twelfth Centuries* (Princeton: Princeton University Press, 1983), pp. 329–62, for the discussion of Saint Anselm's philosophy and, specifically, of the concept of the text, the uses of the text, and their relation to the word.

33. "Now, by 'mental expression' or 'rational expression' I do not mean here thinking the words which are significative of things; I mean, rather, viewing mentally, with the acute gaze of thought, the things themselves which already exist or are going to exist. . . . For example, in one way I speak of a man when I signify him by the name of 'man.' In another way [I speak of him] when I think this name silently. In a third way [I speak of a man] when my mind beholds him either by means of an image of a body or by means of reason— by means of an image of a body, for instance, when [my mind] beholds his perceptible shape; but by means of reason, for instance, when [my mind] thinks of his universal being, viz., rational, mortal, animal." Saint Anselm, *A New, Interpretative Translation*, pp. 85–87; *Monologion* in *Patrologiae*, 185: 159 D–160 A.

34. Saint Anselm, *A New, Interpretative Translation*, p. 91; *Monologion* in *Patrologiae*, 185: 161 B.

35. *Monologion* in *Patrologiae*, 158: 187 B–188 C.

36. This argument was grounded in Plato's *Timaeus* and received a meticulous

(Christian) gloss in the works of William of Conches and Gilbert of Poitiers, as well as Bernard Silvestris's *Cosmographia,* in the first half of the twelfth century. See, for example, Bernard Silvestris, *Cosmographia,* ed. Peter Dronke (Linden, Netherlands: E. J. Brill, 1978).

37. The passage describing the healing of a cripple on Good Friday contains the follow-ing phrase: "[S]ubsequenti nocte Dominicae resurrectionis, *dum sub specie trium mulierum in sepulcro quaereretur corpus Domini Salvatoris,* idem claudus personantibus nervis suis extendit se, et ertectus in pedibus constitit sanus et rectus." [On the night following the resurrection of our Lord, *while the three women were seeking the body of the Lord, our savior, in the sepulchre;* at that time a lame man, with his own tendons crying out, stretched himself out, and, erect on his feet, he stood healthy and straight.] (Emphasis mine.) This statement, however, introduces more questions than it provides answers. When did this miracle happen? Did it happen dur-ing the Easter Mass attended by the lay population? If so, does it mean that the celebration of resurrection was moved from the Night Office? Or did it happen during the Night Office? See *Memorials of Saint Dunstan,* ed. William Stubbs (London: Longman, 1874), p. 231.

38. Margaret Gibson, *Lanfranc of Bec* (Oxford: Clarendon Press, 1978), p. 171.

39. *The Monastic Constitutions of Lanfranc,* trans. and intro. by David Knowles (London: Thomas Nelson & Sons, 1951), p. 1.

40. *The Monastic Constitutions of Lanfranc,* p. 47.

41. See *The Rule of Saint Benedict,* trans. and notes by Dom Justin McCann (England: Stanbrook Abbey Press, 1937), pp. 31–34.

42. Michel de Certeau, *The Writing of History,* trans. Tom Conley (New York: Columbia University Press, 1988), p. xv.

6

Space and Discipline
in Early Medieval Europe

❊

Valerie I. J. Flint

For the organized use of space in early medieval Europe, one movement would be very hard to equal: the monastic movement within the Western Christian Church. From the permanent enclosure of the monastery itself to the number of distinct place-names included within it (welcoming place, guest house, novice house, oratory, dorter, refectory, vestimentary, scriptorium, calefactory, cellarium, kitchen, bakery, infirmarium, garden, and so on), the Benedictine Rule and its customaries seem obsessed with spaces.[1] The monk would be expected to attend to where he was from the first moment of his entry into the community; the place-names would tell him what he should be doing in each space. Space, in framing the monk's activities, seems to sculpture and direct them too. In the *Rule* of Fructuosus of Braga (d. 665), for example, there is striking evidence of a high consciousness of the distance sometimes needed between individuals and of how such distances, or their lack, might affect behavior. Fructuosus rules that there must be at least one cubit of space between the bed of each monk, lest bodily proximity excite desire.[2]

This essay will be based upon such monastic rules and customaries, and I offer within it a proposition, wrapped in a few riddles, inside a suspicion. The suspicion developed as a result of habitually looking up and across from the subject on which I am currently working (in this case pilgrimage) more often than is strictly wise. This suspicion has two parts. First, I suspect that the idea of distancing as *punishment*—putting a

certain amount of public space (sometimes measured) between the miscreant and the community he or she has offended—*may* have developed
as a result of some quite refined thought about the efficacy in general of
space as a means of punishment, refinements that were pioneered in
early medieval European monastic communities and developed in contrast with other existing means. I say pioneered, but perhaps I should
better say institutionalized. My own experience with this kind of punishment as a child (public assignment to a distant and chilly room until
the arts of civilized converse had been recovered) is still very vivid despite
the lapse of time. It suggests to me that the idea was actually pioneered
in families and was generally rather successful, perhaps because it was
preferable, particularly to the culprit, to other kinds of punishment.

The idea of pilgrimage as punishment, then, may have developed
as the result of sophisticated thought about the uses of space in punishment within the early monastic movement. I also suspect that such
methods of punishment, in particular the uses of space and distance
and pilgrimage, actually *impinged* upon secular means of discipline
more often than we have hitherto suspected because they formed such
a contrast with the other sanctions used and were considerably more attractive to some miscreants. They may also have been thought more effective by some. The testing of this second suspicion requires a larger
space than is available at present, and its proof requires more work than
I have done so far. It is, however, one that should be borne in mind, and
I shall return to it at the close.

This discussion will concentrate on exactly *how* the use of space in
punishment came to be institutionalized and will lead to one central
proposition: that the monastic communities of early medieval Europe
were in the forefront of penal reform. It was from the monastic communities that critical views of older and different styles of punishment
filtered into a wider world; a world that was not entirely happy to accept
them because some of these new methods of discipline were incompatible with, indeed destructive of, those of the world outside the cloister.
The riddles in which this proposition is wrapped lie in the sources used.
These are the Rule of the Master (henceforth RM), the Rule of St. Benedict (henceforth RSB), as many of the surviving Benedictine customaries as I have been able to lay hands on, and the recommendations of
other select supporters of monasticism (Cassian, Isidore, Fructuosus of
Braga, Benedict of Aniane, and the like). In addition to these, there are

the ancient prescriptions for public penance (where they can be found) together with the *Libri Penitentiales*. If these do not qualify as riddles, it is hard to say what does. Because de Vogüé's arguments for the chronological priority of the RM over the RSB seem incontrovertible, we may now assume that many of the differences we can find between RM on the one hand and RSB and the Benedictine customaries on the other are deliberate and represent the result of rethinking the Master's recommendations—perhaps a careful one.[3] Internal changes and elaborations of this kind are informative and will be touched upon a little here. They would reward much further work, but my main purpose is how to investigate the many and various early European medieval monastic ways of using its set spaces in the disciplining of ne'er-do-wells.

In all the monastic rules and customaries I have examined, the disciplining of a given miscreant takes place with reference to the most important public spaces of the community: the oratory or church, the refectory, and the chapter house. It is performed by the successive use of these spaces as a means of demonstrating the *moral* distance between the good monk and the bad; a distance the bad monk, it is hoped, will want physically to cross. Take, for example, the RSB's directive (ch. 24) about dealing with the monk who has done something not too seriously wrong:

> If a brother is found to commit less serious faults, he is to be deprived of sharing in the common meal . . . he must eat alone [in the refectory], after the meal of the brethren.[4]

The Eynsham Customary has a variant upon the "eating distance" the Rule of St. Benedict prescribes; the miscreant may eat at the same time as the others in the refectory but not at the common table set in the middle. Instead, he must sit on a stool at the end and have his food put on another stool. To emphasize his disgrace, the stool must be without a tablecloth.[5]

Cassian tells us in his *Institutes* (IV, 16) what some of these "less serious" faults might be. The list is impressive, even inspirational: breaking pots; arriving late for the Opus Dei or chapter; making a mess of singing the psalms; being cheeky, careless, lazy, grumbling, or preferring to read rather than complete an appointed task; taking someone's hand or standing apart with him; speaking to or praying with someone who is already being disciplined; meeting relatives or friends unchaperoned; receiving or writing letters without the abbot's permission.[6] The Eynsham customary adds a good many more (many are taken from Isidore's *Regula Monachorum* and the others perhaps from experience): sleeping too long, talking too much, drinking to excess, swearing, making people giggle in chapter, laughing too much oneself, showing off to juniors and telling them stories (giggling, laughing, and showing off were obviously very common faults, for they appear in many customaries), disturbing the reading or singing, making offensive gestures, leaving clothes around in the dormitory, not putting one's books away.[7] All of this adds up to a pretty infuriating monk and one obviously requiring a measure of control.

This measure is accordingly offered promptly. As well as not eating with the brethren (which, it seems, was invariably the first element is distancing), the erring brother may not intone an antiphon or psalm nor may he read the lesson. This discipline will continue until he makes satisfaction. He may do this by prostrating himself before the abbot in the oratory (RSB ch. 44) until the abbot is prepared to forgive him. The RSB has further thoughts (ch. 43) about punishment for lateness. If late for the night office, the miscreant must take the lowest place in choir or stand "in a place set apart by the Abbot for such careless persons":

> We have thought it best that such persons should stand last, or else apart . . . For if they stay outside the oratory, there may be someone who will go back and go to sleep again, or maybe sit down outside the oratory and gossip.[8]

Distancing from meals in the refectory and from the choir in the oratory for "less serious" faults is a punishment common both to RSB and RM. The latter (ch. 55) offers additional guidance for the *avoidance* of the fault of lateness, one requiring an especial alertness to space and distance (and, it must be said, one's idea of one's own fitness and speed). If the bell rings for the office, says the Master, each monk must check exactly where he is. If he is within fifty paces of the oratory he should proceed there "with gravity". If not, he should just stop and pray on the spot, and he will not then incur a penalty. This provision has been made, the Master adds, because before it monks used to run races to get to the oratory from wherever they happened to be when they heard the bell and thus arrived too puffed to be able to sing the psalms—a venial but still annoying fault.[9] Should someone miscalculate this distance now that the new rule has been made, however, and arrive both late and too puffed to sing the first psalm, the abbot will thoroughly frighten him by shaking his head at him publicly in the oratory. Should he arrive after the third psalm, he will be put outside the door of the oratory to make satisfaction later by prostration (RM 73). A group of eleventh-century German Benedictine customaries (stemming perhaps from Fulda) has a description of the monk's prostration before the oratory that is particularly vivid—he is to lie before the door as the brothers go out, and they are to walk close to his head—but no one is actually to *tread* on it.[10] The RM invokes the fifty pace rule here again. The culprit must lie prostrate at least fifty paces away from the threshold of the oratory. When he has made satisfaction in the above manner, he may be welcomed back into his accustomed place in it.[11]

For any of these less serious faults, the monk is expected to be brought to his senses by means of a clear and shaming use of measured space. He is distanced in the refectory and in the oratory, and his only way back into favor and company is to abase himself in this same public arena.

This disciplinary use of space and of shame within its framework is all the more evident when we turn to the more serious faults and, finally, to the most serious of all—the obdurate refusal to offer satisfaction and reform. Cassian is a good guide to these more serious faults: the inflicting of physical injury, contempt for authority, violent contradiction, consorting with women, fighting, quarreling, arrogating favorite tasks to the exclusion of others, eating secretly and out of hours. Also on the list is *libera et effrenata processio*, which de Vogüé translates as an uncontrolled style of movement, perhaps with sexual overtones. Sodomy is clearly mentioned at this point in the list by Smaragdus.[12] For these faults, distancing of the kind I have described is not considered enough. Such a monk will certainly be distanced from meals and in the oratory (RSB 25), but he will also be left quite alone at his allotted tasks, no one speaking to him or blessing him. The RM (13) makes a point of the fact that, in addition to these exclusions, he will be publicly called a Judas and orders that monks walk past him, obviously ignoring him. If he has to be handed something, no one must make the sign of the cross over it. He is to be quite alone, with only his sin for company. Once he is sorry, the way back is to lie prostrate outside the oratory during the Opus Dei. He may come forward toward the oratory only by set degrees and at a signal from the abbot (RSB 44), prostrating himself before the community at each appointed stage. He can only stop doing this when the abbot allows him to do so. The RM (13) positively dwells on the pleading that must go on outside the oratory before the monk may be readmitted. Between each psalm great sobs must be heard and prayers for forgiveness, specified at length in the Rule. When the abbot has heard enough (and de Vogüé hints that this might have happened quite rapidly, hence its omission from the RSB), he will go out with the seniors, raise the monk up, and bring him in. The culprit must then lie prostrate before the altar uttering a long, tearful prayer (also set out in full in the RM). Finally, having made his satisfaction in this way, he may go with everyone to the common meal.[13] The German customaries I have mentioned increase the element of public humiliation by insisting that the now repentant brother be led back into the chapter house as though he were a novice and that he kiss everyone's feet, including those of the schoolchildren, who are assembled there to watch it all.[14]

But what of the constant serious offender or, still worse, the obdurate one, who will not make satisfaction? Such figures may have been quite common, for they receive attention in all the rules and customaries I have seen. There are, however, differences in the treatment recommended for them that may (de Vogüé thinks do) betoken real discussions and disagreements about the most effective means of treating serious offenders within the monastic community. This evident concern brings us to the central proposition, namely, that monastic regulators were pioneers in the arts of punishment and of questions bearing upon it, and so in penal reform. Was this insistence on space as a means of discipline developed haphazardly, as a result of those spaces that were there anyway in the monastery, and in default of the availability of harsher means (such as severe material or physical deprivation, or mutilation or death)? Or did the use of space in punishment result from careful thought and a good deal of experience in the art of effective punishment, of a kind of punishment that the offender might accept and that might lead, therefore, to his reform and reconciliation? It is hard to know, but on the basis of the evidence that concerns the obdurate offender, there may be reason to believe that this emphasis on discipline through space did indeed spring from real psychological insight and from a particular knowledge of and care for what might actually reform the wrongdoer. Monastic regulators may thereby have fueled a deeper conflict over styles of punishment, a conflict that may—and I have come to think did—often lie at the heart of the battle between "ecclesiastical" and "secular" justice.

We have long known that anxiety about the state of the individual soul runs through St. Benedict's little rule for beginners. Throughout the monastic prescriptions about space and discipline there runs a thread of concern for the style of correction best suited to the *rehabilitation* of the individual recalcitrant monk. The thread may be followed most conveniently by analyzing the use of beating in the rules and customaries—that short-sharp-shock method so beloved of certain medieval, and indeed modern, dealers-out of discipline. Beating was, after all, so economical in time and energy, so easy to mete out, and, so we are sometimes told, so immediately effective.

Beating is specified in the RM, the RSB, and in the customaries as a means of dealing with the truly obnoxious and obdurate, but beating is discussed by some of them in distinct ways and contexts and with wholly differing aims. Some writers recommending it for the correction of seriously erring monks are deeply worried about the place of beating in the process, both of the punishment and of the rehabilitation of such monks.

RM (14) expresses very little worry of this kind. Beating is considered wholly suitable for adolescents and for any adult monk guilty of a serious misdemeanor; it is spoken of, indeed, with a certain zest. Beating is, moreover, acceptable as a final punishment, to be administered for a monk's obstinate refusal to abase himself in the ways and in the places the RM prescribed. It is to be delivered as an immediate preface to throwing the culprit firmly and finally out of the monastic enclosure (RM 13). After a three-day grace period in which he might make satisfaction for his misdeed, he is beaten and out he goes. In the RM, therefore, beating seems to be a judicial sanction, almost a revenge on the part of the affronted brethren for constant and public delinquency. It is a proclamation of the monastic community's power to eject, and, as such, it appears to be rather gleefully retributive than curative. As the devil was thrown out of God's heaven for his pride, so this monk deserves to be thrown out of the haven of the monastery.[15] The procedure emphasizes the rights and expectations of the wronged house rather than those of the individual human culprit.

The RSB is quite different. It too allows beating, but it does so within the strictest limits and without glee. If none of the prescribed forms of distancing has worked, says St. Benedict (ch. 23), then the monk must be beaten.[16] Here, however, beating is clearly a last resort, a substitute of a most unfortunate kind for the use of successive distances of which the saint so clearly approved. Reluctance pervades his words upon the subject; in chapter 30 we see with particular clarity why he is so reluctant to sanction beating. Beating, he says, is only for those who are as yet unable to feel the effect of being cut off by space from their fellows; it is "for boys or youths or others incapable of understanding." [17]

This category of lack of understanding or, perhaps, of intelligence is wholly missing in the RM. Its presence in the RSB, on the other hand, militates against the bodily sanction of beating. Benedict seems to advocate better ways of recalling adults to their senses. The reduction of adults to the symbolic status of children, mentioned in the customaries above, seems to have been one of them. We see here a refinement in the art of punishment—but there is more.

Beating, in the RSB, is not a judicial punishment or a preface to being cast out into outer darkness, as it is in the RM. It is not an act of retribution, nor is it so much an expression of the power of the community as of its failure. Above all, it is supposed to be curative and adjusted to the nature of the miscreant (young, insensitive, or unintelligent) rather than to the offense. It is not a final sanction either. Beating in this rule seems, in fact, to be understood as a sign of how very much more work both abbot and community still have to do on behalf of this obdurate monk. In RSB 28, Benedict dwells on the curative aspects of all of the disciplines he recommends, including that of beating. If everything else has been tried and now it has come to blows:

> If he [the abbot] has made use of poultices, of the ointments of his counsels, of the remedies of Divine Scripture, if he has come at last to the cautery of excommunication [the procedures I have described as 'distancing', that is, to differentiate them from the more familiar understanding of excommunication] and the blows of the rod, and if he now sees that his work is unavailing—let him make use of that which is still greater: his

own prayer combined with that of all the brethren . . . But if even by this means he is not cured, then the abbot must apply the surgeon's knife . . . for fear that one diseased sheep may infect the whole flock.[18]

Here, then, there is to be a large interval of community prayer between the reluctant admission that a medicinal beating may at last have become necessary and the ultimate expulsion of the monk. Furthermore, if this expulsion must happen, it is to be regarded as a medicinal rather than a judicial expulsion—one directed less against the culprit, as culprit, than for the health both of him and of the community itself. The interval of prayer is inserted in the hope that the miscreant can still be saved and the beating averted.

The tenth-century *Customs of Fleury* have vivid passages about the threat of beating and of the community prayer that must precede its administration. In the monastery chapter house (the customs say), a scourge of leather thongs will hang from a peg. In the case of a serious fault a brother will be deputed to stand over the culprit with the scourge while the rest of the community weeps and pleads for mercy. If the brother admits his sin and promises amendment, the abbot will release him and the scourge will be put back on its peg. The presumption is that public communal concern, expressed within the theater of this shared central space, must bring the miscreant to his senses; it is this expressed concern for his true welfare, not the threat of the scourge, which is the secret of his reform. *The Customs of Fleury* also point to the contrast between the threatened beating that the erring adult monk might undergo, but which might be withdrawn, and the simple blows an adolescent may expect to have delivered promptly to his person, in the corner, with the schoolmaster's cane.[19]

The pressure of expressed concern, anxiety, and suffering on the part of the community—a pressure we may rightly describe as psychological—takes precedence, in the RSB, over the threat of a physical beating, just as the successive uses of space also take precedence over this last. The distinction between youth and adulthood, the idea that the abbot and community should continue to care and to pray for the adult wrongdoer and to show that they are anxious to save him and not punish him or take their revenge, are pervasive in this rule and its customaries. The image of the abbot is not that of a disciplinarian but of a doctor of sick souls, forgiver, comforter (on the model of 2 Cor. 2:7), and a good shepherd constantly in search of his straying sheep. The aim of such corrective medicine is to strengthen, not weaken, the wounded limb (this from Fructuosus, copied into Smaragdus's *Expositio* on the RSB, a prime source for the standing of this rule in the ninth century Carolingian Empire).[20] These images do indeed seem to affect, and be affected by, Benedict's own strongly held views as to right and wrong methods of correction:

> He [the abbot] must bear in mind that it is the care of sick souls that he has undertaken, not a despotic rule over healthy ones.[21]

The miscreant is ill and in need, not so much of punishment as of a means of restoration to moral health. No time limit is given in the RSB before which the truly obdurate must make satisfaction or be beaten and excluded, in contrast to the strict limit of three days allowed in the RM. Benedict leaves all such decisions to the abbot, with the strong implication that neither effort, time, nor any other similar sanction must be spared. He seems never to give up hope that the use of space and distance, the care of the abbot, and the charity of the brethren will, together, obviate the cruder penalties and achieve the desired effect.

These reservations about the effectiveness of retributive punishments such as beatings, especially on the intelligent adult, and this insistence that distance, shame, constant concern, and prayer must, in the end, be more effective in correcting the wrongdoer than physical pain or revenge are reflected in many of the surviving early medieval Benedictine customaries. I have cited the *Customs of Fleury*. The German customaries already mentioned (from a nexus of Fulda, Trier, and Melk) rule that when a brother is removed from the common table for a fault, he should still have enough to eat and drink (though he should not have wine). He should have adequate physical sustenance because distancing is a sufficient penalty.[22] Psychological suffering should take precedence over physical suffering. Smaragdus adds that food restrictions should be considered carefully, with due weight given to the individual's bodily needs. After all, he says, the erring monk is to be lifted up to life, not weighed down toward death (*vitaliter elevet non mortaliter gravet*—a phrase that may have reference to the familiar image of the weighing of souls).[23] The wrongdoer should *want* to come back into friendship and good behavior; hunger should not drive him back and tempt him, perhaps by resentment, to enter the wrong side of the scales. The German customaries add exclusion from recreation in the cloister to that from the common table. For more serious faults the brother has to sit alone and silent in the church while others are in the cloister. For those who are so obstinate that they are shut in what one customary describes as a prison, the abbot must send seniors to examine and console them "as St. Benedict says" (a reference to RSB 27—the chapter that insists that the abbot must care for the erring monk and try not to lose a single straying sheep).[24]

Striking a balance between weighing down and raising up is difficult, but the Benedictine Rule and customaries I have examined here suggest that great efforts were devoted to achieving this equilibrium. The idea developed, it seems to me, as a result of extremely careful thought about the effect of a given punishment upon the individual miscreant, of an active preference for the power of exclusion from the preferred spaces within the monastery over other possible penalties, and of a considerable insight into the damage to both community and individual that the power of resentment might cause.

This very careful use of measured, graded, and allotted space; this insistence upon penitential action performed within and with reference to it; this emphasis on the age and mentality of the wrongdoer; this hope that he might be induced, of his own volition, to cross the distance back into the community through a heightened sense of what he has lost; and, finally, this emphasis on time and communal pressure in contrast with retribution, corporal punishment, and confinement, all suggest that monastic regulators gave thought to the psychology of wrongdoing and its correction. The Benedictine rules have something in common with modern ideas on the correction of wrongdoers.[25]

Let us now begin to address the larger questions I posed at the beginning of this paper. How did the Benedictine idea for the rehabilitation of wrongdoers through distancing measure itself against the systems that prevailed outside the walls of the early medieval monastery? And did it reach outside these walls, causing a *frisson* and perhaps even fueling an even deeper conflict between church and state? To answer these questions, I have chosen one obvious source and one period within which to try to test a few hypotheses. The deposit of evidence consists of the *Libri Penitentiales,* or penitential books, especially those coming from the eighth and ninth centuries. The period is the high point of the Carolingian Empire.

We may now, primarily as a result of Cyril Vogel's work, be certain of two facts about the penitential books. First, their origins are to be found in Celtic and Anglo-Saxon monastic circles and may be traceable back to the sixth century, that of St. Benedict himself. Second, the feature that primarily distinguishes these penitential books from older systems of ecclesiastical penance and punishment is their care in linking the type of penance given to each wrongdoer to the type of wrong committed. The *Libri Penitentiales,* in other words, may be characterized as a separate genre of penitential literature by their insistence on "tariffed" penances, on punishments fitting both crime and criminal.[26] Interestingly, these penitentials often preface their lists of tariffs by referring to the need to cure rather than to punish, much in the manner of the Rule of St. Benedict. For the cure to be effective, moreover, the great variety of possible individual wrongs and corrective measures must be addressed, just as the doctor must take account of a whole variety of illnesses and their remedies before his diagnosis and prescription. As wounds are one thing, disease another, tumors and blindness and breaks and burns still others, so must their cures differ too, says a Burgundian penitential book of the eighth/ninth century.[27]

This preoccupation with tariffed punishments and this greater concern for the state of the individual miscreant radically distinguishes the penitential books from the early church's system of public penance, a system that was still current in St. Benedict's time. The essence of the system of public penance was that it made no obvious distinction of degree between the quality of the sin and its punishment (though the bishop did have some measure of discretion). Public penance consisted principally of an undifferentiated accumulation of conditions and prohibitions. The culprit must wear penitential clothes, pray on his or her knees, do laboring work. The penitent may not exercise his or her existing conjugal rights, marry, join the military caste, become a magistrate, engage in trade, or take communion. The sanctions are static, negative, and extremely heavy. They do far better as threats than as promises.[28] Above all, the elements of time and movement and of hope for rehabilitation in this world, all so evident in the monastic system and in the penitential books, are wholly lacking.

Now, the first penalty many of the penitential books recommend (for the most serious crimes, which would have incurred the full rigors of the ancient punitive system) is one of space: the penitential pilgrimage. The penitential pilgrimage derives as an institution from the penitential books. The penitential pilgrimage is quite distinct from the purely devotional one and has long been recognized as such. It is distinct, also, from that voluntary self-renunciation and search for exile that characterized the lives of some early medieval monks, prompting their vocations (though this experience may have fed into the discipline of the penitential books). The use of distance as a means of punishment in the penitential pilgrimage is directed, moreover, to the culprit's rehabilitation. The penitential pilgrimage is a punishment tariffed to certain sins, as the penitential books require, and inflicts the punishment of controlled exile, but controlled exile *with a view to return*. Thus, according to that same Burgundian penitential and echoed in five others of similar date I have examined,

> If a clergyman *[clericus]* murders a near relative *[proximum suum]*, he is to do penance as an exile for ten years (three on bread and water). Then, after he has done his penance, he may be received back into his homeland *[patria]*.[29]

God's punishment of Cain for slaying Abel (Gen. 4:12) is given as the precedent for this particular kind of penitential distancing. As a punishment for the murder of his brother, Cain became a "vagabond and a fugitive on the earth . . . at the East side of Eden." A Fleury penitential in the same group as the Burgundian one and of approximately the same date (late eighth or early ninth century) suggests that the penalty of pilgrimage might be given to laymen as well as to clergy for homicide.[30] The period of exile allotted in the *Libri Penitentiales* varies from seven to twelve years, but the message is a remarkably unified one. Penitential pilgrimage is recommended as the best penalty for serious crime. It is meant primarily, but not exclusively, for the discipline of the clergy. Parricide (the murder of a near relative, on the model of Cain) is the type of homicide most often specified, but murder in general could be expiated in this way. It seems possible to award the penalty of pilgrimage for other types of injury as well, as in the use of distancing in RSB. Three of the minor eighth/ninth century penitentials Kottje edits in his collection award pilgrimage as a punishment for sexual sins within the family.[31] Bishops were supposed to license penitents to travel in this way. Saints' lives mention the licenses such pilgrims carried. A formula for one appears in Marculf's *Formulary*.[32]

Penitential pilgrimage, therefore, is a punishment tariffed to a range of serious wrongs and is contained in penitential books that spring from a monastic setting. Neither penitential pilgrimage nor any other "tariffed" punishment appears in the older systems of ecclesiastical public penance. As those who completed the quotation from Genesis (as the penitential books did not) knew, Cain must not be killed for his offense. Indeed, God marked him in his exile so that he should not be killed in retribution for his act of homicide. Important to the penitential pilgrimage, then, is the idea that, for certain very grave wrongs, space may be a more desirable and effective punishment than revenge extracted in either capital or corporal punishment.

The penitential books echo all the recommendations and anxieties about punishment we have already discussed. The authority given in the penitential books is biblical, but the practice that precedes this authority is monastic. Vogel adds a further feature to the monastic origins and tariff of punishments of the *Libri Penitentiales,* a feature that differentiates them once more from the old system of public penance. The penalties in the penitential books, he says, "seek to make right *(réparer)* the wrong done."[33] Tariffs sometimes right wrongs by compensating the wronged, and some sense of this (though Vogel will allow little) appears in some provisions of the *Libri Penitentiales*. But does pilgrimage? The compensation here, such as it is, lies in getting the wrongdoer out of the community and, thereby, preventing revenge. While pilgrimage is of limited perceived value to the community, however, it is of enormous immediate advantage to the wrongdoer. The "righting" seems to apply chiefly to the culprit. As in the RSB, space seems here to be used less as a means of serving the community, than of saving the wrongdoer and preserving him or her from retribution or physical hurt. The pressure is not corporal, but psychological, directed toward the amendment of his behavior and his eventual return. It appears that the concern for the resocializing of the Benedictine monk spilled over into the ecclesiastical world of punishment outside the cloisters and into the lay world as well. Monastic discipline was adopted more widely—perhaps because it worked.

Finally, did any of these sanctions impinge so seriously upon those outside the monastery as to cause a *frisson* of disagreement? Do differences over styles of punishment help to elucidate the roots of judicial conflict between church and state? We may venture only a short way along this path here, but far enough to discover that, in the late eighth- and early ninth-century Carolingian Empire, penitential pilgrimage certainly did impinge upon state sanctions.

The penalty was apparently allotted heavily. Persons traveling on penitential pilgrimage seem to have been a remarkably common phenomenon in the reign of Charlemagne. The emperor himself mentions it in the *Admonitio Generalis* of 789.[34] The penalty also appears among the canons of the 813 Council of Châlons, and recurs in those of the Council of Paris in 829.[35] Rabanus Maurus tells us in his own first penitential book (written for Archbishop Otgar of Mainz ca. 841–842) that there were large numbers of penitential pilgrims on the roads.

Under the early Carolingians it also made for irritation and conflict. Pilgrimage was being awarded, says Rabanus, to such effect that:

In these modern times parricides are wandering everywhere as vagabonds and indulging themselves in vice and illicit delights.[36]

Early Carolingian rulers appear to have hated the penitential books to a man. The Council of Châlons of 813 condemned them roundly as *certi errores, incerti auctores* (uncertain as to their authority, but quite certainly wrong). Charlemagne, in the same *Admonitio Generalis* of 789, showed himself extremely annoyed by vagabonds posing as penitential pilgrims, vagabonds who claimed they had been lawfully given pilgrimage as a punishment.

It would be a lot better [he says here] if people found guilty of a capital crime were to stay in one place and do penance for it there.[37]

Why were these rulers so irritated? The sanction of penitential pilgrimage—of discipline through distance—was certainly subject to abuse, and such abuse was costly and hard to regulate. But I suspect that a far deeper reason lay behind these objections. The critics of penitential

pilgrimage seek a return to the old sanctions of public penance, sanctions
that penitential pilgrimage seemed, to their minds, to have displaced
wrongly. The *Admonitio Generalis* actually asks for the replacement of public sanctions, and Rabanus, too, specifies some of them with approval—
the prohibitions against military service and marriage, for example.[38] The
irritation reflects, in short, a real dispute about both the cost and the effectiveness of very different systems of correction. A conflict of views
similar to the conflict between RM and RSB had now shifted into the
public arena of the Carolingian state and demanded a change from punishment as an act of power (and as a means of compensation for the
wronged community) to punishment as an attempt to cure, to reconcile
the wrongdoer. This second style of punishment was, however, expensive
to the community in terms of time and effort, and offered, as yet, little
guarantee of success. Thus, I suspect the early Carolingians had neither
the stomach nor, yet, the resources for such refinements.

I have tried to prove that the psychological power of space (a power addressed in many of the other contributions to this volume) was clearly
recognized in the monastic communities of early medieval Europe. I
have also argued that these communities directed their resources toward
solving the problems of effective punishment far more purposefully
than we have suspected hitherto. In choosing to use space and distance
as a primary means of corrective discipline, the monks made inroads
upon other sanctions, both ecclesiastical and secular, and raised questions about the aims of punishment in general that would reach far into
the future.

By the period of the early Carolingian Emperors, the methods that
monks espoused impinged upon those of the state. Recognition grew
that distancing, given certain controls and resources, might work well,
not least because this method of punishment was so different from
other possible sanctions. This very contrast perhaps had added to the
salutary effect it had upon the wrongdoer. Benedictine sanctions looked
to the individual before the rights of a wronged community and to the
power that space had of upholding these rights. Though an attitude of
great sophistication, it was one that as yet found little sympathy in the
world outside the cloister. For all the early opposition to it, however, discipline through distance was here to stay. In the great days of pilgrimage, it would come to prove itself one of the most effective means of

social control the medieval Christian church could offer, and thus set itself up in competition or, just possibly, in cooperation with a hardpressed state. The early monastic use of space in punishment made available a whole new network of peacemaking and control. This network rendered the medieval church, on occasion, a threat in the arts of peaceful government, but a pioneer in these arts too.

NOTES

1. For interesting preliminary remarks upon the question, see P. Noisette, "Usages et représentations de l'espace dans la Regula Benedicti," *Regulae Benedicti Studia, Annuarium Internationale* 14/15 (1985): 69–93. Unhappily, the book then promised has not yet materialized.

2. Nighttime, he adds, is especially attractive to *lucifugas daemones* (demons who flee the light). *Sancti Fructuosus Bracarensis Episcopi Regula Monachorum XVII*, Patrologiae Latina, 87: 1107.

3. For a careful discussion of the differences between RM and RSB in matters of discipline, see *La Règle de Saint Benoit*, ed. Adalbert de Vogüé, 6 vols., Sources Chrétiennes, vols. 181–86 (Paris: Éditions du Cerf, 1971–72), 5: 723–844.

4. *La Règle*, ed. de Vogüé, provides an edition in Latin of the RSB and a translation into French. For an English version I draw upon David Parry, *The Rule of St. Benedict* (London: Longman and Todd, 1984), here, p. 46.

5. *The Customary of the Benedictine Abbey of Eynsham in Oxfordshire*, ed. Antonia Gransden, Corpus Consuetudinum Monasticarum (Siegburg: F. Schmitt, 1963), 2: 86.

6. *Jean Cassien Institutions Cénobitiques*, ed. Jean Claude Guy, Sources Chrétiennes, vol. 109 (Paris: Éditions du Cerf, 1965), pp. 140–43.

7. *The Customary*, ed. Gransden, ch. VI, ii, pp. 83–84. Benedict of Aniane, *Codex Regularum xvi*, Patrologiae Latina 103: 568–69.

8. Parry, *The Rule*, pp. 69–71.

9. *La Règle du Maître*, ed. Adalbert de Vogüé, 3 vols., Sources Chrétiennes, vols. 105–7 (Paris: Éditions du Cerf, 1964–65), 2: 258–61.

10. *Mellicensium Fragmenta*, ed. Willibrord Neumüller, Corpus Consuetudinum Monasticarum, vol. 7, no. 2 (Siegburg: F. Schmitt, 1983), p. 392. For the similarities between this customary and a group stemming from Fulda-Trier, see *Redactio Fuldensis-Trevirensis*, ed. M. Wegener, Corpus Consuetudinum Monasticarum, vol. 7, no. 3 (Siegburg: F. Schmitt, 1984), p. 279. On the influence of Fleury upon such customaries, see L. Donnat, "Études sur l'influence de Fleury au Xième siècle," in *Études Ligériennes d'Histoire et d'Archéologie Médiévales* 18 (1965): 165–74.

11. *La Règle*, ed. de Vogüé, 2: 308–9.

12. *Jean Cassien Institutions*, ed. Guy, ch. IV, xvi, pp. 142–43.

13. *La Règle*, ed. de Vogüé, 2: 44–61.

14. *Mellicensium*, ed. Neumüller, p. 393.

15. *La Règle*, ed. de Vogüé, 2: 46–49.

16. Parry, *The Rule*, p. 45.

17. Parry, *The Rule*, p. 52.

18. Parry, *The Rule*, p. 50.

19. *Consuetudines Floriacenses Antiquiores*, ed. Anselmus Davril et al., Corpus Consuetudinum Monasticarum, vol. 7, no. 3 (Siegburg: F. Schmitt, 1984), pp. 50–51.

20. *Smaragdi Abbatis Expositio in Regulam Sancti Benedicti*, ed. A. Spannagel, et al., Corpus Consuetudinum Monasticarum, vol. 8 (Siegburg: F. Schmitt, 1974), p. 222.

21. RSB, ch. 27; Parry, *The Rule*, p. 49.

22. *Mellicensium*, ed. Neumüller, p. 391.

23. *Smaragdi*, ed. Spannagel, p. 225.

24. *Mellicensium*, ed. Neumüller, p. 392; *Redactio*, ed. Wegener, p. 279.

25. See, for example, the 1988 Carlisle report on the parole system in England, summarized and commented upon by Frank Pakenham (Lord Longford), *Punishment and the Punished* (London: Chapmans, 1991), pp. 182–90.

26. For an excellent summary of the system of "tariffed" punishments and the literature upon it, see Cyrille Vogel, *Les Libri Paenitentiales* (Turnhout: Brepols, 1978).

27. *Paenitentialia Minora Franciae et Italiae Saeculi VIII–IX*, ed. Raymund Kottje (Turnhout: Brepols, 1994), p. 1.

28. For a convenient summary of the prescriptions of public penance, see Cyrille Vogel, "Le Pèlerinage Penitential," *Revue des Sciences Réligieuses* 38 (1964): 114.

29. *Paenitentialia*, ed. Kottje, p. 5. See also pp. 6–8, 56, 60.

30. Ibid., p. 7.

31. Ibid., p. 139. Monetary compensation may, however, sometimes be accepted as a substitute.

32. Vogel, "Pèlerinage," pp. 133–34.

33. Vogel, *Les Libri*, p. 37.

34. Chapter 79 of *Monumenta Germaniae Historica Capitularia Regum Francorum*, ed. Alfred Boretius (Hanover: Hahn, 1883), 1: 60–61.

35. Council of Châlons, ch. 38 of *Monumenta Germaniae Historica Concilia*, ed. Albert Werminghoff (Hanover and Leipzig: Hahn, 1906), 2, no. 1: 281. Council of Paris, ch. 32 of *Monumenta Germaniae Historica Concilia Aevi Carolini*, ed. Albert Werminghoff (Hanover and Leipzig: Hahn, 1908), 1, no. 2: 633.

36. ". . . in modernis temporibus parricidae profugi discurrunt per diversa loca, et variis vitiis atque gulae illecebris deserviunt." *Poenitentium Liber XI*, Patrologiae Latina 112: 1410. He remarks on this again in the Council of Mainz of 847, over which he himself presided, and in his second penitential of ca. 853 also. Here, in his first penitential (with full reference to Cain), Rabanus seems to suggest that penitential pilgrimage was principally awarded for parricide, including the killing of unwanted children, a crime that he singles out for special mention.

37. ". . . melius videtur, ut si aliquid inconsuetum et capitale crimen conmiserint, ut in uno loco permaneant laborantes et servientes et paenitentiam agentes." Chapter 79 of *Monumenta Germaniae Historica Capitularia Regum Francorum*. See n. 34 above.

38. *Poenitentium Liber XI*, Patrologiae Latina 112: 1410.

7

THEATRICAL SPACE,
MUTABLE SPACE, AND THE
SPACE OF IMAGINATION

THREE READINGS OF THE CROXTON
PLAY OF THE SACRAMENT

DONNALEE DOX

Space is an a priori criterion for theater. Theater integrates bodies, objects, and space to represent an alternate reality in performance. Because concepts of space differ across cultures and history, the relationship between bodies, objects, and space cannot be assumed to be consistent. Thus, plays of the past demand inquiry into the concepts of space that governed their performance as well as the concepts of space that govern their interpretation today. The inquiry into medieval theatrical space thus merges two fundamental questions: What concepts of space operated in the historical moment in which the play was performed? What assumptions about theatrical space govern how the play is currently understood as performance?

I will explore three combinations of contemporary and medieval concepts of space that produce radically different readings of the Croxton *Play of the Sacrament* as performance. *Theatrical space* describes stagings of the play based on twentieth-century conjectures and the relationship of bodies and objects in space that produce meanings duplicated elsewhere in fifteenth-century English culture. Traditional European theater's emphasis on realism and linear perspective governs this interpretation of the *Play of the Sacrament* by focusing on the arrangement of bodies and objects in space and finding correspondences between the play's imagery and the East Anglian culture in which it was performed.

Mutable space deals with how the play's themes of Christian order and hierarchy are represented in space. In space, the play's performance literally imitates the narrative's movement from chaos (religious dissent) to order (communal worship led by a bishop). The orthodox message of Christian unity is thus not only told through language and visual imagery but also through the use of performance space.

The *space of imagination* suggests that theatrical performance not only *occurs in* space but also *represents concepts of* space. Space of imagination refers to the development of concepts beyond what the senses can verify (i.e., the imagination). It also refers to a specific domain of space that was conceived by thirteenth-century theologians who challenged the Aristotelian model of a bounded cosmos in order to find a place for the Christian God in the observable universe. The space of imagination offers a conception of space that links performance space directly with belief in God in a way that two-dimensional iconography, nonmimetic performance (such as public preaching), statuary, and even liturgy could not. The space of imagination, unlike the two previous concepts of space, suggests an aspect of space that is not defined by bodies and material objects but by the Christian theological imagination. The concept of imaginary space yields a sophisticated multidimensionality to medieval theatrical performance that resonates with modernist and postmodernist experimentation with theatrical space.

THEATRICAL SPACE:
FILLING EMPTY SPACE TO CREATE MEANING

I can take any empty space and call it a bare stage. A man walks across this empty space whilst someone else is watching him, and this is all that is needed for an act of theatre to be engaged.

PETER BROOK, *THE EMPTY SPACE*

The Croxton *Play of the Sacrament* dramatizes a Host desecration narrative that ends with the conversion of five Jewish characters to Christianity in a quasi-liturgical ritual. The play is of East Anglian origin, dating from 1460 or later. Bury St. Edmunds, Thetford, or one of several towns called Croxton are the most likely sites for the play's performance, if indeed it was performed at all. In the play, five Jewish characters, led by the character Ser Jonathas, bribe Aristorius, a Christian merchant, to steal a Host from a local church. The play shows the Jewish characters putting the Host through a series of tortures to verify through their own (and the audience's) senses, the doctrine of transubstantiation.

In performance, these characters stab the Host with knives, nail it to a post (a mock crucifixion), boil it in a cauldron of oil over a fire, bake it in an oven and also over a live fire. The "crucifixion" episode introduces a Flemish quack doctor whose power to heal is shown to be far less effective than that of the Christian savior. When the Host bleeds after being stabbed in a parody of the eucharistic ritual, Jonathas tries to toss it away. The Host sticks to his hand. The Jewish characters try to detach Jonathas from the wafer by nailing it to a post *(in imitatio Christi)* and trying to pull Jonathas away. In the effort, Jonathas's hand is torn off his body at the wrist to the consternation of his companions, the amusement of the Flemish doctor, and the abject terror of Jonathas himself. Hand and Host are thrown into a cauldron of boiling oil, then into a fiery oven. The last trial proves the doctrine of transubstantiation. The oven bursts open and the figure of Christ, represented as a bloody child, emerges from it. The Christ figure delivers a stock reproach from the cross, condemning the Jewish characters for blasphemy in ancient Christian history and simultaneously for blasphemy in the present moment of European history.

In response, the Jewish characters confess their sins and acknowledge the real presence of Christ. The Jews (following Christian belief in the salvation of a remnant of Jews and the more immediate practice elsewhere on the continent of forced conversion) are then baptized into Christianity by a bishop and assimilated into the Christian community.[1] Aristorius, the Christian merchant, is forced out of the Christian community by the bishop, who sends him on pilgrimage as a penance for stealing the Host. The play ends with audience and players processing together, possibly into a church building, singing the *Te Deum*.

Twentieth-century theater history and criticism have analyzed the performance of this play in the tradition of the European stages of the seventeenth, eighteenth, and nineteenth centuries as part of the development

of theatrical realism from Renaissance notions of *vraisemblance* to nineteenth-century naturalism. In keeping with this materialist tradition, the
imagery produced by the play has been linked to objects, places, people,
and traditions in East Anglian culture as a way of demonstrating the relationship between what is shown in performance space to the "real"
world, which theater is thought to imitate or mirror. The Jewish characters have thus been equated with Lollard heretics in light of Edward I's
expulsion of the Jews and their invisibility in English culture after 1290;
sites mentioned in the play, such as Babwell Mill and Croxton, have been
identified in East Anglia; sites for performance have been suggested
based on sloping hillsides for spectators' sight lines; and the stage tricks
required for the special effects have been described in detail.[2] This approach to the play has revealed its material relationship with East Anglian
culture and its people.

Correspondence between the play's visual imagery and East Anglian
devotional iconography has been one of the most accurate ways to access
how the play might have looked in performance and what devotional
meanings the imagery might have carried. The iconography of the Five
Wounds, for example, showing Christ's severed and bleeding hands and
feet and his disembodied heart, was popular in East Anglia through the
fifteenth century. The play seems to emulate the five wounds of Christ
in the imagery of Jonathas the Jew frantically tearing about the performance space trying to reattach his hand to his bloody wrist, and in the
image of the bleeding Christ. The play draws on the cult of the Five
Wounds with what Gail McMurray Gibson has called the "bloody realism" characteristic of fifteenth-century representation and the audience's devotional response to images of flesh and blood.[3] Similarly, the
image of the *Imago Pietatis*—Christ bleeding and surrounded by the
nails, pincers, whips, and other instruments of torture—resonates with
the play's graphic depiction of the Host tortured with knives, nails, fiery
oven, pincers, and boiling oil.[4]

The link between the play's visual imagery and East Anglian cultural
practices supports a reading of the play as didactic and orthodox. One-to-
one correspondence between medieval dramatic imagery and popular
iconography also emphasizes the idea that performance, as a representational strategy, was striving for a realistic representation of bodies and
objects in space as a way of conveying meaning. The correspondence
between theatrical representation and iconography assumes that the im-

agery itself, rather than spatial relationships, had the most communicative value, and that the performance space itself was static until filled with dramatic imagery.

The idea that the play's textual and visual imagery corresponds to material referents, and that bodies and objects define the theatrical space, is grounded in Western concepts of realistic representation. Theatrical realism implies an understanding of stage space as a reflection of the observable world, be it natural or cultural, and assumes that performance creates an illusion of that reality. This frame has been used to suggest that medieval realism represented "actions and emotions subject to the same laws as our own"[5] and that attention to the realistic display of human emotions paralleled the development of medieval realism out of symbolism.[6]

Interpretations grounded in realism suggest that the *Play of the Sacrament* organized a theatrical space by placing in it props, characters, scaffolds, and scenic elements on the model of the mise-en-scène developed in the intimate theaters of early nineteenth-century Europe. As Stanton Garner has pointed out, theatrical realism is a materialist conception of theatricality, in which stage objects (props) have a dual function. They both link the theatrical world with the "real" (nondramatized) world of the spectator and phenomenologically "constitute privileged nodal points in the scenic field."[7] The arrangement of objects and bodies in an empty space in a "visual pyramid" also has its roots in the conventions of European court and public theaters that presented a "window" into another world (or space). Marked by the introduction of Serlian perspective into the court theaters of Renaissance Italy, box-tier seating facing a raised stage that created the illusion of depth and focal points was the standard social and visual arrangement for theatrical performance.[8] Though critiqued by artists and architects through the nineteenth century (most notably by Richard Wagner's fan-shaped egalitarian Bayreuth Theater), the emphasis on sight lines, visual coherence, and separation of performance space from audience space dominated European theater structures from the late fourteenth century on.[9] These now conventional assumptions about theatrical space focus the action of the *Play of the Sacrament* by placing boundaries around a space designated for representation and analyzing the action and objects within those boundaries that in turn are referenced to observable, material forms (liturgy, literature, preaching, iconography, stage effects such as the boiling cauldrons) and the structure of the medieval town that provided a market square or church as a performance space. Through this lens, medieval theatrical performance represents material, physical phenomena.

Indeed, a large part of what extant medieval scripts offer to contemporary interpretations are indications of the special effects, costumes, visual images, and layout of the playing space for theatrical effect. The spectacular stage effects in the Croxton play indicate the graphic and realistic detail characteristic of fifteenth-century East Anglian iconography. This evidence supports the developmental theory of theatrical representation that suggests a trajectory toward a duplication of material reality in theatrical space.[10] The Croxton play's directions suggest that the performance area, presumably an open place in a town, documented contemporary fifteenth-century, as well as biblical, events with true-to-life accuracy.

As presented theatrically, the play's Host simultaneously represents the historical body of Christ, the liturgical wafer, and an object of violent humor. The tortures presented to the audience were apparently not simulated as fiction, fantasy, or symbol because, according to the stage directions, the performance required actual burning fires for the cauldron and oven. A convincingly real dismemberment, traditionally done with animal blood for effect, was also required for the play to represent the miracle of the Host and the Jews' conversion as realistically as possible.[11]

In addition to the potential affective response a devout Christian might have to these representations of devotional iconography in performance, the public, social playing space itself would have affected the play's devotional or entertainment value. The text offers basic parameters for how the playing space was arranged. The play required at least two scaffolds and an open *platea,* probably with access to a church building. Though the play's themes and imagery were based in Christian ritual and belief, the performance was most likely done in an open place that was not designated for worship. If this place is considered an empty space, waiting to be filled by bodies and objects to convey meaning, then different arrangements of bodies and objects in space, as suggested by contemporary staging conjectures, would have affected how the play was understood as ribald entertainment, serious devotion, antiheretical polemic, or expression of community unity. An analysis of two prominent staging conjectures for this play suggests that the arrangement of the theatrical space has an influence on what meanings are derived from, or assumed to be operating in, modern interpretations of the final communal *Te Deum*.

William Tydeman suggests that traveling players could have performed the play at the Franciscan Priory at Croxton, fourteen miles north of Bury St. Edmunds, perhaps outside a local church.[12] Traveling players would have had no direct connection to the town or townspeople, a monastic order, a guild, or the ecclesiastical hierarchy. Thus, following this reading, the *platea* would have been a commercial space, distinguished from the "real" church into which Aristorius goes to get the Host. Gail McMurray Gibson proposes the market square in the town of Bury St. Edmunds as a site for the play's performance. The market square slopes sharply downward toward the town's Benedictine Abbey gates. Gibson suggests that a Corpus Christi guild or the local society of the Name of Jesus could have supported the play. Such support, which would have given a performance the weight of religious or civic authority, derived from the town of Bury St. Edmunds, the monastery, or local civic organizations.[13] Conjectural arrangements of the playing space suggest different relationships between Christian beliefs and the dramatization itself. Thus, these spatial arrangements have consequences for how the play's performance created meaning.

The play's banns indicate that the play was to be performed on Monday. Monday was a heavy market day for Bury St. Edmunds, and a guild or a troupe of traveling players easily could have raised money.[14] Staging the play in the open square at the base of Angel Hill in front of Bury's Abbey gates (now a parking lot), however, immediately implies an Orthodox agenda for the play's conversionist theme, its anti-Lollard language, and its didactic emphasis on Church hierarchy, rather than the more carnivalesque interpretation suggested in Tydeman's conjecture.[15]

The two conjectures presented here differ most critically in defining the relationship between objects, bodies, and space in the final moments of the play. In the play, the Christian bishop converts the five Jewish characters, who then process with the congregation singing the *Te Deum*. If the procession included both actors and audience, the dramatic performance would end in a ritual space, such as St. James' Church in Bury St. Edmunds. This concludes the play with a devotion that was liturgical rather than dramatic. In other words, the performance would become a communal observance of the doctrine of transubstantiation, and a change in place and a change in the organization and meaning of the performance space would mark this shift. Such a shift would separate the world of commerce, transgression, violence, and miracles from the world of ritualized belief over which the Church hierarchy presided. In contrast, if the entire performance took place outside All Saints' (or any other) Church, the building itself would function simply as another scaffold or, in Renaissance staging terms, a backdrop for the action. The character of Aristorius the merchant would thus have disappeared into a *real* church to obtain a *false* Host, but the performance itself would have remained entirely in public space of commerce, transgression, violence, and, potentially, miracles.

The play's final space presented would thus be organized by the church building and its ritual function: the linear arrangement of the center aisle and transept, and (given the East Anglian locale) the vertical dimension of the characteristic hammer-beam roofs soaring overhead. The impact of entering and being enclosed by such a building after an open-air performance is significant. The structure of the building would have immediately regulated the spectators' and actors' bodies, forcing them into linear patterns of movement requiring sitting, kneeling, or standing, and directing their gaze forward down the aisle toward the altar and ritual image of Christ. The spectators were made aware of the Christian God positioned at the front and center of the church; the ecclesiastical hierarchy defined the order of the Christian world.

Staging reconstructions and interpretations of meaning in the objects the play represents are grounded in concepts of theatrical realism that looks to the arrangement of performance space for meaning and finds that meaning in the visual components of that space. Space is considered a stable receptacle for the objects and bodies that tell a play's story as a reflection of material reality. A major theme in the *Play of the Sacrament*, however, is the *instability* of the material world. This is shown theatrically in the transformation of Host to flesh, of Jew to Christian, and of parody to ritual. As if in imitation of this central theme, the play constantly transforms the performance space as well, refusing to allow the space to remain stable.

In the first part of the play, Jonathas, Aristorius, and the bishop each speak from scaffolds. The scaffolds distinguish the characters' relationships to each other, to the Host, and to the spectators. These fixed positions also fracture the theatrical space to create domains of influence and allow demarcated spaces to signify each character. Characters move in and out of these spaces and in and out of the boundaries of the performance space. The play's objects are similarly unstable. The graphic effects at the center of the play—Jonathas's severed hand, two blazing fires, a boiling cauldron, a bursting oven, and the climactic emergence of the bleeding Christ—also take place in the center of the unlocalized *platea,* not on scaffolds. Thus, the most important doctrinal and structural moments of the play occurred in space that was not identified as a place.[16] The play's theatrical space might also be interpreted as mutable and flexible, depending upon motion in the space, saturation of the space by characters, and entrance of the audience into the theatrical space. Reading the space of performance as flexible and constantly changing, in keeping with medieval performance practices, affects the narrative itself, as the next section of this inquiry will indicate.

MUTABLE SPACE: THE TRANSFORMATIONAL SPACE OF CHRISTIAN ESCHATOLOGY

Space is not a passive receptacle
in which objects and forms are posited. . . .
SPACE itself is an OBJECT [of creation].
And the main one!
SPACE is charged with ENERGY
Space shrinks and expands.
And these motions mould forms and objects.

TADEUSZ KANTOR, "THE MILANO LESSONS: LESSON 3"

Stephen Nichols has suggested that medieval representation was "a means of affirming and describing . . . a world of material reality whose boundaries seem amazingly fluid."[17] Similarly, David Mills has observed a "dissolution of the boundaries of mimesis and sacramental rite, of illusion and reality" in medieval drama.[18] As indicated by the discussion of theatrical space, theater is a material practice. However, the fluid transformation of space, time, and matter inherent in the Christian acceptance of the transformation of matter, as well as radical spiritual transformation, challenges a strictly material reading of theatrical imagery as Mills and Nichols suggest. For medieval plays, modern performance studies that deal with space as mutable (capable of affecting, rather than receiving, objects and bodies), allow for the fluidity between the material world and the nonmaterial domain of Christian religious belief.

The fluidity of matter in space, which the *Play of the Sacrament* seems to assume, is a familiar concept from modernist theater aesthetics. By the third decade of the twentieth century, new developments in physics opened conceptual paths for European visual and performance artists. Einstein's theory of relativity, quantum mechanics, and Heisenberg's uncertainty principle provided new metaphors for theater and visual arts: curved space; time as a dimension of space; the effect of the observer on the thing observed; the relationship between energy, matter, and speed; multiple dimensions; simultaneity of events; noncausal relationships between events; and the impossibility of stable reference points or truths.[19] Thus, in a conceptual domain parallel to that in which theatrical realism emerged and flourished, theater artists such as Wassily Kandinsky, Adolphe Appia, Gordon Craig, Antonin Artaud, and Jacques Copeau sought to represent space as multidimensional and gave light, color, sound, emotional and physical response, and form power equal to that of objects that could be referenced to the "real" world.[20]

If this kind of thinking reflects a twentieth-century fascination with descriptions of space after Einstein and Heisenberg, the pre-Newtonian world may have entertained similar notions of the immutability of space and matter. Certainly, as Clifford Davidson has suggested, medieval concepts of geographic space were at best mysterious:

> Frequently unmeasured in terms of such common units as miles or (as today) kilometers, space as encountered by the traveler often was the unquantified unknown.[21]

If the physical space of medieval performance is conceived as a mutable element in the play's performance, an element literally alive with Christian eschatological images, performance space becomes a space in which any miracle is possible and any historical event immediately available for human experience, whether or not such events could actually happen in the real (i.e., nontheatrical) world.

Medieval theater collapsed space and time by putting the biblical past in material terms, by reinscribing the eschatological teaching of Christ's second coming (the biblical past) and contemporary events constructed by Christian belief (the reported conversion of five Jews in Spain in 1460) simultaneously in the space of the present moment. Thus, it was not necessary for miracles—such as the confession and conversion of five Jews to Christianity after witnessing the transformation of a Host into Christ—to be referenced to material culture. The reference was already present in the Christian imagination. For example, given the expulsion of the Jews from England in 1290, firsthand knowledge of Jews or Jewish conversion would have been rare in England.[22] Still, the play purports to document the "full trewe" existence of Jews and to authenticate the mysterious transformation of the Host and conversion as though the events were taking place in the same space and time as the observing audience, according to a Christian interpretation of those events.

This central idea is intricately connected with the play's requirements for space in performance. If space in the *Play of the Sacrament* is assumed to be mutable, and the narrative structure is organized according to how space and the meanings of space change during the performance, the play begins to generate different meanings. The inconsistencies of tone, style, language, religious reverence, and humor, which have so disturbed literary interpretations of the play, appear as a spatial whole. That spatial whole mimics the play's central theme of the world's conversion from the chaos of unbelief to the order of Christian faith. The chaos of the first parts of the play—shifting scaffolds, tumult in the *platea*, the sudden emergence of the Christ figure—is literally brought into order by the bishop as a representation of the orthodox Church hierarchy, the Church building with its sight lines focusing attention on the risen Christ, and the unity of the final hymn of praise to God. This is not to deny the semiotics of the church building or the impact of positional symbolism. It is to suggest starting with a different idea of space: how the space and the physical performance of the narrative function together.

Assumptions of conversion and transformation as possibilities in the real (nontheatrical) world run throughout the *Play of the Sacrament:* bread converts to flesh, Jews convert to Christians, scaffolds convert to altars, performance converts to ritual, and past converts to present. Indeed, conversion and transformation are fundamental to the medieval Christian tradition, to the extent that the material world was considered to be a mask "for the numinous world of transcendence rather than as a mechanical contrivance explainable by scientifically defined laws."[23] The play in performance thus makes the same assumption in its relationship to space. Conversion is a spatial, as well as a material, condition of medieval performance. The space of Christian theology is not measurable by relative distances, nor is it marked by the bodies and objects that occupy it. As Albert of Saxony would assert some sixty years after the earliest date for the Croxton text:

> God could place a body as large as the whole world inside a millet seed and he could achieve this in the same manner as Christ is lodged in the host, that is, without any condensation, rarefaction or penetration of bodies. Within that millet seed, God could create a space of 100 leagues, or 1,000 or however many are imaginable. A man inside that millet seed could traverse all that many leagues simply by walking from one extremity of the millet seed to the other.[24]

At the center of *The Play of the Sacrament* miraculous spatial (as well as physical and spiritual) transformations take place: an adult figure representing a child inhabits a piece of bread, the biblical past comes alive in the present moment, and Spain is displaced to East Anglia. The play also assumes a deity, located outside the world of the spectators and the play, whose influence can be documented in the bounded, terrestrial space of the performance itself. A performance of the play—that is, the embodiment of these ideas—attests to the "full trewe" miracle of flexibility between space, time, and matter.

Mutable performance space puts the play into yet another configuration. Staging conjectures, as indicated, must allow for at least two scaffolds (localized spaces with representational value) and an open *platea* (unlocalized space) with access to a church (the real space of Christian order).[25] The scaffolds and the spectacles of the boiling cauldron, bursting oven, bleeding Host, and rising Christ organize the space of performance. If space is interpreted as an active participant in the play's performance, in effect the agent that converts belief into material form, the performance space cannot be a static receptacle for bodies and objects but must, like the themes of the play and the core beliefs of Christianity, be able to transform and take many shapes. The issue becomes not how bodies and objects define space, but how space, objects, and bodies affect each other in performance. With this strategy, the Croxton play's narrative structure reveals a striking relationship with the space in which it is performed.

Traditional scaffold staging would identify each merchant, one Christian and one Jewish, with a scaffold from which each "shall make hys bost."[26] Jonathas leaves his scaffold, after the priest and Aristorius confer, perhaps on a journey toward but not reaching Aristorius's scaffold. As the text indicates:

> Her[e] shall Ser Ysodyr the prest speke ont[o] Ser Arystori, seyng on thys wyse to him; and Jonatas goo don of[f] his stage.[27]

Aristorius stays in his place, but his clerk Petre Powle moves between him and Jonathas to make the introductions that precipitate the bribe for the Host.[28] The Christians and Jews meet on Aristorius's scaffold. The Christian invites Jonathas to

> . . . come up and sit bi me
> And tell me wat good ye have to sell
> And yf ony bargeny mad[e] may be.[29]

The bargain for the Host is struck at 100 pounds. The Jews withdraw from Aristorius's scaffold as the priest "commyth home" to Aristorius, where he was last seen. Aristorius and Petre Powle get the priest drunk on "a drawte of Romney red"[30] and "a lofe of lyght bred"[31] so that Aristorius might walk "a lytle waye"[32] to the church and steal the Host for which Aristorius fears a heresy conviction if his thievery is discovered. The conventions of medieval staging and positional symbolism work well to this point in the dramatized narrative.

After this point, however, the play's action redefines the space of performance as a field of action. The second part of the text suggests chaotic motion in the *platea*. The play uses the *platea* as a space of confusion, within which ritual, documentary, and Christian history are collapsed. The center of the play, and certainly the height of its dramatic spectacle, is the torture of the Host. In this section of the play (around line 465), the spoken text diminishes significantly.[33] The mode of presentation shifts to physical farce. The play outlines the dramatic events in language that suggests a great deal of visual drama through movement: "Here shall the four Jewys pryk ther daggerys in [the] four quarters. . . ."[34]

Jonathas must "renneth wood, with the Ost in hys hond."[35] The four
Jewish characters must "Pluke the arme and the hond shall hang styll
wlyth the Sacrament,"[36] beat the Flemish quack doctor out of the playing
space, pluck the nails out of Jonathas's hand, and shake both the hand
and Host into a cauldron boiling with water under which they have built
a fire.[37] At the dramatic apex of the play, the Jewish characters kindle another fire under an oven:

> Here shall Jason goo to the cawdron and take owt the Ost with
> hys pynsonys and cast yt into the ovyn.[38]

at which point

> . . . the ovvyn must ryve asunder and blede owt at the cranys,
> and an image appere owt with woundys bledyng.[39]

The space in this section of the play is saturated with imagery, movement, and noise. The action of the play defines the *platea* as dense and
contained. The dramatic action is focused. The eye must follow complex
action within a small area. The effect of the action on this space is to create a chaotic world in which transgression is possible, in contrast to the
ordered space of the procession and church created by Christian salvation. This is also the space in which Christianity reinscribed its history
along with the history of theological doctrines defining the inevitable
conversion of Jews for blasphemy and doubting.[40]

The third part of the play, beginning with the reproach from the
cross at line 717, organizes the space entirely differently. After the spectacular emergence of the Christ figure, the play returns to an emphasis
on spoken word and narrative structure. The figure of Christ takes the
focus of attention from the Jews and the bleeding Host. This flesh-and-
blood Christ proves the doctrine of transubstantiation and reinforces
the image of the crucifixion and resurrection in the past, the conversion
of the biblical remnant of Jews in the last days, and the ultimate triumph
of Christianity against any heresy or blasphemy in fifteenth-century
East Anglia.

The playing space becomes again a space of journeying, in which all
characters must move to specific locations to fulfill their dramatic functions. Jonathas, with his hand healed by immersion into the cauldron,

confesses: "Here shall the Jew goo to the byshopp and hys men knele styll."[41] Confession is followed by a linear motion that traverses the performance space to the church with the congregation/audience:

> Here shall the merchant and hys prest go to the chyrch and the bysshop shall entre the chyrche and lay the Ost on the auter.[42]

With this movement, the performance seamlessly becomes ritual. The Host is returned to its sacramental physical place, and its rightful place as a sacred object in the Christian imagination.

Thus, the action (as opposed to the placement of bodies and objects) changes the space of performance. The performance space is first saturated with activity and confused in the spectacle of the desecration of the Host, then presented as an open field in which the deity can intervene directly and through the church hierarchy to clarify and order the space. The movement from the undifferentiated *platea* to the church is more than symbolic or liturgical. It is a literal shift from chaotic space to ordered space—the final physical realization of an event and visible documentation of a Christian miracle: the conversion of the Host and the conversion of Jews and the transformation of Christian religious imagination into the material, embodied form of a theatrical performance.

Popular devotional practices, which embellished the magical properties of the Host and emotionally embraced graphic iconography such as the Five Wounds, assumed a correspondence between material representations of the deity and the reality of a divine presence, a tenet of philosophical realism.[43] The material aspects of the performance and the mutable playing space itself together represent a Christian concept of conversion, even as it reinforces Christ's "real presence" in the material world.

The Croxton play presents this intricate interplay by representing simultaneously a contemporary event from 1460 Aragon, the biblical moment of the crucifixion that with the resurrection is the theological essence of Christianity, the parodic representation of the mass by players depicting non-Christians, the history of Anglo-Jewish relations prior to the expulsion in 1290, and the orthodox rebuttal to Lollard heresy. That these can be represented in performance simultaneously in one space as coterminous realities puts theatrical representation on the order of Albert of Saxony's millet seed—all imaginable realities and distances in the space of performance. That space represented a fragment of the observable terrestrial/celestial order, but was mediated by the Christian belief in a mutable, constantly transforming world. As it constantly transformed before the eyes of medieval spectators in the performance of the *Play of the Sacrament,* space was integrated with the bodies and objects that tell the story. As this section has suggested, medieval performance represented more than objects in stable space. It also represented transformations of space, in keeping with the theme of transformation and conversion that is at the core of the narrative and of Christian belief. Postmodern theories of theatrical space suggest that not only is space flexible, but the very act of performance engages concepts of space. These most recent theories of performance consider space not as an independent reality, but as a result of concepts of space. Medieval concepts of space redefine performance by adding a nonmaterial dimension to a seemingly material cultural practice.

SPACE, VACUUM, GOD, AND MULTIPLE WORLDS: THE SPACE OF IMAGINATION

A particular quality of postmodernist theater theory has been the conception of space as an active participant in performance, with a life of its own. Objects and bodies are considered functions *of* space, and matter and energy are recognized as gradations on the same continuum. Theories of performance space have described numerous variations of space, such as found space, plastic space, space of representation, space of memory, simultaneous space, energized space, and saturated space. Thinking of a performance space as fluid, active, saturated with meanings, and always constructing, deconstructing, and reconstructing an imagined reality has become accepted practice in late twentieth-century theater criticism. These theories imply ways of understanding space as nonmaterial, of material objects as forms of space, and of performance as the creation of worlds that do not follow the laws of observable reality in which matter and space are distinct and independent.

Several historical factors have contributed to the perception of performance space as heterotopic domains that need not conform or correspond to reality as perceived by the senses.[44] Theater technology since the turn of the century has made such a conception of space possible with rapidly shifting scenes, intricate light plots that create illusions of shrinking and expanding space, surround sound systems coordinated with light patterns, and computer-generated backdrops that create filmic dissolves—none of which match phenomena observable in the material world.

In late twentieth-century performance theory, the effort to question and deconstruct realism as an ideologically repressive mode of representation has led to performance practices that require theoretical, as well as aesthetic, appreciation of space. In the work of theater artists such as Pina Bausch, Richard Foreman, Robert Wilson, and Tadeusz Kantor, for example, performance space cannot be assumed to represent events, objects, or bodies as they appear in nontheatrical reality. Rather, the work of these artists suggests that space is open to interpretation; it is a concept that can be represented by juxtaposing remembered images from a span of decades simultaneously (Kantor), presenting actors endlessly repeating movements until those movements accumulate and dissolve (Bausch), multiplying dimensions in the performance space visually by, for example, crisscrossing the stage with string (Foreman), or slowing movement in space to alter perceptions of time (Wilson). In these ways, the actions, objects, and bodies these exemplary theater artists transfer into performance treat space not as a void to be filled or an object represented along with bodies and objects, but as a mode of thinking that is inherent in the performance itself. The understanding of performance space as a mode of thinking is as integral to postmodern performance as bodies, objects, and language are to realism.

The understanding of performance space as a mode of thinking may be a quality of medieval performance as well. Concepts of space and its relationship to Christianity were hardly homogeneous in the Middle Ages. While learned theological debates cannot be assumed to be at the forefront of the popular interest in public dramatizations such as the *Play of the Sacrament,* neither can they be dismissed in favor of the assumption that medieval performance was viewed in its time as stable, two-dimensional art or as a form of literary expression. As indicated in the first and second sections, fifteenth-century plays such as the *Play of the Sacrament* represented Christian beliefs graphically with objects drawn from material culture (life-size cauldrons, fires, instruments of torture, dismemberment, the bloody Christ) and presented geographical space as mutable and flexible within set boundaries (as shown in the movements from secular to sacred spaces). At the same time, however, these performances encoded in their presentation ways of thinking about space itself in ways art and literature could not. These seemingly transparent performances of religious belief also represented the very conceptions of space by which the medieval universe was understood. Those conceptions of space were contested on religious grounds, which makes theatrical representation itself (as a practice of space) a contested act. Medieval concepts of space were grounded in both the observable universe organized in the classical tradition and in the effort to reconcile Christian theology with that organization.

The most obvious way to think through medieval conceptions of space and performance as a representation of those concepts is with the Aristotelian theory of the cosmos on which late medieval philosophy and science were based. Aristotle had posited two distinct kinds of space bound to a geocentric, spherical cosmos and based on observation. The terrestrial, or sublunar, region was thought to be composed of the four elements: air, fire, water, and earth. Beyond the terrestrial, extending from the moon outward, Aristotelian theory posited celestial spheres arranged concentrically around the earth with the stars and planets moving on the surface of these spheres in fixed orbits.[45] This cosmos was finite; neither time nor objects existed beyond the two regions of space. The power of this concept of space was its verification by observation.

Following an essentially Aristotelian approach to theatrical space, modern staging conjectures of medieval plays have emphasized the relationship between the spectator/observer and the objects observed and have defined theatrical space as that which encloses the audience/spectators and the performance. Modern conjectures have also stayed within the tradition of distinguishing space and bodies (in medieval terms, dimensionality and corporeality) as separate and incompatible substances.[46] Certainly, fifteenth-century dramatic form, with its graphic stage effects and resonances with the iconography of affective piety, was clearly consistent with the organization of the Aristotelian cosmos, as well as with medieval principles of philosophical realism.[47] The scaffolds, *platea*, and church were fixed in the performance space, representing locations in the "terrestrial" region. Spectators, outside the performance space until the final *Te Deum*, circumscribed the performance area, not representing anything but observing the representation from outside (that is, from the nontheatrical, "real" world).

In traditional analysis, the play's linear narrative is understood to tell its story of divine intervention through objects in space. In this representation of a material world in space, the play's conversions—the Host to flesh and back again, and Jews irrevocably to Christians—are presented as miracles brought about by Christian belief and seen through Christian belief. In this conception of space, theatrical representation was a mechanism by which Christian thought could be made manifest in material form, just as God manifested Himself in material form in Christ.

Medieval theologians, however, had been grappling with the relationship between God, material form, and space since the end of the thirteenth century. Christian philosophy could not accept a two-dimensional description of space and matter if it had to account for the kind of active intervention of a deity in human affairs that the *Play of the Sacrament* represents. Thirteenth- and fourteenth-century thinking about the Christian cosmos and the position of humans within it was thus forced to conceive of a void outside the Aristotelian terrestrial and celestial spheres. The question of whether or not the Christian God could (or did) create worlds beyond those observable by the human senses also had to be addressed. The possibility of a void space—a space without bodies but capable of receiving bodies—in Aristotelian thought came under continual theological scrutiny, even after the Condemnation of 1277 forbade any thought that did not allow for the power of God to create such a void *(potentia absoluta Dei)*.[48] In the effort to reconcile the belief in a nonmaterial deity with a material reality verifiable by the senses, theologians posed numerous arguments that relate directly to the representation of God by means of space, as performance does.

Two arguments emerged during the fourteenth century over the issue of God's power and the extracosmic void. As a metaphor for theatrical space and an alternate model to that of two-dimensional or terrestrial/celestial space, these arguments allow for the extension of performance beyond the imposed boundaries of stage and audience. They allow for the possibility of imaginary domains of space. *The Play of the Sacrament* might indeed have represented this imaginary space in which the play's miraculous transformations were, quite literally, as real as the burning cauldron into which Jonathas's false "hand" was thrown in a spectacular theatrical trick.

John Buridan, one of the most prominent theologians responding to the Condemnation of 1277, considered the possibility that the Christian God could indeed create a separate void space that could receive bodies but was not bound to the problems inherent in Aristotle's rejection of the interpenetration of space and bodies.[49] The standard theory of incorruptibility of the heavens depended on the assumption that the celestial ether could not sustain any matter not of its own form or quality and that a single body could not sustain contrary forms of matter at the same time, as proposed by Albert of Saxony.[50] The *Play of the Sacrament* translated this spatial problem into the earthly world of observable forms in its two central transformations. The transformation of the Host and the conversion of the Jews represent changes of form, an exchange thought to be part of the mechanics of the corruptible terrestrial domain of matter as well a theological necessity. The heavens, however, remained for Buridan the incorruptible domain of God. The celestial region was not, following Buridan's articulation of the Aristotelian cosmos, subject to the laws of contrary forms that allowed for the transformations of matter shown dramatically by the *Play of the Sacrament*. The question of extracosmic space, however, forced a reconceptualization of the essence and organization of space. For Buridan, the authority of the senses and Scripture, if not Aristotle's *De caelo,* posited an extracosmic void as a space of imagination that did not truly exist because it could not be observed:

> we ought not to posit things that are not apparent to us by sense, experience, natural reason, or by the authority of Sacred Scripture. But in none of these ways does it appear to us that there is an infinite space beyond the world.[51]

God could, however, allow more than one body to exist at the same time in the same place, which would make the *Play of the Sacrament*'s transformations possible in spatial terms.[52] In the visual language of the *Play of the Sacrament*'s performance, this argument suggests that the playing space (marked by scaffolds, *platea,* church building, and bodies) represented a bounded cosmos, but one within which God was omnipresent and capable of altering material conditions.

For those theologians whose imaginations did extend into regions of the cosmos not verifiable by the senses, the Aristotelian sensual cosmos proved limiting. The fourteenth-century English Dominican Robert Holkot, for example, posited that nothing existed beyond the known world. At the same time, he suggested the *possibility* of bodies existing beyond the known world, which proved that an extracosmic vacuum, not coextensive with the celestial and terrestrial domains that did not contain matter, did indeed exist.[53] Though many theologians, like Holkot, acknowledged this possibility, a few such as Nicholas Oresme, John de Ripa, and Thomas Bradwardine actually theorized the void (or *imaginary*) space as a reality that God had indeed created. If medieval performance, itself a practice of space, is read through these arguments, medieval plays are shown to be both didactic narratives *and* highly controversial religious statements. Further, by representing spatial relationships, dramatic performance poses questions to Christian theology that religious art, iconography, texts, and sculpture of the period did not.

Thomas Bradwardine was the most prominent among the minority of theologians who proposed a space created by God but inaccessible to the human senses. Bradwardine (d. 1349) conceived of a space beyond the celestial that was both infinite and eternal, which he called *imaginary space*, grounded in the argument that God could exist not only in the worlds observable by human senses but simultaneously throughout both known and imaginary worlds.[54] This imaginary space was not the three-dimensional void that bodies could not penetrate by definition, but a live space extending indefinitely and containing the terrestrial and celestial spheres. For Bradwardine, God's immensity and the imaginary space beyond the observable world were immense and omnipresent.[55] God Himself permeated Bradwardine's space of imagination, not merely the will of God as in the theories of vacuum that Augustine and Aquinas proposed. This space was thus not conceived as a positive or corporeal domain, but a place of spirit or intellect. Though dramatic representation performed amid the increasingly passionate desire for graphic realism of the fifteenth century is grounded in space occupied by matter, the power of this concept of an imaginary space is its assumption of the power of an unseen God to effect miraculous transformations from a realm inaccessible to human sight and mind.

In the context of this debate, the spatial organization of a medieval drama—including the subject-object relationship of spectator to performance that is basic to Renaissance perspective—appears not as the organization of objects and bodies, but as an interrogation of the imaginary space Bradwardine and other fourteenth-century thinkers posited.[56] Pseudo-Siger of Brabant articulated the nuance of the debate particularly relevant to drama by positing that "we can perceive something by our imagination only if it is in a place."[57] That is, perception was dependent upon physical location, sight, and sense. In this way belief in miraculous, sense-defying conversions could be given a place in dramatization and, as the banns of the *Play of the Sacrament* attest, document miracles in material form.

For East Anglian popular piety, the graphic depiction of Christ bleeding and the sensory awareness of His material presence verified the working out of Christian history in the present moment. The possibility of a domain of nonmaterial space, a space of thought, allows for this fluid concept of time. As profoundly as postmodern theater pieces expose space and time as modes of thinking or collapse space and time into a single concept, medieval drama represented the biblical past and the eschatological future of the "last days" in the instant of performance. The *Play*'s linear narrative and physical representation took place in time measured by the movement of objects *(tempus)*, with an Aristotelian beginning, middle, and end. The representation of Christian salvation history playing and replaying out in the present moment was represented in *durati*, or God's time, which was considered to be God's extratemporal "time" of creation and judgment and a conceptual corollary to Bradwardine's imaginary space.[58]

Whereas the opening sequence of events on the scaffolds could be thought of in *tempus* and the terrestrial/celestial space of the observable world, the transformation of the Host and the conversion of the Jews took place in *durati* and the imaginary space of Christian belief in an intervening deity. The play's juxtapositions of contemporary references (e.g., Babwell Mill, Lollard heresy, the Flemish doctor) with national history (the conversion or expulsion of the English Jews) and with Christian belief based in biblical history (the crucifixion and salvation) presented no logical problem for the fifteenth-century East Anglian audience. Quite possibly, the experience of past and future in the present moment as the play was performed paralleled the medieval experience of space. That is, given Bradwardine's argument for a space of imagination, it is possible to read the *Play of the Sacrament* as a representation of both a space made up of and marked by material forms *and* a space of abstract, nonmaterial concepts (such as God) from which material forms were generated. Reading the *Play of the Sacrament* with this imaginary space in mind yields a very different understanding of the relationship between audience and performance, as well as an alternate interpretation of the play's didactic, conversionist theme.

The *Play of the Sacrament*'s final *Te Deum* suggests that medieval performance did not necessarily stop at the edges of a bounded performance area. The performance space extended into the "concentric rings" of spectators, on the model of the Aristotelian cosmos with the earth at the center and the planets in concentric rings. Going further, however, the imaginary space theologians such as Thomas Bradwardine proposed implies a domain of space that was not representational, or at least not represented by material forms. Transferring this model of the cosmos into the terms of performance space, the domain of the performance space empty of representation becomes, literally, the space of the spectators' imaginations. It is a space beyond that marked by the material objects of performance, a space that is a domain of thought. Christian belief defined that space in an omnipresent God outside of but influencing human affairs, in fifteen centuries of Christian history, and in the end of time and space Christian eschatology proposed. In addition to the spaces marked by material objects and bodies in performance, this was a space inaccessible to the spectators' sight and senses, but still inseparable from God.

It is thus possible to conceive of medieval dramatic performance as extending the terrestrial space of performance to the concentric rings of spectators as space marked by bodies, and beyond these observable spaces into an imaginary space where the play's miraculous transformations have their divine genesis. Dramatic performance thus gives the theoretical space of imagination a *place*, in the Aristotelian sense, in the Christian believer's mind. As the site of religious belief, defined in terms of space, the imaginary space was no less tangible than those spaces more easily defined by players and special effects. That very space of imagination made what appear today to be the play's dangerous fictions (the coerced conversion of the Jews) or logical impossibilities (the transformation of bread into human flesh) documents of material realities for fifteenth-century Christianity.

This interpretation of the medieval imaginary space applied to dramatic representation adds a significant dimension to modern understandings of fifteenth-century drama. It allows the Christian beliefs that drive the dramatic narratives (transubstantiation, Jewish conversion in the fulfillment of Christian prophecy, the crucifixion and resurrection of Christ) to actually inhabit a dimension of space. The play in performance represents this space as the relationship between what the Christian mind could imagine (miracles of transformation, such as bread becoming flesh) and what was possible in the material world (the representation of those miracles in dramatizations using theatrical effects such as the representation of Jonathas's dismemberment or the emergence of the figure of Christ from the burning oven). This relationship plays out in the constant transformation of matter in space throughout the play. It is also at the heart of the medieval inquiry into the nature of space and the social problem that unbelief posed for orthodox Christianity.

The theoretical problem of the void or vacuum was its impossible reconciliation with the power of God and the power of the human imagination. At the beginning of the *Play of the Sacrament*, the problem the Jewish characters presented to their Christian audience is not dissimilar: the Jewish characters challenge the conceptual impossibility that bread could become human flesh. The play in performance allows that transformation to occur in the material realm of bodies and objects. The impossible transformation that the bursting oven and emerging life-size Christ challenged was the logic of the observable, material world (much as did Christian religious belief).

The interrogation of material reality that the discourse of the Jewish characters posed is an interrogation into the relationship between objects and the space they occupy. Theater made the possibility of such transformations materially "real," using the imagery of East Anglian popular piety. In the same way that the *Play of the Sacrament* documented Christ's "real presence" in the ritual Eucharist, medieval dramatization suggested the possibility of a space beyond the performance and beyond the ritual of the mass by positing a space of imagination in which these represented events (the transformation of the Host and Jewish conversion) as universal truths. While a dramatization defined a playing space by the relationship between bodies and objects, the medieval concept of space in such a dramatization represented invoked an imaginary realm that was not bound to the laws of observable reality—a heterotopia within which miraculous transformations could logically take place. This analogy suggests that what is "real" about fifteenth-century dramatizations is not the realistic quality of their representation of horrific events, but the Christian imagination that accepted the possibility of such events.

Edward Grant points out that concepts have no spatial and temporal location, motion, kinetic energy, or momentum.[59] As this final inquiry into medieval space indicates, medieval performance can be understood as a representation of imaginary worlds that the Christian mind understood as coterminous with material reality, even if not verifiable by the senses. Taken on faith, as the *Play of the Sacrament* suggests its spectators take the miracle of the transforming Host and converting Jews, God did indeed have the power to construct worlds identical to that which the senses could perceive.

Christian theology's most significant contribution to this discussion of medieval theater may be Bradwardine's link between imaginary space and the omnipresence of God. In addition to affirming Christian dogma and belief, the play affirms the translation of events from one space to another, from the unlimited space of imagination to space that bodies and objects occupied. The "fiediestic affirmation" of popular piety also represents an affirmation of the Christian religious imagination and the possibilities that this imagination created. In the *Play of the Sacrament,* the playing out of the Christian imagination in the conversion of the Jews has had severe ideological consequences. The graphic realism of the conversion from this fifteenth-century drama is perhaps a less critical issue than the force of Christian imaginations that constructed and accepted the dramatic imagery of a deity taking human form and that required the conversion of non-Christians.

As these three readings of the Croxton *Play of the Sacrament* show, concepts of space affect both the understanding of the play's staging and of its religious meaning. While the debates about the nature of the void space might have been remote concepts to a lay audience on market day in Bury St. Edmunds, the defense of God's existence and creative power certainly supports the orthodox orientation of the play. The conception of space as interconnected with the deity offers further insights into medieval thought that are not immediately evident in a reading of extant play texts but that imply a complexity of thought not usually associated with popular civic performance in the Middle Ages.

NOTES

1. Augustinian theology condemned the Jews for their historical rejection of Christ and persistent blindness to Christian salvation. Jews were to be tolerated as witnesses to Christian history, on the principle that the "remnant" of Jews would be saved in the last days of Christian time. Aquinas reconfigured the Augustinian position on the unctio of the Jews in Christian history with emphasis on the daily interaction between Jews and Christians. Aquinas saw Christians as more likely to convert Jews through daily interaction than the reverse, and spoke against forced conversion. See Shlomo Simonsohn, *The Apostolic See and the Jews* (Toronto: Pontifical Institute of Mediaeval Studies, 1991), pp. 5, 27; and Salo Wittmayer Baron, *A Social and Religious History of the Jews*, 2nd ed., 17 vols. (Philadelphia: The Jewish Publication Society of America 1952–1980), 9: 12.

2. See Cecelia Cutts, "The Croxton Play: An Anti-Lollard Piece," *Modern Language Quarterly* 5 (1944): 45–60; Cecelia Cutts, "The English Background of the *Play of the Sacrament* (Ph.D. diss., University of Washington, 1938); Eamon Duffy, *The Stripping of the Altars: Traditional Religion in England, ca. 1400–ca. 1500* (New Haven: Yale University Press, 1992), pp. 65–70; Gail McMurray Gibson, *The Theater of Devotion* (Chicago: University of Chicago Press, 1989), pp. 35–45; Richard L. Homan, "Devotional Themes in the Violence and Humor of the *Play of the Sacrament*," *Comparative Drama* 20 (1986–88): 327–40; Sr. Nicholas Maltman, "Meaning and Art in the Croxton *Play of the Sacrament*," *English Literary History* 41, no. 2 (1974): 149–64; William Munson, "Audience and Meaning in Two Medieval Dramatic Realisms," *Comparative Drama* 9 (1975): 44–67; Ann Eljenholm Nichols, "The Croxton *Play of the Sacrament*: A Re-reading," *Comparative Drama* 22 (1988–89): 117–37; Ann Eljenholm Nichols, "Lollard Language in the Croxton *Play of the Sacrament*," *Notes and Queries* (March 1989): 23–25; Victor I. Scherb, "The Earthly and Divine Physicians: *Cristus Medicus* in the Croxton *Play of the Sacrament*," in *The Body and the Text: Comparative Essays in Literature and Medicine*, ed. Bruce Clarke and Wendell Aycock (Lubbock: Texas Tech University Press, 1990); Stephen Spector, "Anti-Semitism in the English Mystery Plays," in *Drama in the Middle Ages: Comparative and Critical Essays*, ed. Clifford Davidson, et al. (New York: AMS Press, 1982).

3. For other English examples of the cult of the Five Wounds, see Duffy, *The Stripping of the Altars*, plates 50, 85, 99, 100. For the expansion of the Host as a devotional object, see Miri Rubin, "Desecration of the Host: The Birth of an Accusation" in *Christianity and Judaism*, ed. Diana Wood (Cambridge: Blackwell Publishers, 1992).

4. For other examples of Passion iconography and an analysis of increasingly graphic realism in this region toward the end of the fifteenth century, see James Marrow, *Passion Iconography in Northern European Art of the Late Middle Ages and Early Renaissance: A Study of the Transformation of Sacred Metaphor into Descriptive Narrative* (Korrijk, Belgium: Van Ghemmert Publishing Co., 1979).

5. Hans-Jurgen Diller, "The Craftsmanship of the Wakefield Master," in *Medieval English Drama: Essays Critical and Contextual*, ed. Jerome Taylor and Alan H. Nelson (Chicago: University of Chicago Press, 1972), pp. 246, 257.

6. Clifford Davidson, "The Realism of the York Realist," *Speculum* 50 (1975): 272.

7. Stanton Garner, *Bodied Spaces* (Ithaca: Cornell University Press, 1994), pp. 88–89.

8. Erwin Panofsky, *Perspective as Symbolic Form* (Cambridge: MIT Press, 1991), p. 27.

9. For the development and critique of the box-tier arrangement, see Harald Zielske, "Box-House and Illusion Stage—Problem Topic on Modern Theatre Construction Observations and Contemplations Concerning its Genesis," in *Theatre Space: An Examination of the Interaction between Space, Technology, Performance, and Society,* ed. James F. Arnott et al. (Munich: International Federation for Theatre Research, 1977). For departures from this model, see, in the same volume, George C. Izenour, "The Origins, Evolution, and Development of Theater Design since World War II in the United States of America."

10. See, for example, Ann Eljenholm Nichols, "Costume in the Moralities: The Evidence of East Anglian Art," *Comparative Drama* 20 (1986–87): 305–14.

11. For an analysis of the stage directions and their possible reconstruction, see Victor I. Scherb, "Violence and the Social Body in the Croxton *Play of the Sacrament,*" in *Violence in Drama,* Themes in Drama 13 (New York: Cambridge University Press, 1991).

12. William Tydeman, *English Medieval Theatre, 1400–1500* (London: Routledge and Kegan Paul, 1986), pp. 58–59.

13. Gibson, *The Theater of Devotion,* p. 35. The play's connection with the celebration and observance of the Corpus Christi festival remains ambiguous. See Lynette R. Muir, "The Mass on the Medieval Stage," *Comparative Drama* 23 (1989): 314–29; Leah Sinanoglou, "The Christ Child as Sacrifice: A Medieval Tradition and the *Corpus Christi* Plays," *Speculum* 48 (1973): 491–509; and John Coldewey, "The Non-Cycle Plays and the East Anglian Tradition," in *The Cambridge Companion to Medieval English Theatre,* ed. Richard Beadle (Cambridge: Cambridge University Press, 1994). Lynette Muir suggests that the play was not connected to the annual *Corpus Christi* celebration, though its didactic message clearly reinforced the feast's purpose (p. 320). Leah Sinanoglou states that the play was "apparently not performed in connection with the Feast of Corpus Christi" (p. 500). John Coldewey's observation that performances of the play were "only occasional additions to annual Corpus Christi Day or Whitsuntide procession" supports either suggestion (p. 202).

14. John Coldewey, "The Non-Cycle Plays," pp. 203, 205.

15. For an analysis of how the play's language translates as anti-Lollard polemic, see Ann Eljenholm Nichols, "Lollard Language." For the initial proposition that the play was designed to refute Lollard heresies and the proposition that the play's Jewish characters were symbolically Lollards, see Cecelia Cutts, "The Croxton Play."

16. For a detailed examination of medieval interpretations of linear and cyclic time, see Michal Kobialka, "Historic Time, Mythical Time, Mimetic Time: The Impact of the Humanist Philosophy of St. Anselm on Early Medieval Drama," *Medieval Perspectives* 3 (1988): 172–90.

17. Stephen Nichols, "The New Medievalism: Tradition and Discontinuity in Medieval Culture," in *The New Medievalism,* ed. Marina S. Brownlee et al. (Baltimore: Johns Hopkins University Press, 1991), p. 2.

18. David Mills, "Drama of Religious Ceremony," in *Medieval Drama,* ed. A. C. Cawley et al., vol. 1 of *The Revels History of Drama in English* (London: Methuen, 1983), p. 148.

19. See Rosemarie Bank, "Time, Space, Timespace, Spacetime: Theatre History in Simultaneous Universes," *Journal of Dramatic Theory and Criticism* 5, no. 2 (Spring 1991): 65–84. Bank traces the impact of "new physics" on the thinking of artists in theater, literature, and the visual arts through the dissemination of the concepts after the 1927 Solvey Conference held in Brussels. In the same issue, Michal Kobialka discusses the destabilization of the concepts of time and space in eight examples of "quantum realities" defined in the wake of Einstein's special theory of relativity in "Inbetweenness: Spatial Folds in Theatre Historiography." In combination, these two essays summarize major changes in concepts of space that found artistic expression in, for example, cubism, surrealism, and dada.

20. For scenographic changes that articulate new perceptions of time and space, see Stanton Garner, *Bodied Spaces* (Ithaca: Cornell University Press, 1994), pp. 55–58, and for brief descriptions of multivalent theater space and transformational theater space, see Christian Dupavillon, "France and Its Theatre Locations in 1977," in Arnott et al., *Theatre Space*, pp. 73–75.

21. Clifford Davidson, "Space and Time in Medieval Drama: Meditations on Orientation in the Early Theatre," in *Word, Picture, and Spectacle*, ed. Clifford Davidson (Kalamazoo, Mich.: Medieval Institute Publications, 1984), p. 40.

22. For an analysis of Christian representation of Jews in this play, see my article "Medieval Drama as Documentation: 'Real Presence' in the Croxton *Conversion Ser Jonathas the Jewe by the Myracle of the Blyssed Sacrament,*" *Theatre Survey* 38, no. 1 (1997): 97–115.

23. Clifford Davidson, "Toward a Sociology of Visual Forms in the English Medieval Theatre," *Fifteenth Century Studies* 13 (1988): 222.

24. Quoted in Edward Grant, *Planets, Stars, and Orbs: The Medieval Cosmos, 1200–1687* (Cambridge: Cambridge University Press, 1994), p. 171, n. 8.

25. For the distinction between localized and unlocalized playing spaces, see Alan H. Nelson, "Some Configurations of Staging in Medieval English Drama," in *Medieval English Drama: Essays Critical and Contextual*, ed. Jerome Taylor and Alan H. Nelson (Chicago: University of Chicago Press, 1972), pp. 117–18.

26. *The Play of the Sacrament*, ed. John C. Coldewey, in *Early English Drama: An Anthology* (New York: Garland, 1993), p. 281.

27. *The Play of the Sacrament*, p. 283.

28. *The Play of the Sacrament*, p. 284.

29. *The Play of the Sacrament*, ll. 271–73.

30. *The Play of the Sacrament*, l. 340.

31. *The Play of the Sacrament*, l. 342.

32. *The Play of the Sacrament*, l. 358.

33. Richard Homan, "Devotional Themes in the Violence and Humor of the *Play of the Sacrament*," *Comparative Drama* 20 (1986–87): 331.

34. *The Play of the Sacrament*, p. 290.

35. *The Play of the Sacrament*, p. 291.

36. *The Play of the Sacrament*, p. 291.

37. *The Play of the Sacrament*, p. 295.

38. *The Play of the Sacrament*, p. 296.

39. *The Play of the Sacrament*, p. 297.

40. For the *adversus judeos* tradition and policy of protection of the Jews under the *Sicut Judeis*, see Rosemary Radford Reuther, *Faith and Fratricide: The Theological Roots of Anti-Semitism* (New York: Seabury Press, 1974), pp. 117–81. For a detailed discussion of the

position of the Jews in the theology of the Church fathers, see Shlomo Simonsohn, *The Apostolic See and the Jews*, pp. 228–70.

41. *The Play of the Sacrament*, p. 299.

42. *The Play of the Sacrament*, p. 301.

43. Douglas Gray, *Themes and Images in the Medieval English Religious Lyric* (London: Routledge and Kegan Paul, 1972), p. 18.

44. Michel Foucault uses "heterotopia" to describe sites in any culture that "are something like counter-sites, a kind of effectively enacted utopia in which the real sites, all the other real sites that can be found within the culture, are simultaneously represented, contested, and inverted . . . outside of all places, even though it may be possible to indicate their location in reality." See Michel Foucault, "Of Other Spaces," *Diacritics* (spring 1986): 22–28.

45. David C. Lindberg, *The Beginnings of Western Science: The European Scientific Tradition in Philosophical, Religious, and Institutional Context, 600 B.C. to A.D. 1450* (Chicago: University of Chicago Press, 1992), p. 247.

46. For a succinct summary of the medieval efforts to resolve Aristotle's contradictory theories of three- and two-dimensional space, see Edward Grant, "Place and Space in Medieval Thought," in *Studies in Medieval Science and Natural Philosophy*, (London: Variorum Reprints, 1981), pp. 138–39.

47. Jonathan Boyarin, ed., *Remapping Memory: The Politics of TimeSpace* (Minneapolis: University of Minnesota Press, 1994), p. 2; Philip Hefner, "Basic Christian Assumptions about the Cosmos," in *Cosmology: Historical, Literary, Philosophical, Religious, and Scientific Perspectives*, ed. Norriss S. Hetherington (New York: Garland, 1993), p. 348.

48. For historical overviews of the Condemnation of 1277 and its restrictions on any thought that did not acknowledge the Christian God as creator of all worlds, the plurality of worlds, and the debates over the extracosmic void space, see Edward Grant, *Planets, Stars, and Orbs*, pp. 150–77.

49. Grant, "Place and Space," p. 143; Edward Grant, *A Sourcebook in Medieval Science* (Cambridge: Harvard University Press, 1974), pp. 549–50, 551.

50. Grant, *Sourcebook*, pp. 26, 206.

51. Edward Grant, *Much Ado about Nothing: Theories of Space and Vacuum from the Middle Ages to the Scientific Revolution* (Cambridge: Cambridge University Press, 1981), p. 121, n. 27.

52. Grant, "Place and Space," p. 143.

53. Edward Grant, *The Foundations of Modern Science in the Middle Ages: Their Religious, Institutional, and Intellectual Contexts* (Cambridge: Cambridge University Press, 1996), p. 122; Grant, *Planets, Stars, and Orbs*, p. 171; Grant, *Sourcebook*, pp. 548–49, 556, 557–58.

54. Grant, *Foundations of Modern Science*, p. 123.

55. Edward Grant, "Medieval Cosmology," in *Cosmology: Historical, Literary, Philosophical, Religious, and Scientific Perspectives*, ed. Norriss S. Hetherington (New York: Garland, 1993), p. 189.

56. Phillip Hefner discusses the components of myth as "symbolic narrative," described in a "transcendent order," and elaborating "what human action is commensurate with that order." See his "Basic Christian Assumptions about the Cosmos," in *Cosmology, History, and Theology*, ed. Wolfgang Yourgrau and Allen D. Breck (New York: Plenum Press, 1974).

57. Grant, *Much Ado about Nothing*, p. 119.

58. Alan D. Breck, "John Wyclif on Time," in *Cosmology, History, and Theology*, ed. Wolfgang Yourgrau and Allen D. Breck (New York: Plenum Press, 1977), p. 217.

59. Grant, *Planets, Stars, and Orbs*, pp. 58–59.

BIBLIOGRAPHY

Arnott, James F., et al. *Theatre Space: An Examination of the Interaction between Space, Technology, Performance, and Society*. Munich: International Federation for Theatre Research, 1977.

Bank, Rosemarie. "Time, Space, Timespace, Spacetime: Theatre History in Simultaneous Universes." *The Journal of Dramatic Theory and Criticism* 5, no. 2 (spring 1991): 65–84.

Boyarin, Jonathan. *Remapping Memory: The Politics of TimeSpace*. Minneapolis: University of Minnesota Press, 1994.

Breck, Alan D. "John Wyclif on Time." *Cosmology, History, and Theology*. New York: Plenum Press, 1977.

Brook, Peter. *The Empty Space*. New York: Atheneum, 1968.

Coldewey, John C. "The Non-Cycle Plays and the East Anglian Tradition." In *The Cambridge Companion to Medieval English Theatre*, ed. Richard Beadle, 189–210. Cambridge: Cambridge University Press, 1994.

———, ed. *The Play of the Sacrament*. In *Early English Drama: An Anthology*. New York: Garland Publishing, Inc., 1993.

Cutts, Cecelia. "The Croxton Play, an Anti-Lollard Piece." *Modern Language Quarterly* 5 (1944): 45–60.

———. "The English Background of the *Play of the Sacrament*." Ph.D. diss., University of Washington, 1938.

Davidson, Clifford. "Space and Time in Medieval Drama: Meditations on Orientation in the Early Theatre." In *Word, Picture, and Spectacle*, ed. Clifford Davidson. Kalamazoo, Mich.: Medieval Institute Publications, 1984.

———. "The Realism of the York Realist." *Speculum* 50 (1975): 270–83.

———. "Toward a Sociology of Visual Forms in the English Medieval Theatre." In *Fifteenth Century Studies*. Stuttgart: Hans-Dieter Heinz (1988), 13: 221–35.

Diller, Hans-Jurgen. "The Craftsmanship of the Wakefield Master." *Medieval English Drama: Essays Critical and Contextual*, ed. Jerome Taylor and Alan H. Nelson. Chicago: University of Chicago Press, 1972.

Dox, Donnalee. "Medieval Drama as Documentation: 'Real Presence' in the Croxton *Conversion of Ser Jonathas the Jewe by the Myracle of the Blyssed Sacrament*." *Theatre Survey* 38, no. 1 (1977): 97–115.

Duffy, Eamon. *The Stripping of the Altars: Traditional Religion in England ca. 1400–1580*. New Haven: Yale University Press, 1992.

Dupavillon, Christian. "France and Its Theatre Locations in 1977." In *Theatre Space: An Examination of the Interaction between Space, Technology, Performance, and Society*, ed. James F. Arnott et al., 73–75. Munich: International Federation for Theatre Research, 1977.

Foucault, Michel. "Of Other Spaces." *Diacritics* (spring 1986): 22–28.

Garner, Stanton. *Bodied Spaces*. Ithaca: Cornell University Press, 1994.

Gibson, Gail McMurray. *The Theatre of Devotion*. Chicago: University of Chicago Press, 1987.

Grant, Edward. *The Foundations of Modern Science in the Middle Ages*. Cambridge: Cambridge University Press, 1996.

———. *Planets, Stars, and Orbs: The Medieval Cosmos, 1200–1687*. Cambridge: Cambridge University Press, 1994.

———. "Medieval Cosmology." In *Cosmology: Historical, Literary, Philsophical, Religious, and Scientific Perspectives*, ed. Norriss S. Hetherington. New York: Garland Publishing, Inc., 1993.

———. *Much Ado about Nothing: Theories of Space and Vacuum from the Middle Ages to the Scientific Revolution*. Cambridge: Cambridge University Press, 1981.

———. "Place and Space in Medieval Thought." In *Studies in Medieval Science and Natural Philosophy*, 137–67. London: Variorum Reprints, 1981.

Hefner, Philip. "Basic Christian Assumptions about the Cosmos." In *Cosmology: Historical, Literary, Philosophical, Religious, and Scientific Perspectives*, ed. Norriss S. Hetherington. New York: Garland Publishing, Inc., 1993.

Homan, Richard. "Devotional Themes in the Violence and Humor of the *Play of the Sacrament*." *Comparative Drama* 20 (1986–87): 327–40.

Izenour, George. "The Origins, Evolution, and Development of Theater Design since World War II in the United States of America." In *Theatre Space: An Examination of the Interaction between Space, Technology, Performance, and Society*, ed. James F. Arnott, 45–69. Munich: International Federation for Theatre Research, 1977.

Kantor, Tadeusz. *A Journey through Other Spaces: Essays and Manifestos, 1944–1990*, ed. and trans. Michal Kobialka. Berkeley: University of California Press, 1993.

Kobialka, Michal. "Inbetweenness: Spatial Folds in Theatre Historiography." *The Journal of Dramatic Theory and Criticism* 5, no. 2 (spring 1991): 65–100.

———. "Historic Time, Mythical Time, Mimetic Time: The Impact of the Humanist Philosophy of St. Anselm on Early Medieval Drama." *Medieval Perspectives* 3 (1988): 172–80.

Lindberg, David C. *The Beginning of Western Science: The European Scientific Tradition in Philosophical, Religious, and Institutional Context, 600 B.C. to A.D. 1450*. Chicago: University of Chicago Press, 1992.

Maltman, Sr. Nicholas. "Meaning and Art in the Croxton *Play of the Sacrament*." *ELH* 41, no. 2 (1974): 149–64.

Marrow, James. *Passion Iconography in Northern European Art of the Late Middle Ages and Early Renaissance: A Study of the Transformation of Sacred Metaphor into Descriptive Narrative*. Korrijk, Belgium: Van Ghemment Publishing, 1979.

Mills, David. "Drama of Religious Ceremony." In *Revels History of Drama in English, Vol. I Medieval Drama*, ed. A. C. Cawley et al. London: Methuen, 1983.

Muir, Lynette R. "The Mass on the Medieval Stage," *Comparative Drama* 23 (1989): 314–29.

Munson, William, "Audience and Meaning in Two Medieval Dramatic Realisms." *Comparative Drama* 9 (1975): 44–67.

Nelson, Alan H. "Some Configurations of Staging in Medieval English Drama." In *Medieval English Drama: Essays Critical and Contextual*, ed. Jerome Taylor and Alan H. Nelson, 116–47. Chicago: University of Chicago Press, 1972.

Nichols, Ann Eljenholm. "Lollard Language in the Croxton *Play of the Sacrament.*" *Notes and Queries* (March 1989): 23–25.

———. "Costume in the Moralities: The Evidence of East Anglian Art." *Comparative Drama* 20 (1986–87): 305–14.

Nichols, Stephen. "The New Medievalism: Tradition and Discontinuity in Medieval Culture." In *The New Medievalism,* ed. Marina S. Brownlee et al., 1–28. Baltimore: Johns Hopkins University Press, 1991.

Rubin, Miri. "Desecration of the Host: The Birth of an Accusation." In *Christianity and Judaism,* ed. Diana Wood. London: Blackwell Publishers, 1992, 169–85.

Sinanoglou, Leah. "The Christ Child as Sacrifice: A Medieval Tradition and the Corpus Christi Plays." *Speculum* 48 (1973): 491–509.

Scherb, Victor I. "The Earthly and Divine Physicians: *Cristus Medicus* in the Croxton *Play of the Sacrament.*" In *The Body and the Texts: Comparative Essays in Literature and Medicine,* ed. Bruce Clarke and Wendell Aycock. Lubbock: Texas Tech University Press, 1990.

Spector, Stephen. "Anti-Semitism in the English Mystery Plays." In *Drama in the Middle Ages,* ed. Clifford Davidson et al., 328–41. New York: AMS Press, 1982.

Tydeman, William. *English Medieval Theatre: 1400–1500.* London: Routledge and Kegan Paul, 1986.

Zielske, Harald. "Box-House and Illusion Stage: Problem Topic on Modern Theatre Construction Observations and Contemplations Concerning its Genesis." In *Theatre Space: An Examination of the Interaction between Space, Technology, Performance, and Society,* ed. James F. Arnott et al., 23–44. Munich: International Federation for Theatre Research, 1977.

8

Dramatic Memories and Tortured Spaces in the *Mistere de la Sainte Hostie*

Jody Enders

Once upon a time, something happened in thirteenth-century Paris that was so startling and so violent that a Carmelite church was built to honor the site where it had taken place and a play was written to chronicle both the miracle and the formation of a theater guild *(confrairie)* to reenact it. At least so goes the legend of the Jew and the tortured, bleeding, resurrected Host in which a private, Jewish, domestic space is transformed through violence into a public space of conversion and devotion.[1] The play is the little-studied fifteenth-century *Mistere de la Sainte Hostie;* and its compelling combination of memorialization, architectural sites, typology, and violence facilitates a new understanding of the metadramatic role of theatrical space in literary and theological hermeneutics. As the *Sainte Hostie* manipulates space in order to dramatize typology (Judas, Mary, Abraham, Isaac, Christ), and typology in order to dramatize space, it demonstrates that it was possible to encode the theory and practice of medieval anti-Semitism within the space and language of drama. In this essay, I endeavor to crack a code that has not always been broken by New Historicism by laying bare some of the sinister foundations that support anti-Semitism and that are encrypted by an entity that is by no means neutral: theatrical space. I do so not in order to pass judgment upon the Middle Ages but to argue for the relevance in theater history of what David Nirenberg has recently termed "the rare and strange . . . similarity the nightmares of the distant past bear to our own."[2]

In addition to being a story about anti-Semitism, the *Mistere de la Sainte Hostie* is a play about the commemorative epistemology and practice of space. As we shall see, following a brief summary of its plot and an analysis of a particularly dazzling performance from 1513, the play poses special problems for medievalists. A virulently anti-Semitic Host-desecration play, the *Mistere de la Sainte Hostie* celebrates the legend of a fallen Christian widow who wishes to put on her best dress for Easter (her *pâques* and the Jew's Passover [*pâque*]). She cannot do so, however, without first buying back her outer garment *(surcot)* that she has previously sold to the Jew Jacob Mousse for cash. Thus there begins a most unusual play of 1590 verses and twenty-six characters, quite literally around the widow's skirts.[3] To earn back her money, the unnamed widow, designated only as "La Mauvaise Femme," makes a deal with Jacob that prompts the first metadramatic performance of the play. She fakes communion at church and delivers the Host to Jacob, who promptly subjects it to a series of tortures so that he may see for himself whether the Host is truly the embodiment of a Christ with the power of resurrection. So gruesome are its tortures and so persuasive its transformation into the ascending figure of Christ that Jacob's wife, son, and daughter convert at the sight (and the site) of its resurrection. Jacob's son then spreads word of the miracle throughout Paris as that city profits from its own drama of ecclesiastical foundations (the newly consecrated *Mistere de la Sainte Hostie*) in order to lay other foundations for the real and imaginary eviction of non-Christians from the city.[4] Local authorities arrive at Jacob's home and retrieve the Host whose absence from church has been duly noted by three faithful women. Judgment is exacted upon Jacob, who is then executed in a public square normally reserved for the buying and selling of pigs. Jacob's wife and children are baptized and the space of torture becomes a space of devotion within the imaginary and historical space of the play. At that point, "the first drama is over; and a second one begins," because there remains only the delayed retribution against Jacob's accomplice.[5] La Mauvaise Femme has escaped to Senlis and begun her own metadramatic impersonation of a chambermaid in a wealthy household. During her seven-year service there, she is subjected to the graphic sexual advances of the valet, which result in an unwanted pregnancy. After her mistress notices first her maid's swelling belly and then its absence, she demands a confession and learns that La Mauvaise Femme has buried her child alive. Justice is swift here as well, and the evil woman dies at the stake after a public confession.[6]

Like its much better-known English analogue, the Croxton *Play of the Sacrament*, the *Sainte Hostie* exploits the space of its mysterious subject in order to distinguish Jewish from Christian domestic spaces and, more significantly, to create, recreate, and perpetuate a properly Christian space by advocating violence against nonbelievers—wherever they may be. But, when the *Sainte Hostie* alternates between the memory spaces that house violent acts and a metadramatic commentary on the "genuine" or "impersonated" expressions of belief to be inspired or denounced within an audience, it forges a conceptual bond between violence, drama, space, and anti-Semitism that far surpasses the apparent confines of a stage play.[7]

On the one hand, it directs special violence against two particular spaces: the homes of Jews and the wombs of fallen women. In the dramatic remembrance of the miracle, Jacob's home, hearth, and even his bed are associated with the very womb of the perfidious Christian widow as each of the play's spaces of simultaneous creation and mutilation functions as an anti-type for the domestic and ecclesiastical spaces of the Christian family. By the end of the first part of the play, when the usurious Jacob has followed through on his dastardly plot to put the Host to the test with a series of ordeals, his inside life as an infidel and torturer coincides with his outside life as a merchant and usurer—a coincidence that culminates in his public execution at the pig market. Similarly, the vain yet impoverished Christian widow has compromised ecclesiastical space by giving a false performance of true belief in church. An anti-Mary who commits infanticide, she pays privately with her defiled womb and publicly with her child and her life. When both criminals are executed and their polluted spaces exterminated or purified, the *Sainte Hostie* sends a message designed to empower true believers who may invoke just cause to punish the violence of Jews with their own violence.[8] With the same reversal of agent and victim that has been so sensitively analyzed by Elaine Scarry, each time Jacob stokes his fire to torture the Host, he feeds the flames of anti-Semitism in a play that casts the Jews as torturers and doers of violence as the *Sainte Hostie* encourages violence and even torture against *them*.

On the other hand, the *Sainte Hostie* is the commemorative story-in-space of a miracle about space. Inside the space of the Carmelite church, there has ostensibly occurred a miracle of disembodiment and re-embodiment; while outside that architectural embodiment—perhaps upon the very *parvis* of the church—a theater troupe redisseminates a disturbing message about colonizing the domestic spaces of Jews and punishing their misdeeds (which include leading others into sin). Because the two villains of the play both receive very public punishments for their private misdeeds, surveillance becomes an appropriate approach to purifying Jewish spaces and to continuing to exact punishment on Jews for behavior that never was and never will be Christian. Nowhere, moreover, is that moment more compellingly encapsulated than in the play's quintessential scene of torture and conversion that is staged at the hearth of Jacob's home and about which there survives a detailed account from a performance in the city of Metz in 1513. With gruesome and graphic detail, that particular performance of the *Mistere de la Sainte Hostie* employs the ultimate locus of domesticity—the hearth—in order to pack a punch to the moral of the story that Jews and evil Christians should be "homeless." What the violence of the *Sainte Hostie* commemorates and concretizes, then, is a social opposition between the stable, domestic space of the Christian home and the unstable emptiness of the faithless, who are destined to lives of wandering, servitude, and homelessness. Jacob's "false faith" prevents him (but not his eventually converted family) from understanding what it means that the embodiment of Christ in the Host miraculously survives its tortures. A newly homeless man, Jacob pays publicly for a crime committed in private space as his public punishment suggests to witnesses to his execution (and to spectators of the play) that other such crimes may be unfolding at any moment inside any Jewish home. So, once again, surveillance or policing of Jewish spaces becomes a solution that will enable presumably "true" Christians to discover what "false" things are really taking place there.

If theater historian Henri Rey-Flaud has emphasized that "the theater of the Middle Ages seeks not to represent the event but truly to have it relived,"[9] it is reasonable to investigate the precise ways in which the *Sainte Hostie* fulfilled that mission. As the play exalts the tortured drama of what Stanton B. Garner has recently termed "bodied spaces" and Herbert Blau "blooded thought," it thus invites broader speculation about the mediatory status of the theater between remembrance and reality as it questions both the alterity and the modernity of the Middle Ages.[10] It exemplifies Erving Goffman's claim that the "theatrical frame" is "something less than a benign construction and something more than a simple keying." There is nothing "benign" about a theater that exploits space as a means of establishing linguistic and behavioral differences between faith and hypocrisy, torture and retribution, true and false belief.[11] And finally, it offers a concrete medieval antecedent for Bert States's remark in *Great Reckonings in Little Rooms* that "the ritual in theater is based in the community's need for *the thing* that transpires in theater and in the designation, or self-designation, of certain individuals who, for one reason or another, consent to become the embodiment of this thing."[12] In the *Mistere de la Sainte Hostie,* that "thing" was violence, and what a great reckoning takes place within and without the play's "boundaries." Each time a Christian audience gathered in the old familiar places of theater to designate Jews as evil and to self-designate their own communities as virtuous, they witnessed the performance of a play that demanded that Christ's embodiment and disembodiment be mirrored by the disembodiment of the Jews—and that that message was to begin within the space of every home.[13]

In many ways, the *Sainte Hostie* is a play about space and spaces. Among other things, it stains its own setting with blood as it exploits the classical and medieval mnemonic lore that institutionalized a powerful series of violent associations between buildings, bodies, mutilation, conservation, dramatic recreation, and the engenderment of speech.[14] As even the most rudimentary assessment of the plot makes clear, the *Mistere de la Sainte Hostie* displays its characters as types and anti-types while spotlighting the special spaces to be occupied by each type. Opposed to the type of the virtuous Christian widow—(the traditional recipient of special feudal and courtly protections)—is the unnamed "Mauvaise Femme," who strikes a deal with the diabolical Jacob for thirty pieces of silver and becomes the play's Judas figure. Jacob explains her deal as follows:

> Or vien ca. Tu m'as icy dict
> Qu'il est ta pasque et que tu dois
> Recevoir cil en qui tu crois
> Si tu le me veux tout entier

Cy aporter (pour essayer
S'il est vray ce que les chrestiens
Ont un dieu) par quanque je tiens
De ma loy tu auras la cotte
Sans croix, sans pille, et sans riotte:
Si que advise si tu peux
Le m'aporter, et si tu veux
Gaigner trente solz bons a l'heure
(*Sainte Hostie*, fol. 5v°).[15]

[Okay, come here. You've just told me that it's your Easter and
that you must receive him in whom you believe. If you want to
bring him here to me in one piece (so I can see for myself if
it's true that the Christians have a God), then, by the law that I
hold dear, you will have your surcoat without having to flip
heads or tails for it and with no trouble. So that's how it will go
if you can bring him to me and if you want to earn thirty sous
here and now.]

Obsessed with her attire, La Mauvaise Femme fears her alignment with
Judas; but agrees to play her role by merely impersonating the faithful
among whom she moves at church:

Tu me requiers chose trop dure:
Si dieu m'aist que je le vendisse
Comme Judas, haro quel vice:
Mon dieu je serois bien damnee
Que l'hostie digne et sacree
Qui est le corps de Jesus Christ
Pour avoir un peu de profit
Vendisse. Ha, quel horrible chose! (fol 5v°).[16]

[You are asking too hard a task. If God should see me through
to sell Him, like Judas, oh, what viciousness! My God, I would
be rightly damned for having sold for a little bit of financial gain
the noble and sacred Host, which is the body of Jesus Christ.]

Vanity and poverty cause her to concede to the veritable stage directions proffered by Jacob's wife, who is initially complicit in the plot.

The Jewish housewife chastises the widow while assigning her two roles to play: that of Judas, and that of an actress representing someone taking communion:

> Bien es folle d'estre si ferme
> En ta loy chetive meschante.
> Et recoy l'hostie en ta bouche
> Et *de langue point n'y touche*
> Et la metz apres en ta main
> Ou tu la mettras en ton sain
> Et t'en reviens bien coyement.
> On n'en scaura ja rien nullement
> Et tu seras au moins paree
> Sans payer mont ne souldee
> N'esse pas grand gaigne en malheure (fol. 6r°).[17]

[You're really crazy, wretch, to remain so firm in your feeble law. Just go receive the Host in your mouth and don't touch it with your tongue. And then you'll put it in your hand or in your breast and then you'll come discreetly back here. No one will ever know anything about it, and, at least, you'll look nice without paying interest or principal. Isn't that a pretty good deal for someone in your situation?]

The desperate widow accepts the deal, plays her role, and delivers the Host to its tormentor, but cannot bear to watch Jacob's proposed demonstration of Jewish belief, which, in fact, can never take place:

> Adieu: car il nous faut scavoir
> Si le Dieu en qui chrestiens croyent
> Et par qui tant ilz nous haboyent
> Sa vertu, pouvoir, et puissance
> Mettez vous tous en ordonnance:
> Autour de ce coffre et voyez
> Comment chrestiens sont desvoyez
> De croire en une telle oublie:
> En disant qu'elle a sang et vie
> Et que c'est leur Dieu proprement (fol. 8v°).[18]

[Farewell, because now we have to find out all about the God in whom the Christians believe and about whose virtue, power, and strength they're always barking at us. So all of you line up now around this strongbox and see for yourselves how the Christians are misguided to believe in such a Host [offering], saying that it has blood and life and that it is really their God in the flesh.]

The position of the *Sainte Hostie* is, of course, that Jacob's truth is a lie and that his proposed use of torture as a mode of investigation can rightly lead only to the use of torture to investigate and punish *him*.[19]

Jacob's punishment, however, also begins at home as his wife, son, and daughter rise up against him and beg for mercy at each new act of violence that he inflicts upon the Host. A series of vivid stage directions depict the progression as, first, *"Cy prent L'hostie et la cloue d'un clou en une coulonne et le sang en coule a terre"* (He takes the Host and nails it with a nail upon a column and blood runs out upon the ground) (fol. 10r°). Next, Jacob casts it into the fire, where it will not stay *(Il le jette au feu et il ne se y veut pas tenir)*. He then takes a lance and smites the Host against the fireplace *(Le juif prent une lance et frappe L'Hostie contre la cheminee)*, after which he takes a kitchen knife and chops up the Host *(Icy prent un cousteau de cuysine: et hache l'hostie parmy la maison)* (fol. 10v°). At that moment, the miracle of the *Sainte Hostie* is complete when a crucifix appears inside the family's great cauldron and affixes itself to the symbolic architectural embodiment of any home: the hearth *(Icy apert un crucifix en la chaudiere contre la cheminee)* (fols. 11v°–12r°).[20]

The logical conclusion suggested by this event is that a family of Jewish infidels must be dissolved in favor of its rebirth through conversion into a Christian family. Responsibility for that dissolution is shared here by the fallen widow who puts her body on such intimate terms with Jacob that she threatens miscegenation; and by the evil Jacob himself, who participates in the dismemberment of his own family. When they plead with him that he cease and desist his violence against the Host, Jacob threatens to turn his violence against *them:* "Or paix: ou bien je vous battray/ Merdailles. Vous faut-il parler? Paix tout coy sans plus babiller" (Quiet! or I'll beat you, you little shits! Now shut up with no more blabbering!) (fol. 9r°). Indeed, his daughter's prayers that the Christian God intervene are so poignant that father Jacob evicts them all from their home (11v°), at which point the Jewish family becomes complicit in the tale of its own demise. Jacob's good Christian (and bad Jewish) son is both an anti-Isaac and an anti-Christ as he curses his birthright, the father who sired him, and the widow whose very womb will be violated in the second half of the play: "Maudict soit il qui m'engendra / Et la vieille qui t'aporta / Ceans: pour souffrir tel douleur" (May he who sired me be damned along with that old woman who brought You here so that You would suffer such pain) (fol. 12v°). Jacob's family must then abandon their home in order to occupy a different space until such time as their old home can be sanctified by a priest and lose all traces of its Jewishness. "Pour ce," concludes a mother now divorced from hearth and home, "laisseray la maison toute / Pour les meffaictz et les abus" (and that's why I will leave my whole house on account of the misdeeds and abuses) (fol. 12v°). Father Jacob, whose status as an "engenderer" has just been denounced by his son, remains disabled in his bed—or in the space of siring and engenderment: *La femme et les enfans s'en vont, et le juif demeure sur son lict tout enragé* (The wife and children leave; and the Jew remains crazed with rage on his bed) (fol. 12v°).

Such is the "economy" of the spaces of anti-Semitism in the *Mistere de la Sainte Hostie* that Jacob's daughter even goes so far as to invoke the standard register of Jewish usuriousness by predicting to her mother that, "ains qu'il soit minuict / Celuy que mon pere a destruict / Luy en donra *un bon payement*" (before midnight, He whom my father has destroyed will pay him back in kind) (fol. 12v°). Meanwhile, there is another empty space to reckon with. The play goes on to reenact that greatest of all stories of empty space: the *visitatio sepulchri* in which the three Marys visit Christ's sepulcher in the celebrated *quem quaeritis* trope (which stands to this day as an origin of liturgical drama).[21] "Quem quaeritis in sepulchro, o Christicole?," ask the angels of the three Marys of that trope, "Whom seek you, O fearful women, weeping at this tomb?" The women respond, "We seek Jesus of Nazareth who was crucified," and the angels inform them that "He whom you seek is not here; but go swiftly, tell the disciples and Peter that Jesus has arisen."[22] In the *Sainte Hostie*, three faithful women also seek their Savior; but their efforts to worship Him are thwarted by the absence of the Host from their church ("n'est en vostre moustier"). In the same way that the *quem quaeritis* trope is a foundational moment of Christianity and its liturgy, the *Sainte Hostie* interprets that moment literally by retelling and reinventing a narrative

of empty space on which there will be founded both a building—the
Carmelite church—and a "brotherhood" of actors.

   Furthermore, as Sarah Beckwith has recently reasserted of the crys-
tallizing effect of the Council of Constance of 1415, it "helped legitimize
the notion that the Host on every altar was the *same* body of Christ."[23]
Consequently, the Host's absence from a single *moustier* compromises
the sacrament of an entire Christian community. When one of the
Sainte Hostie's three women—the old Martine—demands to know
"what story that Jew has told you" (que vous a ce juif comté?"), the first
woman responds:

>   Il demandoit où nous allons
>   Et nous disons que nous voulons
>   Aller voir dieu, et il nous a dict:
>   Que nostre sauveur Jesus Christ
>   N'est point au moustier (fol. 13v°).

[He was asking where we're going. So we say that we want to go
and see God; and he told us that our Savior, Jesus Christ, is not
in the church.]

"Il se mocque," says Martine of Jacob's son; and threatens to box his
ears. But the lad persists and retells the whole story:

>   Certes, il est en nostre maison
>   N'en vostre moustier n'est il pas:
>   Ne scay si le tenez agas
>   Mais mon père l'a crucifié
>   Et d'un bon canivet percé:
>   Tant que le sang en est yssu (fol. 13v°).

[Verily, He is in our house and not in your church. I don't know
if you take me to be just blathering, but my father crucified him
and pierced him with a good little pocketknife so much so that
blood came out.]

A new metadramatic role begins as Martine invades the Jew's house dis-
guised as a servant in order to rescue the Host from an improper and
unclean space:

Oncques mais je n'ouys comter
Chose qui tel hydeur me fist:
Que cela que ce juif m'a dict.
Par dieu, je prendray ce vaisseau
Qui est (ce m'est advis) net et beau,
Et *feray semblant en maniere*
Que je sois une chambriere
Et que je voyse du feu querre
Pour voir si je pourray enquerre
La verité de ceste chose (fol. 14v°).

[Never have I heard tell of a thing to instill me with such repulsion than that which this Jew has told me. By God, I will take this vessel that seems to me to be clean and beautiful, and I will *pretend to play the role of a chambermaid* and to be off seeking fire so that I might see if I can investigate the truth of this thing.]

In the context of the play, it was, of course, "wrong" for Jacob to have sought his truth by torturing the Host, but it is "right" that Martine seek another truth at the hearth of his "crueux hostel." The truth that endures from the violence committed by Jacob at his hearth is the same truth that foretells his own torture. Martine then brings the Host to a priest as rumors of the miracle start to fall upon Parisian ears everywhere:

Ha sire, regarde,
Mon Dieu que je te présente
Qu'ay trouvé à heure présente
Dedans l'hostel d'un faux juif
Qui dessus le feu l'avoit mis.
Bouillir dedans un chauderon
Et quant j'entray en la maison
Je fus si tresespouventée
Que si je ne fusses armée
Du signe de la croix, sans doute,
Je fusse *contrefaicte* toute (fol. 16v°).

[Oh, my lord, look at my God whom I present to you and whom I found just now inside the home of a false Jew who had placed him upon the fire and boiled him in a cauldron. And when I entered the house, I was so utterly horrified that, had I not armed myself with the sign of the cross, then I would surely have been completely undone.]

Jacob is captured, tried, and burned—but not before retelling his whole story that comes back to his memory ("me vient en memoire") (21v°) as the play brings back the memory of him. He tries to buy himself salvation, volunteers to convert but is refused, and even endeavors to cite the Bible to plead his case. All his efforts fail and lead Jacob instead to an ordeal designed to "pay him back" for that other ordeal to which he (and his forefathers) have subjected Christ. Again denied by his own son—now an anti-Peter—Jacob meets his end when the play exacts public retribution upon his body:

> Si feray je moy par mon âme:
> De son meschef me *souvient* bien
> Je renonce à luy tousjours
> Ha, faux mauvais traicteur,
> Car je vueil estre chrestien (fol. 22v°).

[And thus I too will do it by my soul. I remember well his misdeed, and renounce him for all time, oh, false, evil traitor, for I wish to be Christian.]

Although its head of house was denied conversion, Jacob's family is accepted, and a bishop rehearses their credo with them:

> Et si croyez aussi en somme:
> Que tel comme vous l'avez veu
> En espèce de pain il fut
> Et est transmué dignement
> Par le benoist sainct sacrement
> Que le prestre sacre à l'autel (fol. 23v°).

[And, in a word, this too will you believe: that just as you have seen him here in a kind of bread, he was and is nobly transformed by the blessed holy sacrament which the priest celebrates at the altar.]

Those words of conversion within the play then turn outward to the spectators of the *Mistere de la Sainte Hostie*. The play they have just witnessed is no mere "play" but the real thing. By opposition to the false faith hypocritically acted by false Jewish usurers, they are enjoined to act out truthfully their good faith—which includes lending economic support not to Jews but to the *confrairie* charged with putting on the play:[24]

> Et outre plus mes bonnes gens,
> Si ne soyez pas négligens
> Qui devant voz yeux avez veu
> Le beau miracle: *non pas jeu.*
> S'il vous plaist, *vous le retiendrez.*
> Et de bon cueur le servirez
> En maintenant la *confrairie:*
> Laquelle est bien auctorisée
> *Au propre lieu ou ce fut faict.*
> S'il plaist au doux pere parfaict. . . .
> Amen.
> *La condamnation du faux juif comme*
> *il fut ars et bruslé dehors Paris au marché*
> *aux pourceaux* (fols. 24v°–24r°).

[And what is more, my good people, thus do not be negligent, you who have seen this beautiful miracle before your eyes: it is no game/play. If you please, you will retain it, and you will serve him in good faith by maintaining the *confrérie* which is duly authorized [to perform] at the very site where this thing occurred, if it please our sweet and perfect Father . . .
Amen.
The condemnation of the false Jew and how he was set afire and burned outside of Paris at the pig market.]

Once Jacob has been sentenced to be slaughtered along with the "other pigs" (fol. 29r°), he is further denied the classic spectacle of contrition. He asks for his own holy book and actually dares Christ to try to hurt him (fol 29v°). But Jacob dies with his book and his beliefs as the *Sainte Hostie* exalts conversion and damns an entire race:

Messeigneurs et mes chers amys
Qui avez veu ce beau mystere
Du faux juif et de put aire
Que maudit en soit la nation.

[My lords, and my dear friends who have seen this beautiful
mystery of the false and ignoble Jew, may their whole nation be
damned.]

Once Jacob is dead and the first plot of the *Sainte Hostie* is over, the
play completes its most important conversion of space. Jacob's tormen-
tors—*Affamé* (Famished) and *Maigredos* (Lean-back)—are literally "hun-
gry" to punish him even after death by converting his Jewish home into
a site of Christian worship: "Affin qu'il en soit mention / Et mesmement
dedans Paris / *Qu'en l'hostel du maudict juif / Soit fondé un monastere*
(And so that this be recorded even within Paris, may a monastery be
founded in the home of that damned Jew). Local authorities urge that
the public take heed of the exemplary miracle *(Prenez y tous et toutes ex-
emplaire)* as the starving torturers turn their own hateful proverbial wisdom toward the reputations of Jews as rapacious usurers—which is, of
course, what La Mauvaise Femme should have done: "Il est payé de son
salaire / Ce faux juif de toutes pars. / Luy et son livre sont ars / Fy de luy
et de tous ses artz / Il est payé de son salaire (He has been paid all over
in kind, that false Jew. He and his book are burned. Damn him and all
his arts. He has been paid in kind) (fol. 30v°–31r°). Jacob's family is
then warned that they must learn their new creed well, else be spatially
distanced from their new community through excommunication: "Et
qu'ilz soyent bien endoctrinez: / En la foy premierement / Sur peine
d'excommuniement" (And let them first be indoctrinated into the faith
under threat of excommunication) (fol. 24r°). From the purportedly real
miracle, there thus endures a Christian community, a monument to its
triumph in the space and form of an actual Church available for visita-
tion, and a Christian *confrairie* to rehearse inexorably the violent origins
of both church and community with its own didactic offering of the
Mistere de la Sainte Hostie. Indeed, one particular performance sealed
that fate especially well.

According to eyewitness Philippe de Vigneulles, one of the most
impressive features of the 1513 performance of the play in Metz was the

liberal use of hidden devices or *secrets* that held an abundance of blood—along with some other secrets about the play's anti-Semitism. Philippe's account betrays an implicit wordplay in Middle French between *contre-feu* (fire screen), *contrefoi* (incredulity) and *contrefaire* (to behave hypocritically, to playact, to be undone). In a spectacular piece of staging at the fireplace, the various strands of the *Sainte Hostie* come together as actors "playact" the supposedly real story of the real torture of a real embodiment of a real Christ as a demonstration of real faith—a demonstration whose "reality" depends on the portrayal and vilification of the Jews as the false practitioners of a false faith. So, while there is no phonological or etymological relationship between *contre-feu* and *contrefoi*, it seems more than coincidental that a violent drama concerned with credence and creeds *(contrefoi)* would play out *(contrefaire)* credibly and incredibly at the hearth *(contre-feu)* of a Jewish home:

> Le lundi devant, premiere feste de pentecouste, *fut jué en chambre* le jeu de la ste hostie, laquelle ste hostie est à ste Marie de Paris, et fut un mystère fort biaulx et les secrets moult bien faits. *(Suit l'analyse de la pièce)*. . . . [his ellipsis]. Le traistre juif voulant aprouver s'il estoit dieu, print ladite sainte hostie et la mist sus une tauble et fraipoit d'un coustiaux parmi. Alors par *ung secret,* qui estoit fait, sortit grand abondance de sang et sailloit en hault parmi ladite hostie, comme se ce fut ung enfant qui pissoit, et en fut le juif tout gaisté et dessaigné et faisoit moult bien son personnaige. Aprez non content de ce, il ruoit ladite hostie au feu et par ung engien, elle se levoit du feu et se ataichoit contre le *contre feu* de la cheminée et le traistre la perçoit derechef d'une daigue, et par ung aultre engien et secret, elle jectoit de rechief sang abondamment. Puis ce fait il la reprint et lataichoit avec deux cloz contre une estaiche et la vint fraipper d'un espieu et ladite hostie jectoit arrière sang abondamment et jusques tout emmey le parcque trinçoit *[sic]* le sang *et en fut le lieu tout ensanglanté.* Et alors comme enraigié print l'hostie et la ruoit en une chaudiere d'yaue boullant et elle se elevoit en l'air et montoit en une nueé et devint ung petit enfant en montant a mont et se faisoit tout ceci par engiens et secrets; et s'y fist encore ledit jour plusieurs choses que je laisse. . . .[25]

[The previous Monday, the first feast of Pentecost, there was played on the Place de Chambre, the *Play of the Sacred Host*, which host is at Saint Mary's in Paris. It was a most beautiful *mystère* and the special effects were very well done. (There follows an analysis of the play.) . . . Wanting to test [the host] to see if it was god, the traitorous Jew took the aforesaid Host and put in on a table and stuck a knife through it. Then, by means of a secret place that had been fashioned, there emerged a great abundance of blood, and it shot upwards from the aforementioned host, as if it were a child pissing. And the Jew was all soiled and bloody and played his part very well. Afterward, not content with this, he shoved the aforementioned Host into the fire, and, by means of a mechanism, the Host rose up out of the fire and affixed itself upon the fireguard of the hearth. And the traitor then pierced it a second time with a dagger, and, by means of another hidden mechanism, again it spewed out an abundance of blood. After having done this, he took the Host again and attached it with two nails against a stake and went to strike it with a boar spear, and, from behind, the aforementioned Host abundantly spit out blood until the whole center-stage glistened with blood and the whole place was full of blood. And then, like one enraged, he took the Host and threw it into a cauldron of boiling water, and it rose up into the air in a puff of smoke and became a little child as it rose to the top. And all this was accomplished by devices and hidden places; and there were other things that happened that day that I leave aside. . . .]

The *Sainte Hostie* is, after all, a violent play about credence, creeds, credulity, and incredulity. It is also a play about the opposition between believers who commit noble acts of violence inspired by true faith and nonbelievers *(incrédules)* who commit ignoble acts of violence inspired by false faith or things "against the faith" *(contre la foi)*. There is thus a certain logic to including in its most crucial scene a *contre-feu*, the metal plaque in front of a fireplace that functioned like the modern fire screen. As it happens, that metal implement designed to protect homes from fire had other links to emotion, faith, and belief.

By the thirteenth century, *contre-feu* had a synonym in *contre-coeur*, a term that would come to figure in the prepositional phrase *à contre-coeur*, meaning "halfheartedly", or "against one's will" and *coeur* meaning heart, will, or even courage. That figurative meaning is attested as early as 1393—a good century before Philippe wrote up his memoirs—and is semantically resonant with the term *contrefoi,* which denoted "incredulity" as early as 1260. The representation of faithlessness that lies at the heart and hearth of a Jewish home is then represented and undone *(contrefaite)* before the eyes of an audience by actors doing what they do: play-act *(contrefaire* or *contrafacere).* In other words, in a violent play in which the faithful escape being *contrefaits* by actors whose duty is to *contrefaire,* the entangled resonances of these terms come full circle to another type of *contrafactum* intimately associated with liturgical performance. The etymological ancestor of *contrefaire, contrafacere* calls up an entire performative interplay between secular and ecclesiastical strands not unlike that suggested by the *Sainte Hostie*'s revisited *quem quaeritis* trope. Moreover, *contrafactum* was the musicological term that designated a piece of vocal music in which the melody remained the same but the secular "lyrics" were replaced by sacred ones or vice versa: courtly love lyrics might be voiced over a liturgical melody. Metaphorically speaking, such a replacement also transpires in the *Sainte Hostie* and provides a rationale for the invasion, appropriation, and literal remodeling of Jewish domestic space. Displaced Jews are *contrefaits* while Martine was not; and Jacob Mousse exemplifies a final kind of *counterfeiting.* Portrayed as a moneylender and a purveyor of false behaviors, the Jew is the ultimate *counterfeiter* when he tries to turn against the embodiment of Christ precisely that special brand of torture that was typically reserved for criminals convicted of counterfeiting: boiling and hanging.[26] The *Sainte Hostie* has not only helped to monumentalize anti-Semitism but has encoded anti-Semitic practice within the mental, physical, and philological spaces it creates.

What has been "produced" at the *contre-feu* of the *Sainte Hostie,* therefore, is an anti-Semitism that is grounded in space, in language, and in the language of space. And yet, as contemporary critics draw their own conclusions about that anti-Semitism, there arises a host of new questions about the nonneutrality of space and about the frightening valences of the very language used to designate it. Even in the wake of the most sensitive New Historicist interpretations of medieval culture, anti-Semitism is often "cleansed" or "emptied out" of its violence—a process that has been criticized by Peter Haidu as follows: "in respect to the practices of violence, modernity is medieval: it continues the practices of the Middle Ages, differentiating itself primarily in the amount of violence produced, and in its hypocritical disguisement."[27] Thus, when Rey-Flaud acknowledges the "unheard of sadism" of the medieval stage, he rationalizes its scenes of torture and persecution by assigning to them the exaggeratedly lofty motivation of a Christian "price to pay for collective salvation."[28] He hypercorrects alterity with the assurance that "it is not complicity which medieval men bring to the theater, it is faith."[29] Victor Scherb professes skepticism about the critical tendency to view violence as part of the affective piety of the late Middle Ages— only to conclude of the relentless mutilations of the Croxton *Play of the Sacrament* that "violence is de-ritualized and given bloody form once again so that the action of the play can in effect both *mirror and heal* the divisions within the contemporary Suffolk community."[30] If torture, bloodshed, and anti-Semitism somehow assist in the formation of civilized Christian communities, they do so upon the mutilated bodies of Jews and Jewish sympathizers who are all deemed deserving of their ordeals. Notwithstanding any "mirroring or healing" that might (or might not) have taken place, the formation of the *Saint Hostie*'s Christian community depends on the extermination of another (an other) Jewish community that it unmakes as it remakes itself.[31]

In his reproduction of Philippe de Vigneulles's narrative, Petit de Julleville himself managed to unmake something by concealing through silence an anomaly of the use of violence in the service of Christianity. In the midst of reproducing Michelant's text virtually verbatim, he introduces the long excerpt cited above about "le traistre juif" by signaling a curious ellipsis with the phrase: "(Suit l'analyse de la piece) . . ."[32] Petit de Julleville took the trouble to delete the following twenty-five words: "*car premierement y avoit comment une weve femme de Paris avoit vendu à ung juif celle ste hostie et lui livrait le jour de paicques* et le traistre juif voulant aprower. . . ."" (because first there was the part about how a Parisian widow had sold that holy Host to a Jew and was delivering it to him on the day of Easter. And the traitorous Jew, wanting to test . . .).[33] Why did he do so? One possible answer is that, in the world of the *Sainte Hostie*, the lack of mercy shown to an impoverished and unprotected Christian widow—*mauvaise* though she may be— seemed to him to be just too "unchristian" and too unmerciful on that most sacred day of Easter. Stranger still is the fact that that anxiety ap-

parently needled Petit de Julleville more than it did Michelant or
Philippe de Vigneulles himself.[34]

In light of such textual and extratextual events, it seems reasonable
to submit that medievalists might propose some correctives of their own
to so many early corrections and hypercorrections—perhaps along the
inspired lines elaborated by Louise Fradenburg. In her important essay
on "Criticism, Anti-Semitism, and the Prioress's Tale," she urges that
critics have a responsibility "to engage in what Elaine Scarry calls 'acts
that restore the voice,' that bestow 'visibility' on pain and suffering, that
help the sufferer once again to become available to others through verbal and material artifacts."[35] Fradenburg is extrapolating here from
Scarry's argument that, when torturers produce real pain in real bodies,
they "bestow visibility on the structure and enormity of what is usually
private and incommunicable, contained within the boundaries of the
sufferer's body."[36] However influential Scarry's work has been for the
medievalist, there is something about the notion of a "private and incommunicable" pain that stands at odds with the numerous medieval
spectacles of suffering in public martyrdom, penitence, punishment,
and even in the ritual of transubstantiation as enacted in the *Mistere de
la Sainte Hostie.* Indeed, the very nature of that already public ritual
would become even more public and even more violent during the great
Reformation debate about whether the priest at the altar reenacted the
miracle of the sacrament or merely "represented" it. What is indu-
bitable is that the mysterious illusions and realities of the *Sainte Hostie*
continue to reenact both the violence and the debates surrounding its
foundations.

In the final analysis, what was played out on the Place de Chambre
was an unbelievably violent commemoration (played out believably)
within a bloody theatrical space that imbued the stakes of credulity or incredulity with a clear and present danger. The Parisian space in which a
Jew tortured the Host has thwarted that danger by killing the offender,
converting his family, and reforming the private space of a Jewish home
into the public ecclesiastical space of a Christian community. In that
way, the instructive miracle of how Paris was saved would then stand as
a reminder and an inspiration to any community viewing the play, en-
abling a sinister message of anti-Semitism to be represented, lived, and
relived. That insight is disillusioning, but not merely in the way that
Gustave Cohen had in mind when he reserved a special revulsion for the

medieval prop-masters in charge of violent scenes. They applied all their ingenuity, he writes, "to reproducing horror with the greatest possible realism" and surely carried out the goriest moments "with great technical skill, so as not to lead to too great a feeling of *disillusionment* in the spectator within whom the exposure of fiction would have forestalled the desired emotional response." [37] Much of medieval drama is *"disillusioning"*—especially when the anti-Semitism of its spaces is disillusioned. But if the medievalist fails to engage in the disillusioning interpretation of space, the anti-Semitism encoded in that space risks living on forever.

NOTES

1. For a résumé of the miracle, see L. Petit de Julleville, *Les Mystères,* hereafter *LM,* vols. 1 and 2 of *Histoire du théâtre en France* (1880; reprint, Geneva: Slatkine, 1968), 2: 576. See also editor David Bevington's remark that the English Croxton *Play of the Sacrament,* devoted to an English version of the miracle, apparently dates "from the late fifteenth century, not long after the year (1461) in which the miracle is supposed to have taken place" (*The Medieval Drama* [Boston: Houghton-Mifflin, 1975], p. 756). During the preparation of this essay, I have profited immensely from discussion with several colleagues: Ron Akehurst, William Ashby, Michael Camille, Valerie Flint, Louise Fradenburg, Bruce Holsinger, Alan Knight, Susan Noakes, and Miri Rubin.

2. David Nirenberg, *Communities of Violence: Persecution of Minorities in the Middle Ages* (Princeton: Princeton University Press, 1996), p. 17.

3. See also Petit de Julleville's plot summary in *LM,* 2: 574–76.

4. In that sense, the *Sainte Hostie* participates in the same punitive use of space and distance that are detailed by Valerie I. J. Flint in her contribution to this volume as it poses other historical problems of interpretation. Nirenberg has recently stressed both the fantasy and the reality of the exile of Jews from Paris, as chronicled by the likes of Jean de Saint Victor. Historians, asserts Nirenberg, "are virtually unanimous in declaring that the Jews were expelled from France, at least in part because of their 'crime.' Contemporary chroniclers were more ambiguous. . . . [They] celebrated the exile of the Jews but were unsure whether it had really occurred. Jews left France, but they were apparently never compelled by a royal edict of expulsion" (*Communities,* p. 67).

5. *LM,* 2: 575.

6. My own constraints of space prevent me from devoting to the widow's story the attention it richly deserves. Suffice it to say that her punishments are also localized in the domestic and personal spaces of hearth, home, and womb when she falls victim to the explicit sexual overtures of the household's valet, bears his child, and murders it by burying it alive. She is, however, granted the possibility of confessing her sins—presumably because she is less culpable than the Devil-in-the-form-of-Jacob Mousse, who seduced her into evil.

7. As early as the Fleury Playbook *Herod,* medieval drama regularly invited spectators within its bounds to experience meanings beyond its bounds, as when a didascalic com-

mentary called upon the *populus circumstantem* to participate in the play: "Let them invite the people standing around to adore the child." See, e.g., William Tydeman, *The Theatre in the Middle Ages: Western European Stage Conditions, ca. 800–1576* (Cambridge: Cambridge University Press, 1978), p. 223.

8. Here I allude to the celebrated terminology of René Girard in *Violence and the Sacred*, trans. Patrick Gregory (Baltimore: Johns Hopkins University Press, 1977), p. 37.

9. "Le Théâtre du Moyen Age ne cherche plus alors à figurer l'événement, mais à le faire véritablement revivre." *Pour une dramaturgie du moyen-âge*, hereafter *PDMA* (Paris: Presses Universitaires de France, 1980), p. 18. All translations from the French are mine unless otherwise indicated.

10. For theoretical work on these topics, see their books of those titles: Garner's *Bodied Spaces: Phenomenology and Performance in Contemporary Drama* (Ithaca: Cornell University Press, 1994); and Blau's *Blooded Thought: Occasions of Theatre* (New York: Performing Arts Journal, 1982). For two discussions of the alterity of medieval drama, see Rainer Warning, "On the Alterity of Medieval Religious Drama," *New Literary History* 10 (1979): 265–92; and Hans-Robert Jauss, "The Alterity and Modernity of Medieval Literature," *New Literary History* 10 (1979): 181–227.

11. Erving Goffman, *Frame Analysis: An Essay on the Organization of Experience* (Cambridge: Harvard University Press, 1974), p. 138.

12. Bert O. States, *Great Reckonings in Little Rooms: On the Phenomenology of Theater* (Berkeley: University of California Press, 1985), p. 157.

13. See, e.g., Sarah Beckwith's comment that "the most important, indeed the defining aspect of [Christ's] personhood" was his embodiment in a body that was "loved and adored, but . . . also violated repeatedly," in *Christ's Body* (London and New York: Routledge, 1994), p. 5. Excellent critical approaches to the topic of displaced anger against early Jewish cultures include Nirenberg, *Communities of Violence*; Louise O. Fradenburg, "Criticism, Anti-Semitism, and the Prioress's Tale," *Exemplaria* 1 (1989): 69–115; R. Po-chia Hsia, *The Myth of Ritual Murder: Jews and Magic in Reformation Germany* (New Haven: Yale University Press, 1988); and Elaine Scarry's general discussion of the reversal of agent and victim in the ideology of torture in *The Body in Pain: The Making and Unmaking of the World* (1985; reprint, New York: Oxford University Press, 1987), pp. 50–59: i.e., the *Sainte Hostie* casts its Jews as the doers of violence as it encourages violence against *them*.

14. I discuss at length the violence, pain, performativity, and bodily "architectures" of rhetorical arts of memory in "Emotion Memory and the Medieval Performance of Violence," *Theatre Survey* 38 (1997): 139–60; and in ch. 2 of *The Medieval Theater of Cruelty* (Ithaca: Cornell University Press, 1999). For superb critical introductions to medieval commemorative practices, see Mary Carruthers, *The Book of Memory* (Cambridge: Cambridge University Press, 1990); Frances Yates, *The Art of Memory* (Chicago: University of Chicago Press, 1966); and Janet Coleman, *Ancient and Medieval Memories* (Cambridge: Cambridge University Press, 1992). See also in this connection D. Vance Smith's recent analysis of the ways in which English communities used buildings to navigate their way through violent aspects of history in "Irregular Histories: Forgetting Ourselves," *New Literary History* 28 (1997): 161–84.

15. By Petit de Julleville's account, the *Mistere de la Sainte Hostie* survives in several editions: two undated sixteenth-century Parisian editions in 8°, and a reissue in Aix in 1817

(*LM*, 2: 574). Citations from the play are from one of the two surviving sixteenth-century editions housed in the Bibliothèque Nationale and designated Ris. Yf. 2915. I am indebted to Alan Knight for sharing with me his personal copy of the play when it proved especially difficult to obtain a microfilm. When quoting the text, I have done the following for the sake of clarity: added punctuation and such diacritical marks as accents and apostrophes, substituted "j" for "i" when appropriate, and resolved the occasional abbreviation.

16. The term "haro" was also a standard juridical cry for princely intervention, discussed, e.g., in Thomas Basin's fifteenth-century *Apologie, ou Plaidoyer pour moi-même*, ed. Charles Samaran and Georgette de Groër, *Classiques de l'histoire de France au Moyen-Age*, 31 (Paris: Belles-Lettres, 1974), pp. 259–61.

17. It scarcely seems coincidental that, at Pentecost of 1513, the *Sainte Hostie* was performed in Metz along with another play detailing the perils and torments of "une faulse langue." By the account of Philippe de Vigneulles (to whom I return shortly), the "evil-tongue" could "speak well neither of itself nor of others . . . whence its soul was hanged by the tongue at the heights of hell and the devils inflicted several tortures upon it by throwing fire and hail all over its body" (*LM*, 2: 104). The term *souldee*, moreover, is important because, in addition to designating some kind of reward, salary, or profit, it appears in the expression *aller querre soldes* (to go into service)—precisely the fate of La Mauvaise Femme.

18. In addition to the standard meaning of *oublie* as "forgetfulness," the term denoted an offering, oblation, or sacrifice of a victim. But the use of *oublie* (or *oblie*) is particularly compelling here because, according to Oscar Bloch and Walther von Wartburg (*Dictionnaire étymologique de la langue française* [1932; reprint, Paris: Presses Universitaires de France, 1968], p. 451), it referred specifically to the Host. However, as early as the twelfth century, *oublie* had come to denote a sort of baked good made of light pastry dough that was prepared in the same way as was the Host taken at communion. Thus it is logical that Jacob tortures the Host by using a little pocketknife *(canivet)*, a kitchen implement of the sort used to peel fruit. Elsewhere in this passage, the term *desvoyez* (from the verb *desvoier*) had special spatial resonances by the fourteenth century. Beyond denoting the act of going insane or losing one's reason, it also referred to the demarcation of space, such as the clearing of paths or roads of obstacles.

19. On the blurring of investigation and punishment in medieval torture, see Edward Peters, *Torture* (New York: Basil Blackwell, 1985), p. 28. I explore its special relevance to drama in ch. 1 of *The Medieval Theater of Cruelty*.

20. Compare this scene, e.g., to the analogous scene from the Croxton *Play of the Sacrament* in which the Host is subjected to a series of tortures with a boiling cauldron, a dagger, and a pair of pincers (Bevington, *The Medieval Drama*, pp. 70–73). For two interesting perspectives on that scene, see Donnalee Dox's essay in this volume; and James J. Paxson, "The Structure of Anachronism and the Middle English Mystery Plays," *Mediaevalia* 18 (1995): 321–40.

21. For an example of the trope, "quem quaeritis in sepulchro, o Christicole?" see O. B. Hardison Jr., *Christian Rite and Christian Drama in the Middle Ages: Essays in the Origin and Early History of Modern Drama* (Baltimore: Johns Hopkins University Press, 1965), pp. 231–32, 295, 299. See also the compelling rereadings of its theme of absent presence by Anthony Kubiak, *Stages of Terror: Terrorism, Ideology, and Coercion as Theatre History*

(Bloomington: Indiana University Press, 1991), pp. 51–56; and Helen Solterer, "Revivals: Paris 1935," *Alphabet City* (1995): 74.

22. Hardison, *Christian Rite and Christian Drama*, pp. 299, 231.

23. Beckwith, *Christ's Body*, p. 3.

24. Indeed, the importance of lending economic support to the theater was not lost on Philippe de Vigneulles. He asserts that he was not only an eyewitness to the 1513 performance in Metz but a key financial player in a theatrical production that could not have existed without his efforts: "I, Philip [with the emphatic *Je, Phillippe*], was one of those in charge; and I collected the money that was raised. . . ." (*LM*, 2: 104).

25. *LM*, II: 103–4; emphasis mine. Petit de Julleville's own citation (albeit, with numerous orthographic variations) comes from Heinrich (Henri?) Michelant's edition of the *Gedenkbuch des Metzer Bürgers Philippe von Vigneulles aus den Jahren 1471–1522*, Bibliotek des Litterarischen Vereins in Stuttgart, 24 (Stuttgart: Litterarischer Verein, 1852), pp. 244–45. (A modern reprint has also been published by Rodopi [Amsterdam, 1968]). In my translation, I have assumed a small transcription error by Michelant or by one of his sources: i.e., I read "le parcquE Trinçoit le sang" as "le parcquET rinçoit le sang," a phrase that is rendered in Michelant's version as "le paircque trinçoit le sancq," p. 244. Because the verb *trincer* is not attested in any Old French dictionary I have consulted and the closest thing would be "drinking" blood (by analogy to *trinquer* or to the German *trinken*), this possibility seems more logical. I return shortly to Petit de Julleville's curious use of ellipsis in a text that he has otherwise taken great pains to reproduce in its entirety.

Also pertinent here to the medieval practice of space is the fact that the performance *fut jué en chambre*, a phrase that refers to a specific geographical spot in the city of Metz: the Place de Chambre, named for a military figure named "Chambre." It seems clear, however, that anyone unfamiliar with the geography of Metz or with the exploits of the hero Chambre might well have imagined a different kind of theatrical space: one that resembled not an outdoor but an indoor performance space *en chambre* or *in camera*. Finally, although a 1513 performance is, in the strictest sense, no longer "medieval," I submit that its subject matter is certainly more "medieval" in spirit than, e.g., such French Renaissance offerings as those of Garnier and Jodelle.

26. As F. R. P. Akehurst pointed out during the conference, Philippe de Beaumanoir recommends that all five types of *faus monoier* or counterfeiters "must be hanged, and before that, boiled, and they have forfeited their possessions." See Akehurst's translation of the *Coutumes de Beauvaisis of Philippe de Beaumanoir* (Philadelphia: University of Pennsylvania Press, 1992), section 835, p. 304. More interesting still is the fact that this passage appears almost immediately after Philippe's statement that "a person departing from the faith by disbelief so that he will not come back to the way of truth, or who commits sodomy, must be burned and he forfeits all his possessions" (section 834). Thus, the rich resonances of *contrefaire* are linked to the term *desvoyez* and to the perverse sexuality of the mad Jacob.

27. Haidu, *The Subject of Violence: The "Song of Roland" and the Birth of the State* (Bloomington: Indiana University Press, 1993), pp. 193–94.

28. *PDMA*, pp. 153–54.

29. *PDMA*, p. 19.

30. Scherb, "Violence and the Social Body in the Croxton *Play of the Sacrament*," in *Violence in Drama*, ed. James Redmond, Themes in Drama, 13 (Cambridge: Cambridge University Press, 1991), p. 77. In an essay in the same volume, John Spalding Gatton raises a similar objection against treating spectacular scenes of bloodshed as "examples of Christian fortitude and faith" ("'There must be blood': Mutilation and Martyrdom on the Medieval Stage," p. 78).

31. I refer to the subtitle of Scarry's *Body in Pain: The Making and Unmaking of the World*, which is divided into two parts, "Unmaking" and "Making."

32. *LM*, II: 103.

33. Michelant, *Gedenkbuch*, p. 244.

34. In that sense, drama lags behind in recent inquiries into the ideological agendas of the "fathers" of medieval studies, such as those published in *Medievalism and the Modernist Temper*, ed. R. Howard Bloch and Stephen G. Nichols (Baltimore: Johns Hopkins University Press, 1996). With the exception of Seth Lerer's superb essay, "Making Mimesis: Eric Auerbach and the Institutions of Medieval Studies," pp. 308–33, there are no articles on drama per se.

35. Fradenburg, "Criticism, Anti-Semitism, and the Prioress's Tale," p. 82.

36. Fradenburg, "Criticism, Anti-Semitism, and the Prioress's Tale," p. 27.

37. "Pour ne pas trop désillusionner le spectateur, chez qui une fiction découverte aurait empêché l'emotion cherchée." Gustave Cohen, *Histoire de la mise en scène dans le théâtre religieux français du moyen-âge*, 2nd ed. (Paris: H. Champion, 1951), p. 149.

9

BECOMING COLLECTION

THE SPATIAL AFTERLIFE OF MEDIEVAL UNIVERSAL HISTORIES

KATHLEEN BIDDICK

A SECRET ROOM

On December 29, 1491, the wealthy Nuremberg merchant Sebald Schreyer and his brother-in-law Sebastian Kammermeister signed a contract with the "painters" Michel Wolgemut and Wilhelm Pleydenwurff for the production of the *Nuremberg Chronicle,* a printed universal history conceived to outcompete in sheer size and number of illustrations (1,809 illustrations printed from 654 blocks) a number of other popular printed histories already on the European market. Secrecy was to shroud the printing process. The Nuremberg printer, Anton Koberger, whose printing house was then one of the largest in Europe, was required by contract (March 1492) to "reserve and make available . . . a special room in [his] house, in which . . . [they] are able to put together, arrange, and keep the block for the illustrations . . . to see that nothing of these books and illustrations will be printed, proofed, or taken away in the knowledge and wish of the above-mentioned persons."[1] The secret room intrigues for within it, as I shall show, the "proper" was produced, what Michel de Certeau has called "the victory of space over time."[2] Whose space and whose time becomes the troubling question of this article.

UNIVERSAL HISTORIES AS GENRE

Scholars regard the *Nuremberg Chronicle,* which appeared on July 12, 1493, as a quintessentially medieval artifact. As a universal history it drew on a well-established genre that can be defined as those medieval histories that take the theme of universal history from creation up to the incarnation of Christ (and usually beyond to the time of the author) as their subject.[3] Universal histories divide this expanse of time into six or seven ages. These ages were then cross-correlated (in ever more complicated ways during the Middle Ages) with an array of genealogies pertaining to Jesus, prophets, emperors, and pontificates. Anna-Dorothee von den Brincken has distinguished three styles (albeit permeable and overlapping) of universal history: the *series temporum,* chiefly concentrating on computation of incarnational years; *mare historiarum,* where moralizing the different ages comes to the fore, especially in those histories written during the Investiture Controversy and the Crusades; and finally *imago mundi,* a strand emphasizing geographical instruction.[4]

Universal histories were graphic exercises from their inception.[5] Diagrams and schemata were used to conflate and align the dense information contained in incarnational computation and genealogies. From ca. 1100, as universal histories grew more graphically complex in attempts to render encyclopedic knowledge of geography, *mappae mundi* began to appear as illustrations. These maps depicted the holy city of Jerusalem as the center of the world. The Holy City was the knot that bound together genealogies and time lines and gave them coherency.[6] Printed versions of universal histories, which began to circulate widely from the 1470s, grew even more ambitious graphically.[7] They used the compositional possibilities of woodcuts in print layout to make time lines work like slide rules. Just as a slide rule renders linear logarithmic relations, so time lines in these universal histories helped to make linear their spiraling genealogies. The page layout of the *Fasciculus temporum* by Werner Rolevinck, an incunabulum with over thirty-five printings between 1474 and 1500, demonstrates how the slide rule works (figure 9.1).[8]

Werner Rolevinck ran parallel time lines through the center of each page. On one track he marked "Anno Mundi," time from the Creation marked as year 1 and ascending to the current year. On the other track, he indicated time before and after the Incarnation. These years descend from 6666 to the time of birth of Christ at incarnation year 1 and then begin to ascend to the year of publication. These time lines were cued to genealogies graphically schematized as trees and ran serially throughout the pages of the history. In the prologue Rolevinck described how he imagined his history as a "wall" *(paries)* on which he "painted" *(depinxi)* "holy scripture and other diverse histories" *(sacrarum scripturarum quam diversarum aliarum historiarum)* so that the reader may "diligently observe space and time as they correspond" *(diligenter obseruet spacia et numerum correspondenter)*. These time lines thus worked imaginatively like carbon 14 dating; that is, they sought to produce an independent dating device for biblical history. Scholars commonly regard this printed layout as the perfection of a tradition of medieval graphics.[9]

Such graphic perfection is not the only claim to fame of the *Fasciculus temporum* as a universal history; it also inaugurated the popularity of printed universal histories as a picture books. Its first two printings in 1474 (Cologne) attracted consumers first with four and then with nine illustrations of city views. The entrepreneurial effort to repackage universal histories as picture books began to cohere in the 1480s. Venetian printers, who controlled almost half of incunabular production in Europe by the midpoint of this decade, ardently promoted illustrations in universal chronicles.[10] By the time of the 1480 Venetian edition of the *Fasciculus,*

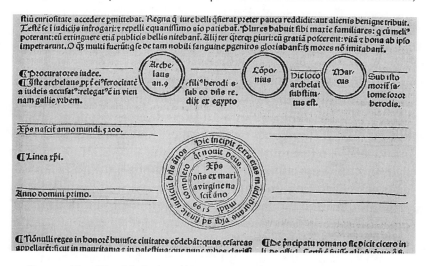

Figure 9.1. The "slide rule" of universal history. Werner Rolevinck, *Fasciculus temporum*, fol. 4v (Radolt, Cologne, 1485). Reproduced from the original held by the Department of Special Collections of the University Libraries of Notre Dame; courtesy of the Department of Special Collections, University Libraries, University of Notre Dame.

the number of city views illustrating the text had risen to forty-four. Another best-selling universal history, the popular *Supplementum chronicarum* of Foresti von Bergamo, first published without illustrations in Venice in 1483 and again in 1485, was furnished with woodcuts in the "third edition" of 1486. Bernardinus Benalius, the printer, used a stock of twenty-two woodcuts for seventy-five illustrations in 1486. Over half of these were of city views. Such views easily exceeded the number of illustrations with theological subject matter. The *Supplementum chronicarum* issue of 1486 thus almost doubled the number of illustrations featured in its rival.

THE CUTTING ROOM FLOOR

It is within this competitive market that leading Nuremberg burghers conceived the *Nuremberg Chronicle* project, printed in 1493. Even as scholars insist on the traditional ("medieval") essence of the *Nuremberg Chronicle*, they also remark, nevertheless, on its exceptionalism: its number of city views surpassed those in other competing histories. This incunabulum featured fifty-two different woodcuts of city views dispersed throughout the text. Scholars have grouped the Nuremberg city views into two categories. "Realistic" views (32 examples) bear some kind of detail that distinguished them as the view of a particular city and they were not reused to illustrate other city views.[11]

A strong association exists between these realistic city views and centers for early printing. The realistic views mostly depict towns that had their own printing presses before 1475 and were often the sites of bishoprics or universities.[12] The blocks of five imaginary city views without distinctive reference to specific cities were also used only once. In style they are indistinguishable from the "realistic" group. The remaining stock of fourteen woodcuts are "generic" views. They differ from each other in detail, but they are not specific to the profile of any "real" city. These generic views could be recycled up to seven times to illustrate for the numerous cities being described in the *Chronicle*.

At first glance, the city views that begin to punctuate printed universal histories in the 1480s might seem to disrupt the working of the slide rule, the graphic paradigm of the universal history. A closer look, however, suggests otherwise. Let me show what I mean by turning to an analysis of a city view from the *Chronicle*. I take as my example the largest city view of the *Nuremberg Chronicle,* a full, double-page spread, which depicts none other than Nuremberg itself, set in the Sixth Age (figure 9.2).[13] The walls of the city extend from horizontal border to border. The foreground occupies about one quarter of the vertical space of the woodcut, an unusually high ratio of foreground to city view, because the majority of the city views in the *Chronicle* start the city walls at the lower frame. This arrangement succeeds in placing at the center of the woodcut the tower of the Frauenkirche, a church built at the mandate of Karl IV over the Nuremberg synagogue that had been cleared by his mandate on November 16, 1349, to make way for a Hauptmarkt.[14] The imperial regalia, including the Holy Lance, were displayed at the Feast of the Holy Lance in a fabric-covered wooden tower, opposite the Frauenkirche, from 1422.

In the left foreground of the view are depicted the tollgates of the city. A very tiny figure makes his or her way to the open city gate. The foreground also features two other human figures: a mounted horseman and a man carrying a pack on his back. These figures are dwarfed by features in the foreground seemingly on the same plane. These include the paper mill of Nuremberg and two road shrines. No inhabitants, as is

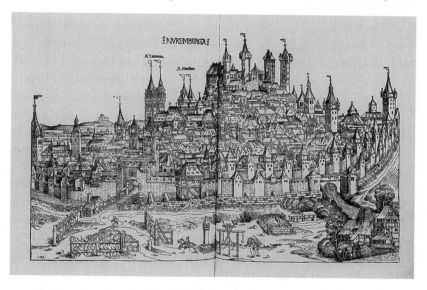

Figure 9.2. Nuremberg city view. *Liber Chronicarum* (Koberg, Nuremberg, 1493), fol. 100r. Photograph courtesy of The Newberry Library, Chicago.

customary of these views, are visible in the spire and rooftop-filled city behind the walls. The woodcut, with its monumental intentions, is the first "sighting" of Nuremberg that the reader would make in the text.

The two-page description of the city begins on page 100v. It first praises the fame of the city and rehearses the debate over its Roman and/or Carolingian origins, opting for the latter based on the opinions of Aeneas Sylvius Piccolomini (Pius II). Some political history follows along with a list of Nuremberg churches and monastic communities. The text celebrates the fact that Nuremberg is the repository of the imperial regalia, whose display with accompanying indulgences proved lucrative to the town. At the end of the description of the city a 4 cm blank ensues, an unusual break for the print layout that, almost without exception, fills up pages.[15] After this break the text engages in an impassioned discussion of the "church militant" that emphasizes the importance of Christ as the cornerstone and Peter as the first apostle. The text bemoans those "cheap cousins" who have "planted the Church with teachers, wonders, images, and bloodshed."[16] When the reader turns the page to 101v, there is a full-page woodcut of Christ enthroned with the apostles; the adjoining text on 102r both tells the story of Pentecost and illustrates it with a woodcut.

The juxtaposition of the Nuremberg city view and description with a scene of Pentecost brings us closer to understanding how the slide rule works in the *Chronicle*. The feast of Pentecost had particular resonance in Apocalyptic thinking in the fifteenth century and enjoyed a rich history of illustration.[17] Exegetes had already begun questioning the relation of Pentecost to Christian history and this temporal argument would vex later Catholic-Protestant debate: Catholic apocalyptic thinking often skipped from Pentecost to the Last Days, whereas Protestant writers regarded church history from the time of Pentecost as crucial to explicating apocalyptic symbols.[18]

Thus far I have described some of the work done by the city view of Nuremberg. But what of the status of Jerusalem, the umbilicus or knot of salvation history, in the *Nuremberg Chronicle*? The Holy City appears only eccentrically in the layout. The printers twice used a so-called "realistic" view of Jerusalem to illustrate the story of Solomon (48r) and the destruction of the temple (63v–64r). An "imaginary" view accompanies the city description that is inserted in the text after the story of Noe. Jerusalem is thus displaced as the spatio-temporal center of universal history in the *Nuremberg Chronicle*. In what time or place, then, is its new center, Nuremberg, to be read? What kind of practice, temporal and/or spatial, is at work in the tactical staging of the city view of Nuremberg, and not Jerusalem, as the navel of history in the *Nuremberg Chronicle?*

Some further clues regarding the representation of realistic city views are needed in order to answer this question. This city view of Nuremberg is the earliest known *stand-alone* realistic view of the city. It is not, however, the first known realistic *depiction* of the city. That distinction belongs to a retable painted by Jadolus Kroll in 1483 for the St. Lorenz church in Nuremberg, in which the walls of Nuremberg form a backdrop to a scene of the Holy Family.[19] Such carefully delineated city views (and also carefully rendered landscapes) become typical in Northern painting in the fifteenth century. Art historians usually read them as background, a reading that implies an implicit relation between the theological subject matter, such as the Holy Family or the Madonna, and the city view. Hans Belting has recently castigated such readings as either a way of refusing the protracted medieval "crisis of the image" or ignoring it by claiming that the so-called history of art begins when city views and landscapes detach themselves from the traditional theological image and come to stand alone, a process we see at work with the city views in the *Nuremberg Chronicle*. Belting insists that it is precisely discontinuities of such carefully rendered city views (or landscapes or still lifes) with their theological subjects that creates the arguments about the crisis of the image within the representation. Belting argues that these city views work like a citation or a quote within the painting, and in so doing they cease to "coexist" with theology and "cut" theological matter. Out of that wound emerges what has been dubbed (naively) by art historians as the "secular" art of the Renaissance.[20]

The Nuremberg city view in the *Chronicle* edited out the theological subject matter still to be seen in the Kroll painting of a decade earlier. Images of the Holy Family or the Madonna, once attached to the city view, now lie on the cutting room floor along with the central image of Jerusalem. These theological cutouts, or outtakes, have their graphic afterlife in the two tiny wayside "shrines" depicted in the Nuremberg city view.[21] Just as the city views of the *Nuremberg Chronicle* cut out theological subjects, so did the universal history qua universal history cut out Jerusalem from the center, the nodal point that threaded together the

temporality of medieval Christian salvation history. What difference
does this make?

The answer is hinted at in the advertisement for the *Chronicle* that
promised its readers "so great delight in reading it that you will think
you are not reading a series of stories, but looking at them with your
own eyes." [22] A moving picture before the invention of moving pictures,
the *Chronicle* made it possible to see time in a new way. The city views,
especially the one of Nuremberg, translate time into place. They act as
the coordinates of this translation process—thus their graphic centrality
in the *Nuremberg Chronicle*. Michel de Certeau would call the work of
cutting out and the act of displacing Jerusalem a "strategy" ("the calcu-
lus of force-relationships that becomes possible when a subject of will
and power [a proprietor, an enterprise, a city, a scientific institution] can
be isolated from an 'environment.'") [23] Not only does the *Chronicle* transform reading practices, its strategies also transform the reader. Through
their excision of Jerusalem as a nodal point, city views also "cut-out" the
links of Christian allegory, a way of binding space and time. With the allegorical link sundered, the city view enclosed the site of the literal and
real. If readers wanted to relink theological time with this new "proper"
space of the city view, they would have to allegorize themselves as readers (imagine themselves as a self that is elsewhere). The new readers
would then fashion themselves as a "type" of an old Christian self whose
links between time and space came preconstituted in the long history of
the redemptive holy image. [24] A famous self-portrait (1500) by Albrecht
Dürer, one of the Nuremberg artists involved in the production of the
Chronicle, is an example of the kind of allegorized "subject" I am imag-
ining reading the Nuremberg city view (figure 9.3). [25] The reader becomes a living icon and the icon becomes proper, that is, isolated as the
afterimage of theological time.

COLLIGITE FRAGMENTA NE PEREANT
(COLLECT THE FRAGMENTS
LEST THEY PERISH)

This chapter could stop here at the layers of scar tissues excreting around
the void created by the excised Jerusalem in the *Nuremberg Chronicle*.
Recall the material strategy of leveling the Jewish neighborhood for a

Figure 9.3. Albrecht Dürer, *Self-Portrait*, 1500.
Courtesy of Scala/Art Resource, New York, and Alte Pinakothek, Munich.

marketplace and building the Frauenkirche over the site of the synagogue, the first cut. Then the symbolic center of Jerusalem is cut out of
the Nuremberg universal history, and, in its place, with the Frauenkirche
positioned over the umbilicus (the knot), appears the city view of Nuremberg. The work of the secret room thus not only synchronized a series of
spatial strategies, it also performed the synthetic work of abstract substitution. Jean-Joseph Goux had drawn our attention to the importance
of such acts of substitution for both signifying and economic processes.[26]
The Nuremberg city image presses us to think about spatial-temporal
circuits of loss and gain at work in its layers of substitutions. Julia Lupton

has insisted on the importance of studying the circuits of loss and gain in these cuts and their substitutions.

The missing link between the circuit of loss and gain in the *Nuremberg Chronicle* is none other than Hartmann Schedel, its editor, and the one partner in the printing project who goes unmentioned in the contractual exchanges. We know from the preserved Latin exemplar used as the layout for the printer that Schedel painstakingly wrote out most of the text of the *Chronicle*. Schedel, a member of the circle of early German humanists, had studied at Leipzig and Padua. He returned to Nuremberg in 1480 where he practiced medicine until his death in 1514. He left behind a library that contained over 370 manuscripts and 600 printed titles. He collected widely in Italian humanism: Vitruvius, Alberti, Petrarch, and Ficino, for example. He possessed a copy of Tactitus's *Germania* and of course a canon of classical authors. He owned the latest works in universal history such as the *Fasciculus temporum* as well as newly printed titles in geography, including Ptolemy's *Geographia*. Also represented are rich collections in medicine, surgery, law, math, theology, and devotion.[27]

It is possible to plug this stereotyped account of a Nuremberg humanist into the circuit of loss and survival circulating in Koberger's secret room by considering one of Schedel's notebooks.[28] Copied in 1504, the notebook includes such diverse material as the first known sylloge of Etruscan inscriptions, drawings of ancient sarcophagi and inscriptions from Rome, literary pieces such as a copy of Annius of Viterbo's *Borgiana Lucubratio* and a version of the poem *Antichità Prospettiche Romane,* as well as some deeply sexualized anti-Italian epigrams composed at a bacchanalian meeting of German humanists that took place in Regensburg in November 1493, just four months after the appearance of the Latin version of the *Nuremberg Chronicle*. The poems are obsessed with Italian humanists as pederasts and sodomites. As one poem puts it: Germans "bang beavers" (futuisse cunnos) and Italians "fuck butts" (culos futire).[29] These poems that Schedel saved inscribe the boundaries of ethnonationalist humanist circles between the vagina and the anus. The poems rehearse deeply felt tensions of nationalism, sexuality, and antiquarianism at stake in collecting literary fragments. They help us read the *Nuremberg Chronicle* against the grain of current scholarship that insists, as I have already mentioned, on its medieval exemplarity. Schedel's fragments help us to understand how the surgery in the secret room was a kind of plastic surgery. As these Nuremberg burghers excised

Jerusalem, they produced Nuremberg as the safely heterosexual civic site of a new, intellectual nationalism.[30]

This economic circuit of survival and loss, described so far, leaves out a critical term. In cutting out Jerusalem, the Nuremberg humanists cut out contemporary Jews who had hitherto been ostensibly protected in medieval Christendom by their allegorical status that bound redemption history with eschatology. The surgery undertaken in Koberger's secret room threw contemporary Jews phantasmatically into a kind of "free fall."[31] In amputating the theological subject matter of the foreground and in relocating Nuremberg as the node of universal history, city views paradoxically "expelled" contemporary Jews not only from space but also from time. By severing the links of Christian allegory, Nuremberg burghers no longer needed Jews to guarantee the apocalyptic teleology of universal history. The pre-Diasporan Jews of the Old Testament (veritas hebraica) became the "real" Jews. The Jews among whom they lived, the "Talmudic Jews" a false species of Jews who could guarantee nothing, became the expelled fragment of universal history. In his humanist panegyric written to Nuremberg that appeared shortly after the Nuremberg Chronicle and three years before the order of expulsion, Conrad Celtis could write of Jews as follows: "there exists no city of Germany to be left immune that their contumely and ignominy would not pollute with this crime, even as they [Jews] have often stolen our sacred hosts and afflicted our sacraments" (Nullam Germaniae urbem immunem reliquere, quam hoc scelere non polluissent, sacris etiam hostiis et sacramentis nostris saepe ablatis contumeliaque et ignominia affectis).[32] Resident Jews would be forced to leave Nuremberg in 1498, not to return until 1850.

Nuremberg printers and artists, as members of the town council pressing the Emperor for permission to expel the Jews and as partakers of civic festivals that included the anti-Semitic productions and publications of Hans Folz, engaged in multiple spatial strategies that condense themselves in the Nuremberg city view.[33] Three anecdotes will suffice to make an exemplary point about the spatial strategies of the "proper" practiced among Nuremberg burghers as they dispossessed Jews materially and symbolically. When the Emperor Maximilian evicted the Jews from Nuremberg in 1498, five years after printing the Nuremberg Chronicle, the town council acquired their houses. Anton Koberger presented one of these houses as a dowry for his daughter in 1500. In his collection of woodcuts and engravings, Hartmann Schedel, the Chronicle's "editor," pasted several of his collected prints onto leaves that had been torn from a late medieval Hebrew manuscript sent to him by a Dominican friend upon the expulsion of the Jews from Bamberg. Finally, Albrecht Altdorfer (a contemporary of Koberger, Schedel, and Dürer, who, like the latter, worked for Emperor Maximilian and who served as an important member of town government in Regensberg) etched in February 1519 two haunting views of the interior of the Regensberg synagogue after the expulsion of the Jews from that town.[34] A voyeuristic fascination with textual and architectural spaces emptied of Jews haunts these stories. That fascination I would argue draws its energy from the undoing of the allegorical knot of ancient Israel *(hebraica veritas)* that bound theological time and space in medieval representation.[35]

ETHNOGRAPHY AND CITY VIEWS

To collect means to exclude time, to use synchronicity as a way of producing the space of collection. It can be said, following de Certeau, that the collection is the "proper" effect of strategies used to deny place and produce space. Thus, we should not be surprised to find the museum collection accreting around the cut made by city views into the cosmology of the medieval universal histories. Collections of city views, which began to circulate in Europe in the mid-sixteenth century as stand-alone graphic artifacts collectible in so-called "modern atlases," trace how such temporal sundering, acts of detemporalization, work as spatial practices.[36] The force of such spatial practices can be grasped by a comparison. Consider, for example, another city view of Nuremberg engraved for the 1575 edition of *Civitatis orbis terrarum* printed by Georg Braun and Franz Hogenberg (1572–1618) (figure 9.4).

When readers bought volume two of *Civitates orbis terrarum* in 1575, they would turn to page 43 for the view of Nuremberg. There they found a fifty-line description of the city backed by a two-page engraved view.[37] No mention is made of the Protestant confession of Nuremberg (no sense in discouraging sales across denominational lines). The account praises the industry of its inhabitants. The view itself (22.5 cm × 34.5 cm) differs markedly from the 1493 view in its handling of the space before the walls. It allows for proportionately more "foreground" and peoples it in

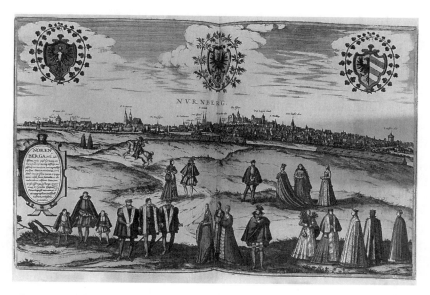

Figure 9.4. Nuremberg city view. Georg Braun and Franz Hogenberg, *Civitatis orbis terrarum* (1575). Photograph courtesy of The Newberry Library, Chicago.

a way that the earlier view did not. Starting with the lower border, the reader sees four views of different stages of formal dress and hairstyle of a richly clad young woman. The front, side, and back views emphasize details such as the fall of fabric, the border designs of hems, the braiding of hair. Another woman (a servant?) also in this group, is depicted in simpler dress. She holds a basket, a bouquet of flowers, and a vase with flowers. Behind this grouping poses yet another group consisting of a mustached man sporting a sword and an elegantly clad woman attended by two young women. Again the reader is invited to linger on the carefully delineated textures of fabric cladding the women as well as the "architecture" of dress trains and tubular hats. Moving along the foreground the reader encounters a mixed group of two women and a man, each elaborately dressed; a group of three elegantly dressed, bearded "city fathers" carrying swords; an elegantly dressed man with (presumably) his two young sons, whose hands he holds. As the reader's eyes scan the center ground, they behold a man with feathers in his cap talking to a simply clad woman with a basket under her arm. Further back there is depicted a horseman and two women standing with their backs to the reader.

This Nuremberg view from the *Civitates orbis terrarum* maps in its foreground what I want to call a "local ethnography," that is, a "collection" of various views and perspectives on local aspects of gender, age, class, dress, fabric, hair. Sartorial in its emphasis, this ethnography recalls the sumptuary concerns of sixteenth-century cities. The Nuremberg city walls have become the backdrop to its local ethnography that has displaced the city wall farther back into the view. The suturing of the ethnographic foreground to the background of the city view renders the foreground figures proportionately as big as city walls.

The 1575 view in *Civitates orbis terrarum* brings the 1493 woodcut of Nuremberg full circle. The center of the sixteenth-century view crosses not through the Frauenkirche, but rather through the empty space of a field in front of the walls. The amnesia signified by that empty space has enabled figures to reestablish themselves in the foreground. The empty space at the center of the sixteenth-century view forgets the cut of 1493 that opened a "great parenthesis" between past and present and severed ancient Israel from a "present" that "Talmudic Jews" inhabited. The spatial strategy to place Jews in a "proper" time other than the present of Christendom has now cleared the way for figures to reestablish themselves. These figures cannot be read, however, as the return of the theological subject. Rather, in their occupation of what Walter Benjamin has called the "empty time" of history, these figures need to be read as ethnographic in that they signify a purely spatial effect, a collection.[38]

My story of the city views of Nuremberg tells a tale of the "proper." By cutting out Jerusalem from the center of universal history and by excising theological subject from the space of the city view, Nuremberg burghers transformed place and its temporal contingencies into space. From the voided space of the foreground gradually emerged a new, ethnographic subject, a subject that is "proper" and frozen in empty time. Enter the collection.[39] Enter what Julia Reinhard Lupton has brilliantly described as the "the crafting of myths of modernity precisely out of the religious material that formed such an important part of [their] early modern daily vocabularies."[40] Regard the collection as the afterlife of medieval universal history, haunted by its evocation of Jews as that which is unconscious to Christianity, that is, "what remains radically repressed by and hence disturbingly internal to it, the imploded husk of a previous representational system."[41]

NOTES

1. Adrian Wilson, *The Making of the Nuremberg Chronicle* (Amsterdam: Nico Israel, 1976), p. 52. Maximilian I held his Reichstag in Nuremberg in 1491 and resided there for six months. His imperial presence undoubtedly inspired the grandiose *Chronicle* project.

2. This essay seeks to contribute to current critical work on epistemological genealogies of the "secret"; see Eve Kosofsky Sedgwick on the "open secret" in her *Epistemology of the Closet* (Berkeley: University of California Press, 1990) and Stephanie Jed's study of the secrecy of mercantile writing with its jealously guarded hidden spaces in her *Chaste Thinking: The Rape of Lucretia and the Birth of Humanism* (Bloomington: Indiana University Press, 1989). I am trying to link the secret space of print production to what Michel de Certeau has called the "proper," that is, "the victory of space over time," and its corollary, the "place": "A place *(lieu)* is the order (of whatever kind) in accord with which elements are distributed in relationships of coexistence. It thus excludes the possibility of two things being in the same location (place). The law of the 'proper' rules in the place: the elements taken into consideration are beside one another, each situated in its own 'proper' and distinct location, a location it defines" (de Certeau, *The Practice of Everyday Life*, trans. Steven Rendall [Berkeley: University of California Press, 1988], pp. xix, 117).

3. Karl Heinrich Krüger provides an overview and a beginning bibliography in his study *Die Universalchroniken* (Turnhout: Brepols, 1976). For a nuanced contrast of universal history with prose chronicles, see Gabrielle M. Spiegel, "Genealogy: Form and Function in Medieval Historical Narrative," *History and Theory* 22 (1983): 43–53. See also these indispensable introductions: Anna-Dorothee von den Brincken, "Mappa mundi und Chronographia: Studien zur imago mundi des abendländischen Mittelalters," *Deutsches Archive für Erforschung des Mittelalters* 24 (1968): 118–86; Anna-Dorothee von den Brincken, "Die lateinische Weltchronistik," in *Mensch und Weltgeschichte: zur Geschichte der Universalsgeschichtsschreibung*, ed. Alexander Randa, Internationales Forschungszentrum für Grundfragen der Wissenschaften Salzburg (Salzburg: Anton Pustet, 1969); Hans-Werner Goetz, "On the Universality of Universal History," in *L'Historiographie médiévale en Europe*, ed. Jean-Phillipe Genet (Paris: Editions du Centre National de la Recherche Scientifique, 1991).

4. Von den Brincken, "Die lateinische Weltchronistik."

5. The graphic design of universal history has been discussed brilliantly by Gert Melville, "Geschichte in graphischer Gestalt: Beobachtungen zu einer spätmittelalterlichen Darstellungsweise," in *Geschichtsschreibung und Geschichtsbewusstein in Späten Mittelalter*, ed. Hans Patze, Vorträge und Forschungen 31 (Sigmaringen: Thorbecke, 1987).

6. For a general introduction to *mappae mundi*, see *The History of Cartography*, vol. 1, ed. John B. Harley and David Woodward (Chicago: University of Chicago Press, 1987); for recent surveys of *mappae mundi* that have Jerusalem inscribed as the center of the world, see Iain Macleod Higgins, "Defining the Earth's Center in a Medieval 'Multi-Text': Jerusalem in *The Book of John Mandeville*," in *Text and Territory: Geographical Imagination in the European Middle Ages*, ed. Sylvia Tomasch and Sealy Gilles (Philadelphia: University of Pennsylvania Press, 1998); Kerstin Hengevoss-Dürkop, "Jerusalem—Das Zentrum der Ebstorf-Karte," in *Ein Weltbild vor Columbus: Die Ebstorfer Weltkarte: Indisziplinäres Collo-*

quium 1988, ed. Hartmut Kugler and Eckhard Michael (Weinheim: VCH, 1991); Hartmut Kugler, *Die Vorstellung der Stadt in der Literatur des deutschen Mittelalters* (Munich: Artemis Verlag, 1986); Bianca Kühnel, *From the Earthly to the Heavenly Jerusalem: Representations of the Holy City in Christian Art of the First Millennium,* Römische Quartalschrift für Christliche Altertumskunde und Kirchengeschichte Supplementheft, 42 (Freiburg im Breisgau: Herder, 1987); the essays in *Jerusalem, Rome, Constantinople: L'Image et le myth de la ville au Moyen-Age,* ed. Daniel Poiron, Cultures et Civilisations Medievales 5 (Paris: Presses de l'Université de Paris-Sorbonne, 1986); and Franz Niehoff, "Umbilicus Mundi: Der Nabel der Welt," in *Ornamenta Ecclesiae: Kunst and Künstler der Romanik,* ed. Anton Legner (Cologne: Stadt Köln, 1985).

7. Anna-Dorothee von den Brincken, "Die Rezeption mittelalterlicher Historiographie durch den Inkunabeldruck," in *Geschichtsschreibung und Geschichtsbewusstein im Späten mittelalter,* ed. Hans Patze, Vorträge und Forschungen 31 (Sigmaringen: Thorbecke, 1987).

8. Margaret Bingham Stillwell, "The Fasciculus Temporum: A Genealogical Survey of Editions before 1480," in *Bibliographical Essays: A Tribute to Wilberforce Eames* (Cambridge: Harvard University Press, 1924).

9. Melville, "Geschichte in Graphische Gestallt," p. 82.

10. For both the *Supplementum Chronicarum* and the *Fasciculus,* city views were simply added to an already existent text; see Achim Krümmel, *Das "Supplementum Chronicarum" des Augustinermönches Jacobus Phillipus Foresti von Bergamo,* Bibliothemata 6 (Herzberg: Bautz, 1992). Krümmel, who has undertaken exhaustive study of the *Supplementum Chronicarum,* doubts that Foresti von Bergamo had input into the choice and placing of the illustrations for the 1486 edition (p. 151).

11. See V. von Loga, "Die Städtansichten in Hartmann Schedels Weltchronik," *Jahrbuch der königlich preussischen Kunstsammlungen* 9 (1888): 93–107; 184–96; Elizabeth Rücker, *Hartmann Schedels Weltchronik: das grosste Buchunternehmen der Durer-Zeit* (Munich: Prestel, 1988).

12. Severin Corsten, "Der frühe Buchdruck und die Stadt," in *Studien zum städtischen Bildungswesen des späten Mittelalters und der frühen Neuzeit,* ed. Bernd Moeller, et al. (Gottingen: Vandenhoeck and Ruprecht, 1983).

13. This view appears on 99v and 100r.

14. See Gerhard Pfeiffer, *Nürnberg, Geschichte einer europäischen Stadt,* (Munich: Beck, 1971).

15. Significantly, there is a deliberate blank of three pages (folios cclviii, cclx, cclxi) left between the sixth age and the seventh age of the Last Days in the Latin edition of 1493.

16. "Sie haben diese kirchen mite lere, mit winderzaichen, mit even pilder und mit plutvergissen geplantzt" (fol. 101r, facsimile German edition, 1493).

17. Here it is interesting to note the resemblance drawn between Pentecost and printing in the next century by John Foxe in his *Acts and Monuments* (1583, last edition of Foxe): "Notwithstanding, what man soever was the instrument, without all doubt God himself was the ordainer and disposer thereof; no otherwise than he was the gift of tongues, and that for a singular purpose. And well may this gift of printing be resembled to the gift of tongues: for like as God then spake with many tongues, and yet all that would not turn the Jews; so now, when the Holy Ghost speaketh to the adversaries in innumberable sorts of

books, yet they will not be converted or turn to the Gospel." This text is cited in Anthony Kemp, *The Estrangement of the Past: A Study in the Origins of Modern Historical Consciousness* (New York: Oxford University Press, 1991), p. 103.

18. Kemp, *Estrangement of the Past;* Richard Kenneth Emmerson, *Antichrist in the Middle Ages: A Study of Medieval Apocalyptism, Art and Literature* (Seattle: University of Washington Press, 1981), p. 236.

19. See François Robin, "Jérusalem dans la peinture franco-flamande (XII–XVème) siècles): Abstractions, fantasies et réalités," in *Jerusalem, Rome, Constantinople: L'Image et le myth de la ville au Moyen-Age,* ed. Daniel Poiron, Cultures et Civilisations Medievales 5 (Paris: Presses de l'Université de Paris-Sorbonne, 1986).

20. Hans Belting, *Likeness and Presence: A History of the Image before the Era of Art,* trans. Edmund Jephcott (Chicago: University of Chicago Press, 1994); see especially pp. 470–78. I am joining this critique of Belting to the work of Julia Lupton in her *Afterlives of the Saints: Hagiography, Typology, and Renaissance Literature* (Stanford: Stanford University Press, 1996).

21. See Christopher S. Wood, *Albrecht Altdorfer and the Origins of Landscape* (London: Reaktion, 1993) for meditations on these traces of voided theological subject matter in the landscapes of Albrecht Altdorfer.

22. A translation of the Latin text that appeared on the advertising flyer for the *Nuremberg Chronicle* is given in Wilson, *The Nuremberg Chronicle,* p. 209.

23. De Certeau, *Practice of Everyday Life,* p. xix.

24. These thoughts try to link some aspects of iconoclasm in these city views with later "confessional" versions of these. In a brilliant study entitled *The Interpretation of Material Shapes in Puritanism: A Study of Rhetoric, Prejudice, and Violence* (New York: Cambridge University Press, 1986), Ann Kibbey has shown how the relations of sound with meaning were reconfigured by reforms of late fifteenth and early sixteenth centuries and how this acoustical rhetoric intersects with the iconoclastic notion of the "living image." In her words "Because iconoclasm concerned the significance of human beings as material shapes, because it sanctioned material harm, and because it thrived on the confusion between people and objects, the iconoclastic dimension of Puritanism strongly influenced the development of prejudice" (p. 44). The recent, brilliant study of Thomas H. Luxon also bears directly on the iconophobic problem I am trying to delineate here for city views; see his *Literal Figures: Puritan Allegory and the Reformation Crisis in Representation* (Chicago: University of Chicago Press, 1995).

25. Albrecht Dürer worked in the workshop of Michael Wolgemut during the time Wolgemut was involved with designing the woodcuts for the *Nuremberg Chronicle;* see Zahn, pp. 193–206. For a brilliant study of this self-portrait, see Joseph Koerner, *The Moment of Self-Portraiture in German Renaissance Art* (Chicago: University of Chicago Press, 1993); for another example of such self-allegorization, see Lisa Jardine's brilliant study of Erasmus's calculated efforts to stage himself as the "figure of trans-European learning" (*Erasmus, Man of Letters: The Construction of Charisma in Print* [Princeton: Princeton University Press, 1993], p. 147).

26. Jean-Joseph Goux, *Symbolic Economies: After Marx and Freud* (Ithaca: Cornell University Press, 1990), p. 4.

27. Richard Stauber, *Die Schedelsche Bibliothek* (1906, reprint, Nieuwkoop: B. De Graaf, 1969).

28. On the spines of his notebooks Schedel would inscribe the motto "Collect the fragments lest they perish" (Colligite fragmenta ne pereat), von Loga, "Die Städtansichten, p. 102.

29. Ingrid D. Rowland, "Revenge of the Regensburg Humanists," *Sixteenth Century Journal* 25 (1994): 307–22.

30. For an overview of the "translation" of Italian humanism in German cities, see Lewis W. Spitz, "The Course of German Humanism," in *Itinerarium Italicum: The Profile of the Italian Renaissance in the Mirror of Its European Transformations*, ed. Heiko Oberman with Thomas A. Brady Jr., Studies in Medieval and Reformation Thought 14 (Leiden: Brill, 1975). Conrad Celtis' panegyric to Nuremberg, *Norimbergae* (1495), can be read in a facsimile edition edited by Albert Werminghoff, *Conrad Celtis und sein Buch über Nürnberg* (Freiburg im Breisgau: J. Boltze, 1921).

31. I am working out this argument in much greater detail in my forthcoming *Cut of Ethnography* (Philadelphia: University of Pennsylvania Press). The collaboration of humanistic and scholastic circles in the detemporalizing of Jews is addressed in my essay, "The ABC of Ptolemy: Mapping the World with the Alphabet," which appeared in *Text and Territory: Geographical Imagination in the European Middle Ages*, ed. Sylvia Tomasch and Sealy Gilles (Philadelphia: University of Pennsylvania Press, 1998). Luxon writes brilliantly about ancient Israel as the knot between allegory and typology in Puritan "reading" practices. For intensifying practices of anti-Semitism in Germany and environs in the fifteenth century see Heiko A. Oberman, "Discovery of Hebrew and Discrimination against the Jews: The Veritas Hebraica as Double-Edged Sword in Renaissance and Reformation," in *Germania Illustrata*, ed. Andrew C. Fix and Susan C. Karant-Nunn, Sixteenth Century Essays and Studies 18 (Kirksville, Mo: Sixteenth Century Journal Publishers, 1992); Alexander Patschovsky, "Der 'Talmudjude': Vom mittelalterlichen ursprung eines neuzeitlichen Themas," *Zeitschrift für Historische Forschung*, Beihefte 13 (1992): 13–28; Charles Zika, "Hosts, Processions, and Pilgrimages: Controlling the Sacred in Fifteenth-Century Germany," *Past and Present* 118 (February 1988): 25–64; R. Po-chia Hsia, *The Myth of Ritual Murder: Jews and Magic in Reformation Germany* (New Haven: Yale University Press, 1988); and R. Po-chia Hsia, "The Usurious Jew: Economic Structure and Religious Representations in an Anti-Semitic Discourse," in *In and Out of the Ghetto: Jewish-Gentile Relations in Late Medieval and Early Modern Germany*, ed. R. Po-Chia Hsia and Hartmut Lehmann (Cambridge: Cambridge University Press, 1995). For specific Christian initiatives against Jews in their last decade in Nuremberg (expulsion: November 7, 1498), see *Germania Judaica*, Band III/2 (1350–1519), ed. Arye Maimon and Yacov Guggenheim (Tübingen: J. C. B. Mohr, 1995); Michael Toch, "'Umb Gemeyns Nutz und Nottdurfft Willen': Obrigkeitliches und jurisdiktionelles Denken bei der Austreibung der Nürnberger Juden 1498/99," *Zeitschrift für Historische Forschung* 11 (1984): 1–21; and Arndt Müller, *Geschichte der Juden in Nürnberg 1146–1945* (Nuremberg: Stadtbibliothek Nürnberg, 1968).

32. Werminghoff, ed., *Conrad Celtis und sein Buch über Nürnberg*, p. 199.

33. See the article by Toch and *Germania Judaica* for the strategies of the town council to expel Jews from the 1470s. For background on Hans Folz, see the following essays:

David Price, "Hans Folz's Anti-Jewish Carnival Plays," *Fifteenth Century Studies* 19 (1992): 209–28; Aaron E. Wright, "'Die gotlich sterk gab daz der teuschen zungen': Folz, Schedel, and the Printing Press in Fifteenth-Century Nuremberg," *Fifteenth Century Studies* 19 (1992): 319–49; Edith Wenzel, "Zur Judenproblematik bei Hanz Folz," *Zeitschrift für Deutsche Philologie* 101 (1982): 79–194; Edith Wenzel, "Synagoga und Ecclesia: Zum antijudaismus im deutschsprachigen Spiel des Mittelalters," *Internationale Archive für Sozialgeschichte der deutschen Literatur* 12 (1987): 57–81; Hans Walther, "Hans Folz: Altes und Neues zur Geschichte seines Lebens und seiner Schriften," *Zeitschrift für Deutsches Altertum und Deutsche Literatur* 29 (1966): 212–42.

34. See Wilson, *The Making of the Nuremberg Chronicle*, p. 176; Béatrice Hernad, *Die Graphiksammlung des Humanisten Hartmann Schedel* (Munich: Prestel, 1990), p. 66; for a reflection on the Altdorfer etchings, see Kathleen Biddick, "Paper Jews: Inscription/Ethnicity/Ethnography," *Art Bulletin* 78 (1996): 594–98.

35. Kibbey extends this discussion to the New World and traces how Protestant notions of icons worked to produce the decision to annihilate the Pequots in New England in 1637.

36. Svetlana Alpers, "The Mapping Impulse in Dutch Art," in *Art and Cartography: Six Historical Essays*, ed. David Woodward (Chicago: University of Chicago Press, 1987); Thomas Frangenberg, "Chorographies of Florence: The Use of City Views and City Plans in the Sixteen Century," *Imago Mundi* 46 (1994): 41–64; Jürgen Schulz, "Jacop de'Barbari's View of Venice: Map Making, City Views, and Moralized Geography before the Year 1500," *Art Bulletin* 60 (1978): 425–74.

37. The descriptions and views could also be marketed separately without the edifying frontispiece and didactic address to the reader written by one of the editors, Georg Braun. See R. A. Skelton's introduction to the facsimile, *Braun and Hogenberg: Civitates Orbis Terrarum* (New York: World Publishing Company, 1966).

38. See Walter Benjamin, "Theses on a Philosophy of History," in *Illuminations*, ed. Hannah Arendt (New York: Schocken, 1968), p. 255. For further explication of this move toward ethnography see, Biddick, "ABC of Ptolemy."

39. Paula Findlen underscores how such collections in the early modern museum did the work of bringing together "pieces of a cosmology that had all but fallen apart in the course of several centuries." She writes further, "organizing all known ideas and artifacts under the rubric of museum, collectors imagined that they had indeed come to terms with the crisis of knowledge that the fabrication of the museum was designed to solve" (Paula Findlen, *Possessing Nature: Museums, Collecting, and Scientific Culture in Early Modern Italy* [Berkeley: University of California Press, 1994], p. 50; also Krzysztof Pomian, *Collectors and Curiosities: Paris and Venice, 1500–1800*, trans. Elizabeth Wiles-Portier [Cambridge, U.K.: Polity, 1990]). Pomian views the early-modern collection as a "replacement" (p. 38) of medieval treasure-houses and relic collections. See also Anthony Lane Shelton, "Cabinets of Transgression: Renaissance Collections and the Incorporation of the New World," in *The Cultures of Collecting*, ed. John Elsner and Roger Cardinal (Cambridge: Harvard University Press, 1994).

40. Lupton, *Afterlives of the Saints*, p. xxi.

41. Lupton, *Afterlives of the Saints*, p. xxviii.

10

POETIC MAPPING

ON VILLON'S "CONTREDICTZ DE FRANC GONTIER"

TOM CONLEY

In a chapter entitled "Textual Space," located near the conclusion of *La Mesure du monde*, the late Paul Zumthor paints a comprehensive picture of medieval extension. He remarks that literary space in the Middle Ages can be studied from three concurrent points of view. The first looks at both the page and its written inscriptions and the shape of the book or manuscript in which they are located. The second considers the spaces described in and through the writing. These are the "literary representations of physical space," in other words, the imaginary areas a reader obtains through the referential material. Included here are the description and mention of place-names or itineraries in a given document. They can be what authors imply to be the content or areas "signified" in the texts or pictures of their signature.[1]

The third category that Zumthor places under the title of "poetic space" seems to defy the area he is plotting to define. Because it escapes Zumthor's categorical ambitions, it becomes, as in so many studies of space of recent vintage, something that remains indiscernible.[2] It cannot be contained in language, nor is it a term that falls easily between the demarcations of form and content or the subject and his or her world. Zumthor's reflections beg more questions than they answer. What is poetic space? How is it prehended? Can it be tracked in the relation of the so-called "author" and his or her "text" in dialogue with a "reader"?

The very terms that require the author to set "poetic space" between inverted commas become no less problematic than the space Zumthor would like his designation either to signify or, more likely—given the delicate relation of language and extensions that he is exploring—to occupy. Much of the chapter is written to venture toward a formulation that requires the author to appeal to poetry in order to aim at the object of his reflection. When required to put in words what stands at the crux of his book, the author seeks a poetic idiom to define medieval space. The latter is no longer that of the historian or the semiotician. Another voice intervenes. In response to the question he tenders to himself about how to define poetic space, Zumthor asserts that it is characterized by

> Regard et désir, élan vers un autre révélé par l'opération même du langage, mais irrémédiablement *là-bas;* la poésie, volonté de migration, exil, nomadisme sans fin; le poète, chevalier errant de la forêt sans repères. N'est-ce pas là (sous le couvert de l'anecdote, prétexte au déchaînement verbal) la conception inexprimée qui anime l'art des troubadours et de leurs disciples, dans toutes les régions de l'Occident? Poésie et musique ensemble, chant pur, le *trobar* (c'est ainsi qu'il se nomme) confie à la voix humaine le soin d'ouvrir, au sein de l'espace empirique où elle résonne, l'entrée du jardin clos: l'*aizi* (en occitan), qui est le lieu de l'amour, l'*ais* (en ancien français), mots où survit le latin *adjacens,* l'endroit d'à-côté, terme d'une appropriation nécessairement différée. (pp. 377–78)

> [A gaze and desire, a thrust toward another revealed by the very operation of language, but inevitably *over there;* poetry, the desire to migrate, exile, endless nomadism; the poet, the errant knight of the boundless forest. Now isn't that (under the mantle of anecdote, a pretext for verbal release) the unexpressed conception that animates the art of the troubadours and their disciples in all areas of the West? Poetry and music together, the pure song, the *trobar* (so it is named) confides the human voice with the desire to open, at the very origin of the empirical space in which it resounds, the entry into the closed garden: the *aizi* (in Occitan), that is the site of love, the *ais* (in Old French), words in which the Latin *adjacens* survives, the sidelong spot, the end of a forcibly deferred appropriation.]

The object of his reflection, a working and forever provisional definition of poetic space, hinges on the image of the "errant knight of the boundless forest." It sums up the rich pages dedicated to adventure in an earlier chapter (pp. 206–12), in which Zumthor imagines the medieval poet writing of imaginary travels of heroes and heroines into areas whose imagination has not yet been deforested; where space moves toward, within, and about the wanderer at the same time he or she wanders into it; where the unknown is confused at once on the horizons of the knight's quest, in the aura of a language that turns about and around its object, without ever attaining it, and which resides in the very bends and turns of the calligraphic or typographical letters conveying narratives of movement.

For Zumthor poetic space is forever animated and in perpetual dialogue with the poet. Far from that of the age of the Renaissance, medieval space does not exist outside of the subject or remain in a passive condition that invites conquest or control. It is not "other" to the degree that some crushing or menacing alterity incites the traveler, whether out of fear or desire, to place it under colonial rule.[3] It is eco-logical, its raison d'être assures who or whatever lives in it to respect and honor its own life. Space can even be an intimate friend, a world companion whose limitless wealth is discerned in or illuminated about every slightest object. In his or her desire to travel "over there," "far away," in "high places" (p. 378), the poet avows that written and spoken languages convey the shapes of world maps on which voyages lead the writer and reader to the limits of a space that paradoxically travels with them.

That the extension of the courtly novel seems so mysterious and boundless betrays the fact that the notion of adventure compensates for a world shrinking under the effect of accelerated spatial and temporal compression.[4] Throughout *La Mesure du monde*, Zumthor adduces the point by marking the effects of deforestation that had razed much of the European continent by the end of the twelfth century. The space of the courtly novel and literature that follow the great waves of deforestation had been attesting to "a discomfort falsifying our thoughts and action, connoting the bad conscience we betray in the pursuit of our aggression against the Earth" (p. 410). Let us not, he adds, treat medieval space in the sense of a nostalgic return to professional enclosures in which we confine ourselves in order not to divulge the deeper complicities we share with a politics of geocide. Rather, what we discover in poetic space of medieval lyric can serve as a measure for action in our time.

In the very extension of the title, *La Mesure du monde,* Zumthor tells us that the medieval poet was inhabited by a soul assured of—but not always threatened by—the environing world. He or she who knows *la mesure du monde* also has *l'âme sûre du monde.* The poetic space and its broader economy that Zumthor seeks to describe are echoed in the title. In a similar fashion, in medieval poetry we hear not only expressions of wonder and marvel about the soul of the "forest" in the courtly novel, but also echoes of the plaintive cries of Nature violated and sullied that resound in texts both of the twelfth century Renaissance and, three centuries later, of the flamboyant age, in Franco-Burgundian poetry. In Jean de Meung's *Roman de la rose* and Villon's *Grant Testament,* it is common knowledge that the force of nature is reclaimed to show how an immanence can be shared by subjects in and with their environment. Both Jean de Meung and Villon craft a poetic space in which a healthy and dynamic order of the world is sought. In their works it exists independently of a perceiving body and can thus be understood as something both organic and inorganic, something procreative and perpetually active and always copresent with consciousness.[5]

In what follows I would like to examine how a similar coextension of poetic space and nature are virtually mapped through the ballads of *Le Grant Testament.* Much of the space created in the poem of Villon's signature is further animated by the transitional or intermediate—indeed, a physically dialogical—condition of the text. What Zumthor calls "textual space" is discerned in the movement of meaning that flows between the shape of a manuscript and a printed book.[6] The spaces of the *Testament* become multifarious in that they are at once textual, referential, and creative of worlds of a measure common to two different media. The textual spaces make manifest a literary representation of a sense of *res extensa* of the time of the writing and editing of the poem (1450–1490), but they are also nascent maps in both the fixed form of the ballads and in their relation to the topographical and cosmographical dimensions of the broader lines of the *Testament.* It might be said that *Le Grant Testament* coordinates its representation of a cosmographical space of the world and time with that of Paris and local sites that fall within the greater purview. The local spaces do not quite fit in any schematic design that a philosophy of space or a cartographical convention would supply. Reflecting a greater sum, each poem nonetheless calls into question the idea of a totality. An infinite space is opened, but it is riddled with social conflict. Only fragments or flashes of greater forms strike the eye and ear. Local spaces are folded into a broader world picture, but there prevails a sense of subjective isolation and exclusion that emerges from a doubt about the seamless nature of the parts of the world said to reflect the greater creations of God.

A national space, which seeks to be a French dominion, is created in the first half of the *Testament*. In the later poems emphasis is placed on topographical description that seems to separate from the cosmography and scatter into singular entities, poetic islands set adrift in the work, that are bereft of specific coordinates that would fix them in a rational order. The celebrated Ballad of the Ladies of Yesteryear (which, in his 1533 edition of *Le Testament*, Clément Marot entitled "La Ballade des femmes du temps jadis") invokes a future of France in a procreative space that will succeed the miseries of the Hundred Years' War. It synthesizes in the poetic reach of its meanders a memory that reaches back to ancient Rome and to timeless nature ("Flora, la belle rommaine . . .") and a drive to bring nature back to French soil and, thus, to define a national character that supersedes chronological history. Other ballads in the first half of the poem ring with similar echoes. In the ballads that fill out the second half of the *Testament*, a topography seems to replace the cosmographic vision in which the future of France is sought. Here poetic space tends to be marked by cartographical value ascribed to areas where the lyrical intensity is conveyed by a voice underscoring the paradox of being at once in and excluded from the spaces it describes.

The text focalizing the paradox is the ballad that Marot crowned with the title "Les Contredictz de Franc Gontier" [Franc Gontier's Counterdeeds]. The ballad offers a summary cartography of social contradiction and, in its overall effect, leads to an exclusion of the human animal from the world in which it lives. The poem plots a nonspace that displaces the ostensive voice (that would be speaking the poem or emanating from or through its graphic characters) onto a margin where all symbolic or redemptive occupation is eradicated. The deliberative and satirical registers chart a subject's exclusion from the *habitus* being described. On a limited register the poem argues for a wisdom of modesty through a refrain that reiterates how we best ought to avoid stress in our lives. On another, it uses the topos of the antagonism of the country and the city to map out the copresence of two irreconcilable worlds. Between the two is drawn a line of demarcation and rupture that sums up several centuries of spatial phantasies about the city as a site of salvation or damnation in which, here, Paris would be either a modern Jerusalem or a Babylon.[7]

In contravening the rustic ways of Franc Gontier, the poem heralds the beauty of an urban non-place.[8] Paris stands at the origin of the poetic space by virtue of the way, similar to other ballads, the text of the "Contredictz" falls and nestles into the folds of the surrounding world of toponyms and highly localized anthroponyms. It displaces and is displaced by its environs. It is mapped as a piece of writing, its crimped and scrambled surface suggesting a cartography that projects a *locus amoenus* of oral, olfactive, erotic, and visual delight. Yet its vocables constitute unforeseen possibilities for furnishing other territories or other spaces that inhere in the art of the poem's failure to distinguish an urban dystopia from a rural utopia.

The ballad can be read as a map, a city-view, or even an urban landscape:

> Sur mol duvet assis ung gras chanoine
> Lez ung brasier en chambre bien natee
> A son coste gisant dame Sidoine
> Blanche tendre polye et attintee
> Boire ypocras a jour et a nuytee
> Rire jouer mignonner et baisier
> Et nud a nud pour mieulx des corps s'aisier
> Les vy tous deux par ung trou de mortaise
> Lors je congneuz que pour dueil appaisier
> Il n'est tresor que de vivre a son aise
>
> Se Franc Gontier et sa compaigne Elayne
> Eussent ceste doulce vie hantee
> Doignons cyvotz que causent forte alaine
> Nacontassent une bise tostee
> Tout leur maton ne toute leur potee
> Ne prise un ail je le dy sans noisier
> Silz se vantent coucher soubz le rosier
> Lequel vault mieulx? Lit costoyé de cheze?
> Qu'en dictes vous? Faut il ad ce muser?
> Il n'est tresor que de vivre a son aise
>
> De groz pain bis vivent d'orge et d'avoyne
> Et boyvent eaue tout au long de l'annee
> Tous les oyseaux de cy en Babiloyne
> A tel escot une seulle journee

Ne me tendroient non une matinee
Or s'esbate de par Dieu Franc Gontier
Helayne o luy soubz le bel esglantier
Se bien leur est cause n'ay qu'il me poise
Mais quoy que soit du laboureux mestier
Il n'est tresor que de vivre a son aise

Prince jugiez pour tost nous accorder
Quant est de moy mais qu'a nulz ne desplaise
Petit enffant j'aoy oÿ recorder
Il n'est tresor que de vivre a son aise[9]

[On soft down is seated a fat canon / By a sizzling fire in a neatly natted room / By his side lay supine Lady Sidoine / White, tender, tanned, in elegance groomed, / With mirthy wine, day and night consumed, / They laugh, play, tickle, and cackle, / Flesh on flesh so better their bodies shackle / I saw the two through a hole in mortared wall / When I knew that to abate sadness to befall / The only treasure, life in ease, carries for all.

If Franc Gontier and his friend Elaine / Lived a sweetened life of this grain / With breath smelling of chive and onion / They wouldn't be worth a piece of toast / Nor soup, curdled cheese, nor a roast, / Even a sliver of garlic, I say not to boast: / If they want to sleep by a bed of roses, / What's better, what's worth the most? / The only treasure, life in ease, carries for all.

With fat loaves baked with barley and oats / They eat and drink water till kingdom come / All birds from here and heaven to Babylon / For their diet of a day wouldn't be my own / Or wouldn't tempt me for even a morn / So, by God, let Franc Gontier shun renown, / Laying with Helen under her rosebush / Their life doesn't make me blush, / But whatever the work of the plow, all in all, / The only treasure, life in ease, carries for all.

Prince, decide now, and once and for all! / As for me, now, if you might allow, / A child, yes, I once heard recall, / The only treasure, life in ease, carries for all.]

For David Kuhn the poem is a presentation of a scene lived through the point of view of an observer who speaks in the voice of the first person.

The text becomes the object for deliberation by comparison with a similar scene in Philippe de Vitry's poem about Franc Gontier.[10] Initially the fat canon's sensuous life leads us to conclude that "the city has invented refinements of pleasure unknown to the rustic" (p. 362) and because we cannot procure anything of what is spied upon we must be happy to live the modest lives we lead. Hence, "Il n'est tresor que de vivre à son aise." If urban pleasures win over country ways, it is because the poet has known both modes of existence. Villon treats his subject obliquely, showing Vitry that Franc Gontier's vision "has nothing to do with current realities of peasant life" (p. 366) in that he "seems to live in a country without seasons, lacking winter" (p. 368), even if both Villon and his source, Le Roman de la rose, draw from Ovid's Metamorphoses (ll. 8355–60; 9493–96; 9521–35). Vitry sins by omission of realism and by the narrowness of his philosophical views. Kuhn notes that Villon's assertions leave for the reader a "negative knowledge" that comprises the "ironic lesson" (p. 369) of the ballad and a sense of the poem that replaces Vitry's pedagogy of honest provincial ways with an eristic vision that knows no easy conclusion. The poem reaches an undecidable state in the choice that cannot be made between two impossible conditions. In its imitation of a legal document the Contredictz means a "contradictory response designating at once the act of responding and the object being responded to" (p. 395) such that the poem, like the meaning of contredit, can be an "obstacle, resistance, and objection" in both concrete and figural dimensions.

The poem generates a poetic space as do few of the other ballads in the Grant Testament, perhaps with the exception of two of its counterparts in the first half of the work, "La Ballade des femmes du temps jadis" (ll. 329–56) and "La Priere pour nostre dame" (ll. 873–909). The Contredictz leads us back to an uncanny representation of a primal scene in the aftermath of the debate over the comparative virtue of urban and rustic ways. A city view in the first stanza blends into that of an intermediate area in the second (that can be either city or country), while the third, more directly idyllic and bucolic, shifts to a nature bereft of seasonal change. The first seven lines depict an interior of warmth in winter insulated, it is revealed, by a wall through which the narrating voice reports seeing what has just been described. The image of a fireside scene of fulsome pleasure that continues night and day leads the narrator to correct a perception of envy and that of his own exclusion—were he only in the place of the *gras chanoine* with *dame Sidoine*—by coming to the realization that an easy life is the best remedy to melancholy or anguish of exclusion if, indeed, *deuil* connotes the trauma beneath the subject's vital discovery of his or her gratuitousness in the social order.

In the second stanza, when the country gentleman of the famous poem of Philippe de Vitry, "Les Ditz de Franc Gontier," is imagined in the place the canon occupies "sur mol duvet," it is presumed that he would never have been drawn to identify with what the poet has evoked above. But when, in the third stanza, a life of leisure is imagined in the paradise of a golden age of pastoral life, under the wild rose bush *(le bel esglantier)*, it too is called into question.

In the envoy addressed to the nobleman, the primal scene that was initially conveyed in a visual sketch returns in the sound of the inner speech of memory. Hence, "petit enfant j'ay oÿ recorder" (it is only a treasure to live in ease); the loose syntax suggests that in his childhood or as an infant he heard the truism that the child related. The child, who might indeed have been the poet himself within his own memory, returns to elucidate the debate. The urban image returns from within the narrator's past where previously it had been focalized when the poet-as-voyeur saw the fat canon on the soft down through the hole in the wall.

In its most simple and reduced formulation, in the space between the first stanza and the envoy, the ballad tells us that the most precious lesson in any deliberation over social contradiction is an experience of social conflict that leads to physical and intellectual rejection of any kind of ease. The life of the upper crust in Paris of winter is as impossible to imagine as the stasis of classical figures in the warm nirvana of classical eclogues. The poet moves away from what he first describes with envy. Only the impressions gained through the creation of a dialogue in language, what indeed plots out the space of conflict, gives rise to the vital experience of exclusion.

The poem thus varies on the intensity of the refrain, "Il n'est tresor que de vivre à son aise," from its initial affirmation (l. 1482) to its summoning at the end of the second stanza (l. 1492). There, as an implied question appended to the four points of deliberation immediately above ("[Est-ce qu'] Il n'est tresor que de vivre à son aise? . . ."), the assertion is suddenly bathed in doubt, anticipating the intensification of the irony of anyone living at ease when and wherever the heavy duties of country life or continuous transgression of adultery beg for fallow time (l. 1502)—

what today might be called "discretionary spending" of erotic energies—until, in the last line, the childish figure has gumption enough to hear the pun, It is a *tresor* ("très ord" or "very filthy") to live in leisure. The inversion leads the reader's eye to speculate on the cutting edge of a murderous axe (*ais* in *aise*) that would be at once the farmer's tool, a stiff phallus, or the fulcrum of an intellectual problem that cannot account for the contradiction.

The poem maps out spaces of difference at once within itself and within the context of the greater form of the *Grant Testament*. It pushes the narrator to a liminal space that affords, if nothing else, an equivalence between the performance of the poem and the creation of a symbolic area that the poet can occupy for the duration of its reading. In the same way the ballad is marked by latent wind roses that plot an itinerary defined by recurring points of contradiction. The optical center of the poem is occupied by the strange tourniquet that shifts from I *(je)* to an English homonym, a slice of *ail* (garlic), that reiterates the othering of the self. Seen and heard at this focal point is a proto-Rimbaldian "je est un autre" conveyed as "*I* as a sliver of garlic." The implied equivalence is the first spatial description of a *locus amoenus,* the *rosier* recalling from the ballad the source and counterpart in Philippe de Vitry, a place "under green leaves, on a bed of grass," where "birds chirped" and the couple held themselves in amorous congress.

The *rosier* economizes and intensifies the description by threading through its form three principal figures of the debate. At an equivalent point in the first stanza the bodies of the canon and Lady Sidoine are "nud a nud pour mieulx des corps s'aisier" (1419), set in place better to seize and be in ease with each other. The "rosy" picture contrasts the bucolic scene in which Gontier and Elayne take pride in lounging beneath the trellis. At the very same point in the third stanza we are led to wonder if the same couple feels bliss "soubz le bel esglantier" (under the wild rose bush) that was commonly known to bear thorns and, for that reason, to carry a popular doublet in the name of a *gratte-cul.*[11]

Three sites of pleasure, all set at identical intervals in the poem, establish a seasonal contrast with climate and geography. In each a rosy aura of eternal warmth is contravened. In the same line a contrast is established with the outdoors of the place where "ilz se vantent coucher soubz le rosier" and the inner space of a kitchen, in the aroma of onions and chives, where bread is toasted, meat is baked and roasted, and milk and soup are simmered. Within the description are the winds of change. *Une bise tostee* could refer to bread and meat on the stove.[12] Also present is the oxymoron of a warm north wind, an unsettling breeze *(aura brisa)* of nature that magnifies the "strong breath" *(forte alaine)* of the preceding line. The eros of a life of buttered toast and kisses visibly folded into the signifiers is threatened by climatic convection. In "S'ilz se *vantent* couchier soubz le rosier," the equivocation on wind and suckling duplicates what is seen in the reiteration of the figure of bread in the final stanza,

> De groz pain bis vivent d'orge et d'avoyne
> Et boyvent eaue tout au long de l'annee. (ll. 1493–94)

The winds of change seem to bring forward the migratory patterns of birds that seek temperate climates by going to and from Africa and France.[13]

Four kinds of wind blow through the text. One, in the first stanza, is the performative breath that describes the scene in the whisper that leads to the initial utterance, a silent rumination, of the refrain. The second is the warm wind of an illusion, of "ceste doulce vie hantee" of exhaled breath of onions and garlic, in which atmosphere is synonymous of life itself, *vie hantee* being the mannequin-formula of a body *v . . . antee,* of a thing molecularized. The illusion is also echoed in the pride Gontier and Elayne take ("ilz se vantent . . .") in living by a bed of roses. Herein "Elayne" rhymes with "alaine," the breath containing the sign of garlic exhaled from the mouths of the dubious models of country wisdom. The third is the wind of nature or of climate, of the reality of temporal life that is charted according to geographical patterns. Implied are the Mediterranean winds on which fly birds to and from Babylonia. The fourth, that haunts the cloacal regions of the text, is the pestilent wind originating in the southern climes or the lower end, both of the ballad and the *Testament* as a whole. "Helayne," the woman of breath, is counterpoised to the *esglantier.* It is announced by a south wind, known on wind maps, that comes form the entrails of the world and seems to be underscored in the allusion to Babylonia to the southeast and to the *gratte-cul* of the wild rose.

The sense of a space that changes with the four seasons attests to the experience of growing contradiction in the movement of the poem from each of its stanzaic "seasons" to the other (winter → spring → non-time). What was felt to be an inner and private world of exclusive pleasure barred to the poet and reader, situated in Paris in winter, is set adjacent to the equally impossible time of the "laboureux mestier" of the farmer, or the illicit fornicator, who can never find a time to live in ease, be it physical or moral. "Prince, jugiez pour tost nous accorder!" (l. 1503): the equivocation allows *tost* to refer to the quick resolution of a problem, such as the coming of spring on the heels of winter or the slicing of an argument, like that of a loaf of bread, that will afford the poet enough crumbs—figured indirectly in the homonym of *toast* and *tost*—that would be awarded for his poem. Agreement would take the form of a creative tension in the musical *accord* of the various winds of the poem: of nature, of the collective *I* of the ballad, and of the climate in which change amounts to life itself. Now the recall of childhood in the last lines swells with impressions of plenitude—perhaps a life of teething on biscuits and suckling at a breast—that exists only in the most simple ring of the refrain, in which the breath and voice of mother nature are felt immediately in the regression to an originary moment of separation, a vitally traumatic moment that shatters the poet into consciousness of the world and its social contradictions.

In every event the geography of wind and the odor of toasted bread and hot victuals in the "Contreditz de Franc Gontier" establishes vital ties with other cartographical poems in the *Grant Testament,* most notably "La Ballade de la Grosse Margot" (ll. 1591–1627). Kuhn inaugurated his reading of that ballad by remarking that hardly by chance does the "Contredictz" recall "Fat Margot" (p. 361) in the turns of phrase that ask us to evaluate one mode of life in contrast to another. In both poems an allusion to bread recalls the summer of torture the poet endured in deprivation, in which he was sodomized by Thibault d'Aussigny and forced to live on water and crumbs ("Peu m'a d'une petite miche/Et de froide eaue tout ung esté [Fed me with crumbs/And cold water for a whole summer] [ll. 13–14]). But, Kuhn adds, the ballad seems to fit in a greater list that makes up the infernal regions of the inner and subterranean geography of the poem. "The kinship of the ballads of Franc Gontier and Grosse Margot is patent. . . . They are opposed to and complete each other, both in their meaning and in their stylistic resemblance, just as they are split by their intention" (p. 375). They fit in a quadrant that includes "one of Villon's magnificent lists," the ballad of "envious languages" (ll. 1422–56), that gives way to Gontier, which in turn announces the ballad of the "good beaks" of Paris (1515–38) before that of Fat Margot (ll. 1591–1627). "This arrangement is not absolute insofar as all three ballads are interlinked to crisscross and confound a symmetry of this order" (p. 375).

Close reading allows us to surmise that any arrangement can be made because a cartographical latency uses the loose listings of octostiches and ballads to order the text according to a pattern of parataxis. A spatial rhythm inhabits the poem and constitutes its geographical aspect. Yet, at the same time, the local, urban, and specifically Parisian geography of this region of the *Testament* (ll. 1422–1627) sets in relief a topography that constructs the more properly cosmographic spaces plotted in the "Ballad of the Women of Yesteryear" (ll. 357–84) and the "Prayer for Our Lady" (ll. 873–909) that dominate the first half of the work. As is so typical in Villon, what becomes increasingly specific in descriptive detail also carries a cosmic inference of total space, volume, and biological time. By contrast, the sweeping views of history and nature in our memory of the earlier ballads acquire a more local aspect that confers them with a paradoxical sign of chorographic immensity.

There is, however, no redemptive reflection of the one on the surface of the other. The connections are more implied, thus mobile and continuously folding and ever invaginating, shifting in shape in the context of the poems in which they are seen. Further, the comparison of "Gontier" to "Margot" (ll. 1591–1627) makes manifest the spatial dilation and closure. The latter resembles "Gontier" not only on deliberative grounds, as Kuhn notes so well, but it does so in its graphic treatment of winds and seasons, the very basis of early cartographical consciousness.

In its clockwork construction the ballad tells of the twenty-four-hour day of two sex workers, a well-endowed prostitute and her servant. The ballad reproduces the deliberative frame of the "Contredictz" by inaugurating a question to the effect that in the report that follows the reader will have to wonder if the activities of the poet merit inculpation. Must he be tried for making the avowal about life in the lower depths? Depiction of life in the brothel-theater ensues until, in the envoy, a second question asks the spectator who has followed the narration about which of the two parties is superior. It's a life of cat-and-mouse. No matter how vile their life may be, the lines conclude that when the wind blows, when rain turns to hail, and when the moral issues are treated "in the final analysis," it is better to be nurtured on cooked bread *(pain cuit)*. The wind that begins the refrain is convected from the lady who, before passing a grandiose fart *(pet)*, is more distended than a "velimeux escarbot" (poisonous or poisoned scarabee). The explosion brings peace *(paix)* to the establishment. In the irony of that auratic moment is contained an irenic eternity. "Tous deux yvres dormons comme un sabot" [Drunk together we sleep snugly as in a shoe]. When they arise the wind returns, "Quand le ventre luy bruyt," or when a monstrous rebirth of the world is about to take place. Her belly grumbles with signs of a miraculous birth of an unearthly being. Nonetheless, the poet emphasizes, it is better to be inside the space of the *bordeau* than outside.

The inversion of the spatial condition of the "Contredictz" shows that rather than looking in from without, the poet is confining himself to the laws and rules of the *bordeau,* where he lives in a place whose perimeters are felt in the multiple inflections of the four repetitions of the refrain that describe the tavern as a brothel, a port, a world (or *polis*), and a wooden panel on which is engraved the poem or an icon (or map) of the space of its action. In the narration of a world being engendered from the *ventre,* within the *bordeau* recurs the figure of the wooden sign that, like Margot's belly, flattens the poet-servant as might either a plank or a *mappa mundi* in the style of the didactic image that appeared in a first printed edition of Isidore de Seville's *Etymologiae.*[14] Or, it can be inferred from comparison with the *Contredictz* and its source that it is an axe *(ais),* a flat wedge of iron.

The articulation of the climatic disturbances and the cold that follows the seasonal changes of the poem (in which the first stanza, as spring, leads to summer in the second, etc.) yields a warmth of an inner space protected from the winter, wherein "Tous deux ivres" (l. 1615) (the two protagonists) sleep for the duration of the winter *(ivre),* snug as a bug in a rug, close to the optical center of the poem. The protective warmth of the interior gives way to a spatial arrangement of circular enclosures that move from the *omphalos* of the *ventre* to the world-*bordeau* that seems to have no borders. For that reason the comparison of Margot to a creature more swollen than a *velimeux* or *venimeux escarbot* requires study in terms of its spatial and cartographical latency.[15]

At issue is the creation of a world from a universal condition of corruption, in which the cloacal residue of the world is stored up in the space surrounding—but also within—the body of the bloated scarabee.

In their prudent reading Rychner and Henry, noting that "several texts attest for *escarbot*," the unquestioned sense of the "shit-beetle" (coleoptera that lives in dung), it can perhaps be admitted that the scarabee can be "swollen, stuffed with excrement," in that its gluttony is well known."[16] It would be pointless, as legions of critics have shown, to wonder if the simile of the insect to Margot's belly is licit simply because the spatial register of the text causes its grammar to exceed its borders. The scarabee is evoked as both the insect and its world, its inner matter and its food for rumination being of the same essence. In lines 1611–1613 are the contours of the phantasm of the world-as-dungheap or, no less, as a mountain of concentric circles of excrement dropped by a monstrous or divine creature above.

An orography or a relief map of the earth's lower depths is obtained from the image produced of the poem as world. In "Margot" a cartography of poetic space is given from the relation of a center and a periphery of a caricatural world-theater in which the poet lives. His world is all at once a local space (a *bordeau*), a city at the edge of the sea, and a map panel. There is no escape from its confines, even if it englobes cosmographic space at large. By contrast, the world of "Franc Gontier" is one of exclusion into which the poet has been confined. As in "Margot," it articulates the city and the country in accord with the seasons and their winds. We witness the creation of an uncanny poetic area, which might be called a subjective orography, in the inflections of the relation of the poet to the space from which he seeks isolation or into which he burrows.

Unlike poetry that imagines topographical spaces in its referential field or drafts pictures of nostalgic retreat, as does much of Philippe de Vitry's poem that is recalled through Villon, in *Le Grant Testament* the ballad itself becomes a mapped form of non-places. The ballads that give order to the form by way of punctuation are not merely machines that reiterate a refrain and end with an envoy but are especially, in the overall cosmography that is being drawn as a whole, evidence of a latent but surely affective cartography. To explore further the impulse that maps out subjectivity in Villon's poem, it would be necessary to navigate along the lines that tie the more properly geographical ballads of the beginning to the network, in which figure "Gontier" and "Margot," to other poems that plot the ground of a national and local space in a future envisioned to be less denatured than that of the present.

Nonetheless "Gontier" and the ballads with which it is associated are inflected by emotive intensity that originates in the expression of exclusion from or incarceration in a latent map. Such is the effect of a poetic space whose arena is a field of tension born of a paradoxical separation from the space created in the process of writing. Such, too, is Villon's "Petit enffant j'ay oÿ recorder: Il n'est tresor que de vivre a son aise." Zumthor had evoked the "aiz" or the closed space of the paradise garden to be the vanishing point at which adventure and lyrical drive are aimed. In "Franc Gontier" it is flattened and local, a space of exclusion, which invokes the drama of being severed into the vital process of living with the world and encountering it as a helter-skelter of zones and heterotopias. In this way the poem seems to crystallize much of what at the outset of this paper was fathomed about the relation of medieval space to adventure. Adventure, understood after the twelfth century as a new movement of enterprise in the garb of chivalric ideals,[17] was also an effect of compensation for, if not a denial of, the domestication of alterity. In this light adventure could be fancied as what would control and pacify areas of fear extending between the imagination and the physical apprehension of the world. The forest, a figure that harbors the unknown and the pleasures and fears of alterity, was the *arrière-pays* toward which the enterprising knights set forth. In Villon's poem the illusions of that other space are felled with an axe of irony. With it comes new paths and itineraries we can make by way of cultivating medieval space in the world in which we move.

NOTES

1. Paul Zumthor, *La Mesure du monde: Représentation de l'espace au Moyen Age* (Paris: Seuil, 1993), p. 363. Further references to this work will be made in parentheses.

2. Henri Lefebvre, *The Production of Space*, trans. David Nicholson-Smith (New York: Basil Blackwell, 1991), stands as a benchmark for a history and anthropology of space. The central chapter on "differential" space seems to work out Michel Foucault's vital treatment of heterotopias, published as "Des espaces autres" in his *Dits et écrits: 1954–1988*, ed. Daniel Defert and François Ewald, 4 vols. (Paris: Gallimard, 1993), vol. 4, pp. 752–62. It appears that Lefebvre's remarks on literature and space derive much from two of Foucault's seminal essays of 1964, "Le Langage de l'espace," and "La Folie, absence de l'oeuvre," in *Dits et écrits*, vol. 1, pp. 407–511; 412–20. In the former text, Foucault anticipates much of what Zumthor states about poetic space. Space, he argues, is not just a metaphor in literary language, but it is what is transported or translated in language. A reasoned critique of

Lefebvre and his tradition is offered in Michael Curry, *The Work in the World: Geographical Practice and the Written Word* (Minneapolis: University of Minnesota Press, 1996), pp. 175–209.

3. Zumthor himself shows how the space of the New World inspired fear and how, as a result, it had to be domesticated and controlled. "After 1500, most of Columbus's followers will be men as much of science as of adventure. The stakes of their expeditions no longer include a correct knowledge of the globe, but a confirmation of human mastery over Creation, of the domestication of extension" (p. 253). In *The Darker Side of the Renaissance* (Ann Arbor: University of Michigan Press, 1995), Walter Mignolo shows how the unknown had to be integrated into a language of everything that was known. Mignolo argues that Johannes Ruysch's map of the new world of 1508 betrays an "unconscious arrogance and deep belief that what for him was not known had to be, of necessity, new; that whatever was not known to him, naturally did not exist" (p. 264). In a study of Montaigne's "De Cannibales," in *Heterologies: Discourse on the Other*, translated by Brian Massumi (Minneapolis: University of Minnesota Press, 1986), Michel de Certeau has shown that Europeans' fear of the savages derives from their nomadism: they lack a place or space that can be tagged with a name and hence precipitate a collapse of boundaries (pp. 70–72) that the colonizer will have to remap according to policies of domination. See also Jean-François Lyotard, *The Inhuman: Reflections on Time* (Stanford: Stanford University Press, 1991), p. 119.

4. Here the author recoups some of the general hypotheses about spatio-temporal compression studied in David Harvey's *The Condition of Post-Modernity* (London: Basil Blackwell, 1989). The conclusions here are close to those of Yi-Fu Tuan in *Topophilia* (1974; reprint, New York: Columbia University Press, 1990), pp. 129–49, in which the flattening of the world's volume in planispheric representations marks the shift from "cosmos to landscape." A similar tension, it will be shown below, inheres in Villon's poetic space.

5. A. M. F. Gunn, *The Mirror of Love: A Reinterpretation of "The Romance of the Rose"* (Lubbock: Texas Tech University Press, 1951); Ernst Robert Curtius, *European Literature and the Latin Middle Ages*, trans. Williard R. Trask (reprint, Princeton: Princeton/Bollingen University, 1973), pp. 117–27; and especially David Kuhn, *La Poétique de François Villon* (Paris: Armand Colin, 1965), to which this study will make copious reference. The concept of "passification" in the name of things irenic or pacific belongs to Jacques Lacan and is alertly glossed in Teresa Brennan, *History after Lacan* (London: Routledge, 1993), pp. 12–15.

6. Pierre Guiraud argues for the permanently transitional state of the text in *Le Testament de Villon, ou Le Gai savoir de la Basoche* (Paris: Gallimard, 1970), pp. 113–15. Its mobility owes much to the concurrently scriptural and typographical character of the verse.

7. Jacques Le Goff, *L'Imaginaire médiéval* (Paris: Gallimard, 1974), pp. 130–36.

8. "Non-place" is chosen to invite comparison of the places cited in *Le Testament* to what Marc Augé calls *non-lieux* of our age. The latter are zones to which one gains access but that are uninhabitable. "Places" have identitarian value, and are relational and historical in quality, whereas the non-place resists anthropological analysis and, contrary to Baudelairean modernity, "does not integrate older places," in *Non-lieux: Introduction à une anthropologie de la modernité* (Paris: Seuil, 1992), p. 100.

9. The transcription is taken from Jean Rychner and Albert Henry, eds., critical edition of *Le Testment Villon*, 2 vols. (Geneva: Droz, 1974), 1: 117, ll. 1473–1506, and adapted

according to Kuhn's orthography in which modern punctuation, in order to approximate its status as a manuscript or in an incunabular book, is reduced to a minimum.

10. Studied in Kuhn, *La Poetique*, pp. 372–80. He reproduces de Vitry from A. Piaget, *Romania* 27 (1898): 63–64:

> Soubz feuille vert, sur herbe delitable
> Lez ru bruiant et prez clere fontaine,
> Trouvay fichee une borde portable.
> Ilec mengeoit Gontier o dame Helayne
> Fromage frais, laict, burre, fromaigee,
> Craime, matton, pomme, nois, prune, poire,
> Aulx et oignons, escaillongne froyee
> Sur crouste bise, au gros sel, pour mieulx boire.
>
> Au goumer beurent et oisillon harpoient
> Pour resbaudir et le dru et la drue,
> Qui par amours apres s'entrebaisoient
> Et bouche et nez, polie et bien barbue.
> Quand orent prins le doulx mès de nature,
> Tantost Gontier, haiche au col, ou boys entre;
> Et dame Helayne si met toute sa cure
> A ce buer qui queuvre dos et ventre.
>
> J'oy Gontier en abatant son arbre
> Dieu mercier de sa vie seüre:
> 'Ne sçay', dit-il, 'que sont pilliers de marbre,
> Pommeaux luisans, murs vestus de paincture:
> Je n'ay paour de traïson tissue
> Soubz beau semblant, ne qu'empoisonné soye
> En vaisseau d'or. Je n'ay la teste nue
> Devant thirant, ne genoil qui s'i ploye.
>
> 'Verge d'uissier jamais ne me deboute,
> Car jusques la ne m'esprend convoitise,
> Ambicion, ne lescherie gloute.
> Labour me paist en joieuse franchise;
> Moult j'ame Helayne et elle moy sans faille,
> Et c'est assez. De tombel n'avons cure.'
> Lors je dy: 'Las! serf de court ne vault maille,
> Mais Franc Gontier vault en or jame pure.

[Under green leaf, on a cushion of grass,/Noise sounding and near a clear fountain/I found erected a portable sign./There Gontier was eating with Lady Helen/Fresh cheese, milk, butter, yogurt,/Cream, pudding, apples, nuts, prunes, pears,/Garlic and onion, curdled milk on toast with sea salt in order better to drink./At the meal they drank and birds chirped/To inspire the lover and his beloved,/ Who in their frolics then kissed about/Their mouths and noses, polished and nicely bearded./When they were filled with the sweet goods of nature/Then Gontier, his axe hanging from his collar, enters the woods/And Lady Helen takes a cloth to wipe him clean/Of the sweat covering his back and belly./I hear Gontier, felling his tree,/Thanking God for a life so secure./"I can't say," he says, "what marble piers may be,/Shiny newels, walls clothed with paintings./I fear not treason woven/Under good looks nor being poisoned/By golden vessels. My head is never bared/Before a tyrant, nor is my knee bent in homage./The writer's plume doesn't bother me/Because I covet nothing/Of ambition or gluttonous lechery./Plowing the earth fills me with joyous freedom;/I love my Helen and she, without fail, me./And that's enough. Of a tomb we have no need."/And so I say, "Alas! Serfdom in the court is worthless,/But Franc Gontier is worth pure gold and gems."]

11. The profane figures are held in the text to remind the reader of the spatial dialectic that links national and corporeal space in the final lines of the quatrain Villon pronounced at the foot of the gallows.

> Or d'une corde d'une toise
>
> Mon col saura que mon cul poise,

is here figured in the visual contiguity of the *gratte-cul* to the recurring verb playing on the gravity of the debate. In line 910, following the refrain of the *Priere pour nostre dame*, the legator leaves to his love "une chiere rose," a silken (but also shitful) object.

12. Jean Dufournet translates *une bise tostee* as a "roast" in his edition of the *Poésies* (Paris: Garnier/Flammarion, 1984), p. 229.

13. Kuhn, *La Poetique*, p. 372, remarks that this ballad counts among those whose wealth owes to the changing meanings of the refrain. The shadings confer the poem with a "spacious truth" comparable to the ballad in "Old French" (ll. 388–412) that brings similar variety to the poetic texture. In this poem he shows that the images are so delicious that "everyone knows it is easier to be gone with the wind by being taken up by the picturesque" dimension (p. 374). He does not study the wind that blows in the paragrammar.

14. The figure of the world-as-panel is reviewed by Rychner and Henry, eds., *Le Testament Villon*, 2: 226. Rodney Shirley includes a figure of Isidore's *mappa mundi*, in *The Mapping of the World* (London: The Holland Press, 1983), p. 3.

15. Pierre Levet's edition of 1489 prints "venimeux" in place of "velimeux." Because orthography is mobile and because variation of season is one of the enduring elements of the textual reason, both connotations can be read together. The poem defies the unilateral reading imposed by Rychner and Henry that tends to betray editorial habits, inherited from the tradition of the critical edition, moving in the direction of a lexical cleansing of the text.

16. Rychner and Henry, eds., *Le Testament Villon*, vol. 2, p. 225.

17. See Michael Nerlich, *The Ideology of Adventure: Studies in Modern Consciousness*, trans. Ruth Crowley, 2 vols. (Minneapolis: University of Minnesota Press, 1988), ch. 1 and material pertaining to Chrétien de Troyes.

CONTRIBUTORS

KATHLEEN BIDDICK is professor of history at the University of Notre Dame, where she also teaches in the Gender Studies Program. Her book *The Shock of Medievalism* considers the intersections of disciplinarity, periodization, and pleasure in medieval studies.

CHARLES BURROUGHS is associate professor of art history and director of the Center of Medieval and Renaissance Studies at Binghamton University (SUNY). He has published diverse studies of early modern Italian architecture, urbanism, and visual culture, including *The Italian Renaissance Facade: Structures of Authority, Surfaces of Sense,* a book on the anthropology of the architectural facade in Italy from the fourteenth through the sixteenth centuries.

MICHAEL CAMILLE is Mary J. Block Professor of Art History at the University of Chicago. His latest books include *Mirror in Parchment: The Luttrell Psalter and the Making of Medieval England* and *The Medieval Art of Love: Objects and Subjects of Desire.* He is currently working on gargoyles and a study of street signs in medieval France.

TOM CONLEY is professor of Romance languages at Harvard University. He is the author of *The Self-Made Map* (Minnesota, 1996) and *Film Hieroglyphics* (Minnesota, 1991), and he has translated several works, including Michel de Certeau's *Culture in the Plural* and Gilles Deleuze's *The Fold,* both published by the University of Minnesota Press.

DONNALEE DOX is assistant professor of theatre history at the University of Arizona.

JODY ENDERS is professor of French at the University of California at Santa Barbara. She has written extensively on the interplay of rhetoric, medieval literature, performance theory, and law. She is the author of *The Medieval Theater of Cruelty* and *Rhetoric and the Origins of Medieval Drama.*

VALERIE I. J. FLINT is currently G. F. Grant Professor of History at University of Hull, U.K. Among her many publications are the books

The Rise of Magic in Early Medieval Europe and *The Imaginative Landscape of Christopher Columbus.*

BARBARA A. HANAWALT is the King George III Professor of British History at Ohio State University. Her books include *Growing Up in Medieval England: The Experience of Childhood in History* and *"Of Good and Ill Repute": Gender and Social Control in Medieval England.* She has edited numerous books for the Medieval Cultures series.

MICHAL KOBIALKA is associate professor of theatre at University of Minnesota. He is the author of a book on Tadeusz Kantor's theatre, *A Journey through Other Spaces: Essays and Manifestos, 1944–1990,* and a book on theatre and drama in the early Middle Ages, *This Is My Body: Representational Practices in the Early Middle Ages.* He is the editor of *Of Borders and Thresholds: Theatre History, Practice, and Theory* (Minnesota, 1999).

ANDRZEJ PIOTROWSKI is associate professor in the College of Architecture and Landscape Architecture at the University of Minnesota. He is coeditor, with Julia Williams Robinson, of the forthcoming *Discipline of Architecture* (Minnesota, 2001). He focuses on the interconnections between representation, epistemology, and architectural design and is currently working on a book tentatively titled *Space and Image.*

DANIEL LORD SMAIL is assistant professor of history at Fordham University. He has published on various subjects related to medieval law and society and is the author of *Imaginary Cartographies: Possession and Identity in Late Medieval Marseille.*

MEDIEVAL CULTURES

Index